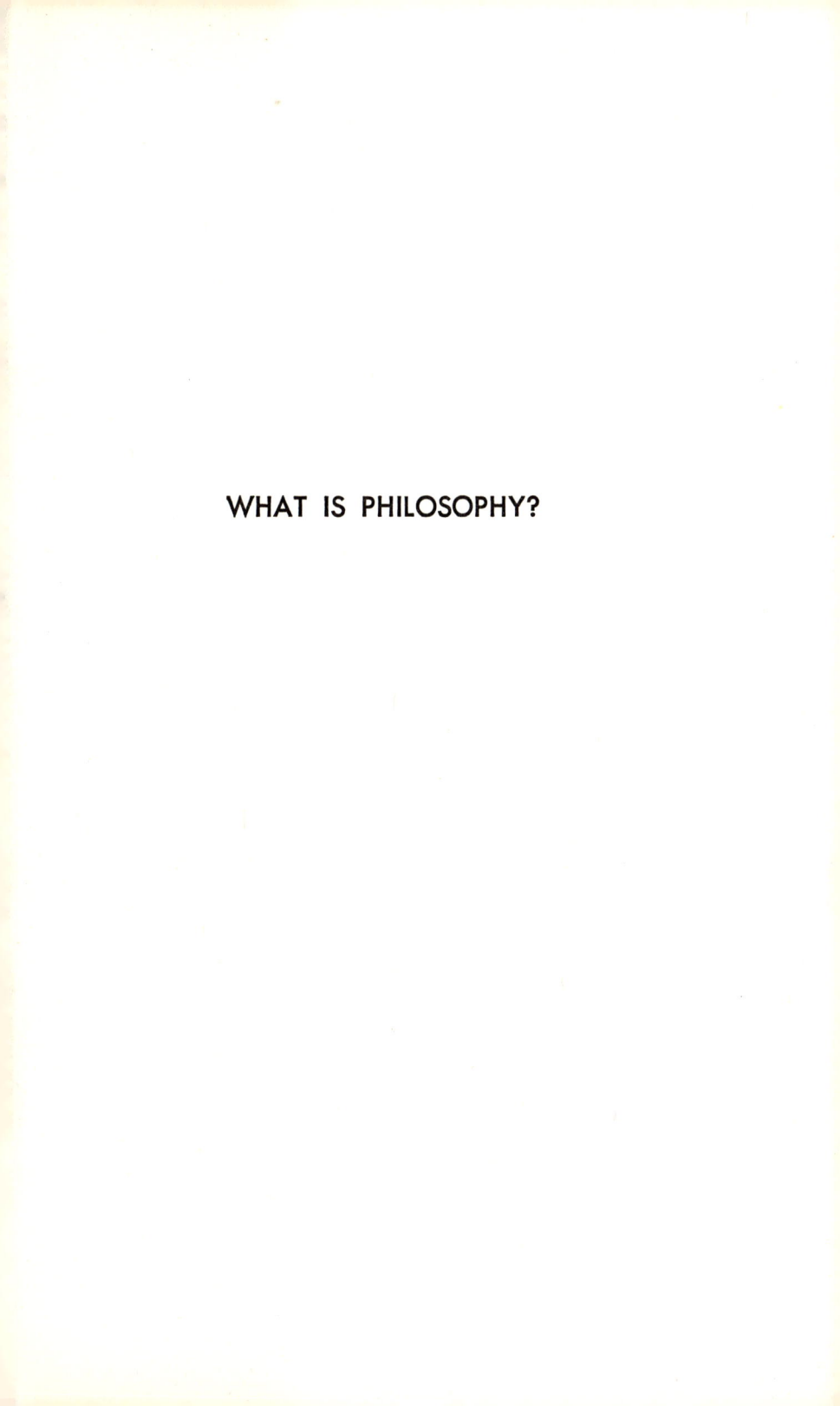

WHAT IS PHILOSOPHY?

WHAT IS PHILOSOPHY? is one of the volumes in a new series, IMPACT BOOKS, designed to bring to the modern reader the significant achievements of scholars, both Catholic and non-Catholic, in the fields of Scripture, Theology, Philosophy, Mathematics, History, and the Physical and Social Sciences. IMPACT BOOKS will explore these realms of human knowledge in order to give the average man some idea of the work being carried on today within them and in order to lay a basis for fruitful dialogue between men of different interests and persuasions on questions vital to all mankind.

WHAT IS *Philosophy?*

DIETRICH von HILDEBRAND

THE BRUCE PUBLISHING COMPANY
MILWAUKEE

NIHIL OBSTAT:
John A. Schulien, S.T.D.
Censor librorum

IMPRIMATUR:
✠ William E. Cousins
Archbishop of Milwaukee
March 20, 1960

Library of Congress Catalog Card Number: 60–12647

© 1960 The Bruce Publishing Company
MADE IN THE UNITED STATES OF AMERICA

ACKNOWLEDGMENTS

I want to thank wholeheartedly my dear friend and colleague, Dr. William Marra, Professor of Philosophy at the Fordham School of Education, for making this publication possible. With great care and painstaking efforts, he translated a former epistemological work of mine, written in German and published by Hanstein, Bonn. Several chapters of this translation were incorporated in this book, although in a modified form. He also was very helpful in the elaboration of the new chapters, and moreover, corrected them from a linguistic point of view. I am very indebted to this outstandingly gifted philosopher, who, I am proud to say, was once my student.

It is difficult to formulate what I owe to another colleague, Dr. Alice M. Jourdain of Hunter College, who was for many years my collaborator in the writing of my books, and who is today my wife. I dare say there is not one problem dealt with in this book which I have not discussed with her, and in the clarification of which she did not have a great share.

CONTENTS

Acknowledgments v

Introduction 1

Introductory Remarks 11

I. Knowledge in General 13
   1. Knowledge as a primary datum. 2. The specific features of taking cognizance of something.

II. Basic Forms of Knowledge 26

III. The Nature of Philosophical Knowledge in Contrast to Prescientific Knowledge . . 38
   1. Naïve prescientific knowledge. 2. Theoretical prescientific knowledge.

IV. The Object of Philosophical Knowledge . 63
   1. The characteristics of apriori knowledge. 2. The many meanings of the concepts: apriori and experience. 3. Genuine essences are capable of being grasped intuitively. 4. Epistemological characteristics of genuine essences which can be grasped intuitively. 5. The object of philosophy.

V. Objectivity and Independence . . . 152

VI. The Two Basic Themes of Knowledge . 172

VII. **Distinguishing Mark of Philosophical Knowledge and Inquiry** 185

1. The dominant themes of philosophic inquiry. 2. The depth dimension and depragmatization of the philosophical knowledge of essences. 3. The positive relation of philosophy and scientific knowledge. 4. The method of philosophy. 5. Phenomenology.

VIII. **The Meaning of Philosophy for Man** . . 227

Index 239

WHAT IS PHILOSOPHY?

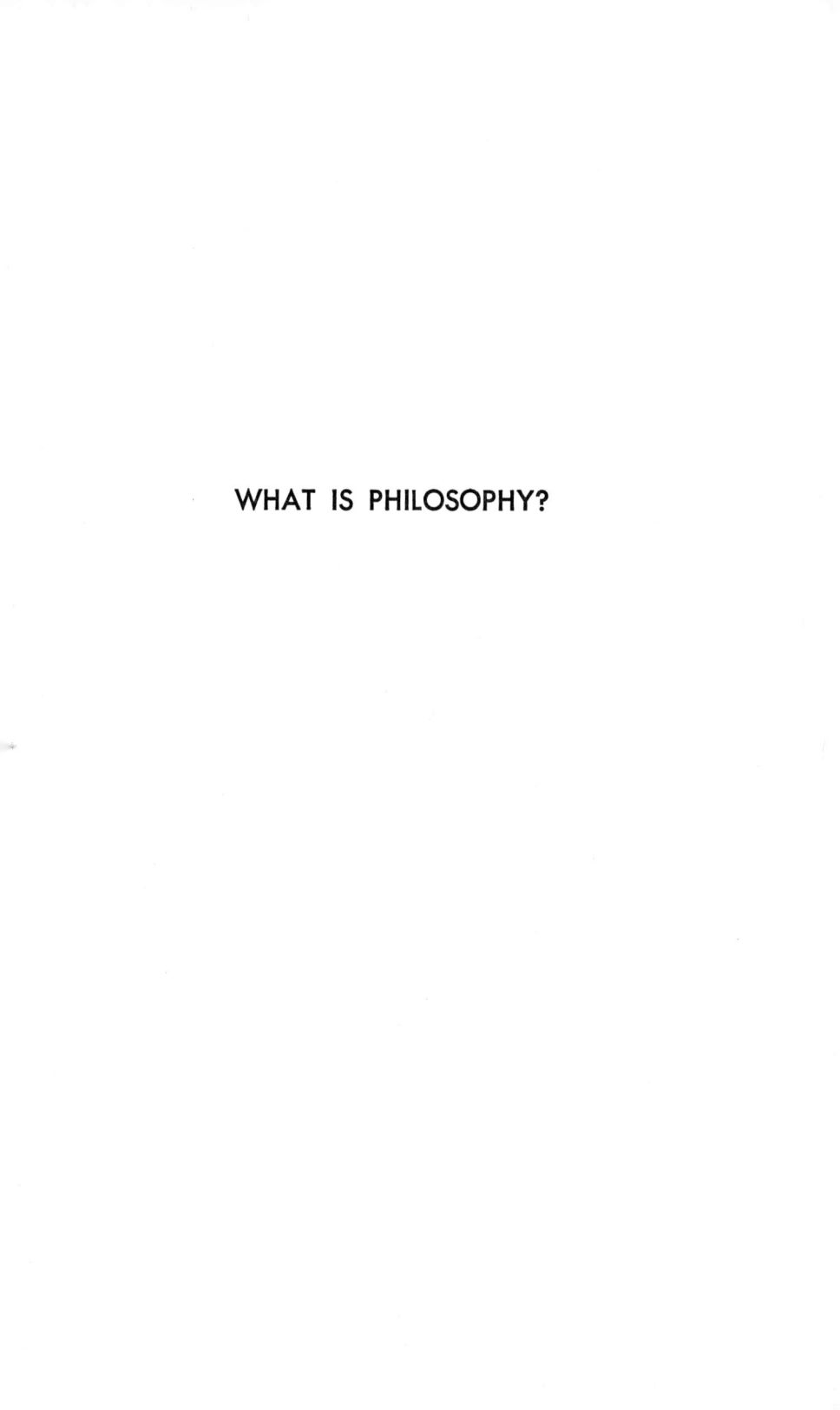

INTRODUCTION

If we consider the philosophy generally predominant in the universities of today, we are struck by the miserable role that many philosophers themselves consign to philosophy.

We are thinking of positivistic and relativistic philosophies of every kind, logical positivism, empirical sensism, and the like. We are thinking of all those professors of philosophy who look upon science as something incomparably superior to philosophy, who have difficulty in proving that philosophy has a right to exist, who actually betray the very nature and role of philosophy.

Reduced to its essentials, the philosophical creed of such men, logical positivists and semanticists, for example, actually amounts to a denial of philosophy. Sometimes this denial consists in restricing philosophy to the role of a mere handmaid to the sciences. Sometimes it involves the dissolution of philosophy, and the handing over of its objects to science. Thus ethics is often made an anthropological or sociological topic, or even a field for psychoanalysis. Epistemology and aesthetics are interpreted as parts of experimental psychology. And, as a matter of course, metaphysics is denied absolutely.

The striking feature about the men who thrive in this philosophical climate, when compared with the relativists and skeptics of former days, is their attitude toward science. The skepticism of the Greek Sophists extended consistently to all knowledge, philosophical as well as scientific (insofar as we can speak of scientific knowledge as distinct from philosophical knowledge in the fifth century B.C.). When the Sophists denied objective truth, they gave to philosophy a decisive and supreme role. It was philosophy which gave the verdict about all kinds of knowledge; their philosophy, negative though its content may have been, claimed to be queen in the sphere of knowledge.

If we examine the relativistic or skeptical philosophies in former times, we find that they did not refuse to grant philosophy an important role. They showed no tendency to favor science at the expense of philosophy. Even Hume's skepticism was directed just as much against science as it was against philosophy.

Today, on the contrary, there is a boundless respect for, and an unwavering faith in, science exhibited by the very philosophers who deny objective truth and profess, as philosophers, complete relativism and subjectivism. Unlike the skeptics of older times, they have an inferiority complex with respect to the role and importance of philosophy. Yet strangely, this does not hinder them from manifesting an arrogant, snobbish attitude toward all the actual topics of philosophy, toward all metaphysical realities, toward morality, and toward religion.

But at the same time they look upon science as something incomparably superior, as something which is not at all affected by the denial of objective truth which they profess. What are the reasons for this surprising attitude?

First, we must realize that these men, although they call themselves philosophers and are recognized as such by their contemporaries, have abandoned the very method of philosophical research. As a matter of fact, positivism in its various guises is not a wrong philosophy for the simple reason that it is not a philosophy at all. Positivism borrows the methods of certain sciences to deal with philosophical topics. Methods and approaches which are legitimate, and even the only adequate ones in certain sciences, are applied to the exploration of philosophical topics, for which they are absolutely inept.

There are many wrong philosophies, for example, subjective idealism, or solipsistic psychologism, that can still claim the name of philosophy, however erroneous, for despite their errors they are nevertheless the result of philosophical speculation, construction, and argumentation. The characteristic feature of positivism, however, is that it attempts to deal with philosophical topics in a radically unphilosophical manner. It approaches the data of morality, beauty in art and nature, the spiritual life of the human person, free will, love, and knowledge in a way which bars any contact with these data from the start and necessarily leads to overlooking them and replacing them by something else.

We must realize that all beings are not on one level, that one kind of object can differ from another to a tremendous degree, and that completely different intellectual "organs," each suited to the kind of object in question, must be called into play if we are to grasp the existence and nature of the many and varied beings given in experience.

Certain facts and data are readily accessible and may be grasped by anyone if only he is not absent-minded or slipshod in his approach. Thus, we may confidently expect that any normal person can give us a correct account about the number of persons in a room. We may likewise expect that a man will be able to give us a correct answer about the result of a chemical experiment if he has learned how to perform it.

But obviously we cannot expect a person to be able to inform us in the same way about the difference between purity and the absence of sexual instincts, or between the experiences of a moral prohibition and a psychological inhibition, or between something merely sad and something tragic. It would be foolish to expect a true answer, an answer which corresponds to reality, from a person who is simply attentive and reliable. Such qualifications are not sufficient here. The person in question must actualize other intellectual "organs" in order to grasp the objects about which we inquire. He must, moreover, have the intellectual courage to stick, in his answer, to what he grasps, and he must have the philosophical talent to express and formulate his discovery adequately.

In order to count the number of red and white corpuscles on a slide, a man need only look through a microscope and count accurately. To describe a tissue under a microscope or to perform a chemical experiment is likewise within the capabilities of an orderly, attentive person — he can just go ahead. No special intuition, no specific understanding is required, and still less a philosophical *prise de conscience*.

If we expect the difference between a moral prohibition and a psychological inhibition to reveal itself in the same way as the number of red corpuscles on a slide, or the number of persons in a room, we shall never discover this difference. We have to realize that a great part of reality, and certainly not the least important part, is open to us only in a way completely different from that in which objects such as the number of corpuscles and the design of a tissue are accessible. To grasp these other realities, to state truths about their existence and nature, we must actualize, as it were, another intellectual key.

Ernst Mach made a humorous sketch of himself in search of the "ego." He claimed that after observing without prejudice everything about himself that was manifest to himself, he could not find the "ego" but could find only his body. This is symbolic of the approach to philosophical matters taken by the positivists.

The positivist considers as reliable, serious, and systematic only that knowledge which has the character of blunt observation. Not only does he identify systematic and critical knowledge with scientific knowledge, but he even uses only one part of scientific knowledge, namely, pure empirical observation, seeing in this the pattern of knowledge as such. Many things which, in his naïve approach to being, in his existential experience, are the most immediately and undoubtedly given, are excluded as merely subjective aspects, as illusions, as soon as the positivist places them under the "microscope" of a so-called

INTRODUCTION 5

sober, realistic, serious intellectual analysis. Granted his approach to philosophy, the positivist's exclusion of these realities is understandable. Yet we must realize that this intellectual analysis, arrogating to itself the name of philosophy, is in reality a bad copy of certain methods essential to science and implies an approach which forces us to look in a direction where these elementary data will never be found. From the very beginning this approach restricts the given as such to a specific type of accessibility. It erects an arbitrary frame and summarily denies the existence of everything not found within this frame.

The positivist confuses this type of accessibility, this form of tangible verification, with evidence. He overlooks the fact that something may be unequivocally given, that it may be a continuously presupposed fact, and that, nevertheless, it may not be possible to subject it to this tangible type of verification. The intrinsic evidence of certain principles, of the existence of moral values, of the difference between an inferiority complex and humility, of the difference between mind and brain, is in no way altered by the fact that all these realities cannot be recognized by mere, blunt observation, but have to be "understood." They presuppose the actualization of another intellectual "organ" than do the things which can be verified by blunt, tangible observation.

Philosophy essentially and necessarily implies the actualization of this higher spiritual "organ," and the realities which are the very topic of philosophy can only be verified in a way which, far from being inferior to the tangible, incomparably surpasses it in its certitude and evidence.

Hand in hand with this unphilosophical or antiphilosophical way of research and knowledge goes the reduction of one thing to another, which I mentioned in the Prolegomena of my Ethics.[1] The "nothing else but" formula, which may be legiti-

---
[1] Cf. Dietrich von Hildebrand, *Christian Ethics* (New York: McKay, 1954), pp. 6, 7 ff.

mate and adequate in science, is meaningless nonsense when applied to the intelligible data which are the special domain of philosophy. The main characteristic of positivism, which is not so much a philosophy as a pseudo philosophy, is the application of the "nothing else but" formula to all those data which form the classical topics of philosophy. It thereby reduces them to beings which are of concern to the sciences.

That certain self-styled philosophers make philosophy an intellectual outcast is partly explained, therefore, by their abandoning the truly philosophical approach in favor of an empirical method of blunt observation. But there is a second reason why these men look upon philosophy as a pariah that must beg crumbs from the table of science. Most of them are very poorly gifted as philosophers. They lack the talents and gifts indispensable for a true philosopher. This does not mean that they lack intelligence. On the contrary, some of them, especially logicians and semanticists, possess a very refined type of formal intelligence. They have a mental sharpness and agility akin to that required of mathematicians. But they are wanting completely in specifically philosophical powers. As Maritain once very rightly said, the main difference between one philosophy and another seems to hinge on this, namely, whether the particular thinker sees certain things or does not see them.

To discover in a philosophical *prise de conscience* those data which are not accessible to blunt observation, though they are most certainly immediately given, to delve into the mysteries of being, to have the courage to cling steadfastly to the data reached in a prephilosophical experience, and to penetrate these data and do justice to their nature — these are the specifically philosophical gifts. In vain shall we look for this gift in the average professor of philosophy today.

Yet in facing the contemporary intellectual situation, we are confronted with a paradox. On the one hand, philosophy is discredited by reason of the poor and lowly place which the

INTRODUCTION 7

average philosopher bashfully grants it. On the other hand, there lives in the soul of modern man a passionate thirst for the true answers to real philosophical problems.

Positivistic, relativistic, and nominalistic pseudo philosophy gains more and more influence as an official philosophy in colleges, implanting an attitude of excessive awe toward science in the mind of the average man. Paradoxically, an increasing unrest and longing for true philosophy is engendered by the fact that this "philosophy" simply ignores all the vital problems of man, his life as a personal being, his happiness, his destiny. It is engendered by the unrealistic, nonexistential, and insipid character of this "antiphilosophical" philosophy.

This pseudo philosophy, in which science takes the place of metaphysics and religion, more and more corrodes the life of man, making him more and more blind to the real cosmos, in all its plenitude, depth, and mystery. It imprisons man in a universe deprived of its true light, of the features which give meaning to everything, such as good and evil, true and false, right and wrong; it locks him in a universe which is dehumanized, reduced to a "laboratory," stripped of all color, a universe in which all the great and fundamental realities of a personal human life are ignored, ousted, or denied. Today we are witnessing an inner revolt against the deformation expressed in this pseudo philosophy, a revolt which dramatically manifests itself.

The great number of suicides, greater than in any previous period of history, the great number of mental diseases, the frightening increase of juvenile delinquency, all eloquently disclose the inner revolt against positivism, with all its metaphysical boredom and suffocating dullness. Never was the need for a true philosophy more urgent; and by "true" is meant: first, a genuine philosophy instead of a philosophy which has abandoned the very character of philosophical knowledge, and, second, a philosophy which does justice to reality in its content. Never was philosophy more of an existential vital need, because never before has the naïve approach of man to being been so corroded by a pseudo philosophy which makes a fetish of science. Whatever may have been the philosophy of an earlier day and its conception of love, for example, never before have men in their life denied the reality of love between man and woman, never have the poets ceased to sing about it and praise it. It is only now that theories reducing love to a sublimated sex instinct are beginning to corrode the living approach to love. Not only love, but truth; not only truth, but beauty, art, authority, and happiness — all have begun to wither, thanks to the corroding influence of theories which confuse them with other things or which deny them outright because they are not accessible to blunt observation and "empirical verification by a community of neutral observers."

We do not claim, however, that there are lacking today philosophers in the true and full sense. In the recent past, thinkers like Bergson, Husserl, Scheler, and Blondel have eloquently and magnificently demonstrated that the stream of true philosophy has not run dry. This stream, which runs deeply through all centuries, appears again in these men. Again, even if we take no account of the representatives of a Christian philosophy and of all those in whom lives the spirit of the *philosophia perennis*, if we prescind from those who constantly deal with classical problems and enrich the philosophical conquest of being with rich and valuable insights (we are thinking of a Marcel), we find that those contemporary thinkers who deal with philosophical topics in a philosophical way merit the title of philosophers. For instance, Heidegger's works, whatever be the merit of their content, display a real philosophical method. They have absolutely no bashfulness about the role of philosophy in its relation to science. Philosophy holds its sovereign place and dares to deal with fundamental philosophical and metaphysical problems. Above all, they fully emphasize the vitality and dominance of philosophical problems for man.

This book is dedicated to a rehabilitation of philosophy. It aims to elaborate upon the true nature of philosophical knowledge, the true topic of philosophy, its epistemological dignity and its existential vitality. We also hope that it may become an efficient weapon in razing the fortress of those who make a fetish of science, and serve to reopen the gates to the authentic universe, to the cosmos in all its height, breadth, and depth.

This book will seek to expound the classical role of philosophy in man's life. The author fully realizes the opposition this book will encounter. He foresees the ironic smiles on the faces of many positivists, who will consider this work an expression of an obsolete reactionary mentality. He expects to be condemned by those who worship science, who will consider this book as superannuated, naïve, and unscientific.

With this book, I consciously and gladly throw the glove into the arena. I am fully aware of the insufficiency of my contributions in comparison with the depth and grandeur of my topic, and I am under no illusion that this book can do full justice to the enormous task it undertakes. I am, however, unshakably convinced of the imperative necessity of fulfilling a great and timely task by rehabilitating philosophy and declaring war on positivism and relativism.

It would be a complete misunderstanding to see in this book any revolt against science as such, or any lack of respect and full appreciation for its enormous and admirable achievements in physics, chemistry, biology, and medicine. No. War is not to be waged against science. That would be a ridiculous and futile enterprise. But it is to be waged against those who look upon science as some sort of a magical charm and attempt to deal with topics of philosophy in the same way as they proceed legitimately in science. War is to be waged against replacing, by a pseudo scientific method, the authentic philosophical analysis of those topics which are accessible only to the "philosophical organ." We say pseudoscientific, because the same method which is adequate in the framework of scientific research is inept and useless when applied to topics which are by their very nature inaccessible to this method.

Certainly, to convert a champion of positivism or relativism or logicism, more is needed than strict arguments and convincing proofs. From the start he places himself outside the range of this discussion. His blindness to reality will blind him also to the objective validity of our arguments and unambiguous elaborations.

But all those who, although nourished by these pseudo philosophies and perhaps infected by them, have nonetheless preserved their *"anima naturaliter philosophica,"* who still long for answers which only true philosophy can give, may find in this book deliverance from the prejudices of philosophical relativism combined with the fetishism of science.

Militant as this introduction is, we must emphasize, however, that the main character of this book is neither apologetic nor polemical. The rehabilitation of philosophy will be accomplished by a thoroughly objective, sober analysis of the true nature of philosophy and by an elaboration of the true character of apriori knowledge, or, as we prefer to say, of the *veritates aeternae* — the eternal truths.

This book is not concerned with polemics and with refuting the errors of fashionable pseudo philosophy. Purely positive insights concerning the nature of philosophical knowledge and the topic of philosophy will unmask the betrayers of philosophy. The main contents of this book are purely positive, and the author hopes above all that he has contributed new insights in the field of the theory of knowledge which have value and importance even when considered apart from the present philosophical situation, with its discrediting of philosophy and its need for the rehabilitation of philosophy.

INTRODUCTORY REMARKS

There are attitudes in man which disclose quite clearly the character of his earthly situation as being a *status viae*. Such are questioning, longing, and hope. They are not confined simply to this *status viae* as are weariness and illness, among others, in the vital sphere. On the one hand, they show us that man is a being ordered toward eternity and that his life transcends mere animal existence; on the other hand, they manifest the unfulfillment and incompleteness of his earthly situation. They simultaneously demonstrate both the finitude of man's existence and his relation to the infinite. Man in *statu viae*, in this earthly journey of existence, is a questioner. This basic, classical role of questioning, as a component of earthly existence and the transcendent character of man, reveals itself above all in the fundamental questions concerning the meaning of the world, the meaning of life, the destiny of man, and especially concerning the ultimate root of being, i.e., the absolute questions which live in the heart of every man — however deeply they may be buried, however much man tries intentionally to put them out of his way.

The basic questions of every man are thus religious and philosophical. A philosophical question is not the idle concern of a sophisticated mind, nor does it possess only a specialized interest for an academic mind. On the contrary, it is a fundamental component of the human mind.

We intend to investigate the meaning and nature of philosophical inquiry.

The meaning and nature of a certain type of questioning is determined by the very object about which one inquires and, again, by the kind of knowledge one wants to obtain. An investigation which would treat of the nature of philosophical inquiry must include, therefore, an analysis of the nature of the philosophical way of taking cognizance of something, of the kind of knowledge desired in philosophy, and of the objects of philosophy. Ultimately, philosophical inquiry makes sense if there is a kind of knowledge which is able to fulfill this inquiry, i.e., to answer it. If such knowledge is nonexistent, then philosophical inquiry is meaningless. The main clarifications of the nature of philosophical inquiry will ensue as soon as we grasp the nature and meaning of taking philosophical cognizance of something as well as of the object of philosophy. This being so, not only must we begin the investigation with an analysis of taking philosophical cognizance of something in its essential relation and contradistinction to prescientific, extrascientific, and scientific knowledge, but we also must give it the broadest position in our discussion because it is most basic. In such a way we shall advance step by step to the understanding of the meaning of philosophical questioning itself.

CHAPTER I

KNOWLEDGE IN GENERAL

1. Knowledge as a primary datum

The act of knowledge is an ultimate datum which cannot be reduced to anything else. Therefore, we cannot "define" it; we can only point to it indirectly. The true nature of knowledge can be grasped only in itself and not through anything else. In order to fix our spiritual eye unequivocally on this datum we must distinguish the act of knowledge itself from all neighboring data, such as judging and being convinced. To deepen our grasp of the nature of knowledge, and to see it in greater clearness, we must, furthermore, endeavor to behold its characteristic features. We must, however, avoid the error of thinking that the apprehension of the special features and properties of knowledge can replace the direct grasp of the datum itself. On the contrary, these features can be understood only on the basis of a living, intuitive contact with the act of knowledge.

If we consider the human person, we are struck by the fundamental role that knowledge plays in his life. The unique capacity for the individual person to partake in the existence of the entire remainder of the world, which knowledge in all its forms represents, from a simple perception right up to an insight into a state of facts, is the basis of our whole spiritual life. All our willings and strivings, our loves and hates, our joys and sorrows presuppose knowledge. They presuppose a consciousness of the object of willing, striving, loving, a knowledge of it, an understanding grasp of it. Causality links us, as it does nonpersonal beings such as a stone, a plant, an animal, to the total world which surrounds us, beginning with the physical, spatial, colored, sounding world, full of material things and events, and going on all the way to the people about us. But in addition we are linked to these in the entirely unique way of a spiritual grasping of the world, an intentional participation in it, a spiritual comprehension of it; and this is knowledge. If we can say that the being of a person cannot be thought of without including his capacity for knowledge, so, too, must we say that knowledge cannot be conceived without including the spiritual person, a *conscious* being, who has an intentional structure and a capacity for transcending the limited sphere of the self. Knowledge is a wholly unique contact in which one being touches another and possesses the other in an immaterial manner. This cannot possibly be similar to a merely causal contact between different objects of any kind. Rather, it essentially presupposes that one being is a personal subject, a conscious being.

Knowledge, moreover, is a one-sided contact in which the object is grasped by the subject, that is to say, a contact which implies a change only in the subject knowing and not at all in the object known. But this change in the subject must not be interpreted to mean that the known object becomes part of our personal being. Just as the object is not changed in its own objective being when it is known, so it does not become, when we know it, a real part of our personal being. Certainly, knowledge represents a participation of the subject in the object which is known. When we see the color orange, we truly partake of orange in a unique way. We possess it spiritually insofar as we have a consciousness of it. But this intentional contact must be fully distinguished from a real, physical participation in the being of the object. We do not "become" orange when

KNOWLEDGE IN GENERAL 15

we see it. The partaking of our minds in the being of the object which is known is neither the transformation of our being into that of the object nor a real incorporation of the known object into our personal being.

When we rejoice we really live this joy; the joy is a real constituent part of us: we are joyful. Likewise the act of gaining knowledge of something is a real constituent part of us, an act of our person. In such a case, we are perceivers. But the *object* which we grasp in the act of gaining knowledge, simply because we are grasping it, in no way becomes a real part of our personal being. We remain really and fully distinct from it, although we "penetrate" it in a very marked way and the object is — in some way — "incorporated" in us. We embrace it, as it were, spiritually from above.

The overlooking of this basic fact has been the central error of the various forms of psychologism. It comes about through the equivocal use of the notion "content-of-consciousness." It must certainly be evident that we are concerned with two wholly different things, when (1) we have a consciousness of an object and, when (2) something is itself a *conscious being*, such as an act which we accomplish, for example, the act itself of taking cognizance of something.

2. The specific features of taking cognizance of something

From the start we must understand that taking cognizance in the widest sense is a unique contact with an object, a contact which only a spiritual person can accomplish and which is different from every real "becoming" on the part of the subject. Taking cognizance of something is essentially a "receiving." Every theory of knowledge which sees it as a spiritual "producing" of something misunderstands taking cognizance of something in its most essential nature. It belongs to the very meaning of taking cognizance that an object, such as it really is, is grasped by the person, becomes understood and known, that the object discloses itself and unfolds before our spiritual eyes. The idealistic interpretation of taking cognizance of something as a spiritual building up out of an amorphous stuff and as a creation of the object of knowing is, therefore, equivalent to denying knowledge. Moreover, the misunderstanding of this basic meaning of taking cognizance of something necessarily travels in a vicious circle. Let us see why this is true. Transcendental idealism interprets taking cognizance of something as a construction of the object and thereby denies that we are able to grasp a real object such as it is. Yet it claims that philosophy describes the real nature of knowledge. It is perfectly clear that transcendental idealism does not consider its own interpretation of knowledge as a mere construction and that it claims it to be the disclosure of the authentic nature of knowledge. With this claim it tacitly presupposes and silently reintroduces the real nature and true notion of taking cognizance, namely, the grasping of an object such as it is, and not the constructing of an object. This intrinsic contradiction in transcendental idealism is, however, inevitable. For the genuine datum of knowledge and taking cognizance of something is so elementary that every attempt to deny it or to interpret it as something else necessarily leads to a vicious circle. Taking cognizance, as the genuine receiving and grasping of a being as it is, is really so elementary and inevitable a fact that it silently comes back into the picture and regains its rightful place even when a person tries to explain it away as something else.

Idealism declares that what presents itself to our naïve understanding as knowledge is in reality something completely different. The failure to distinguish between taking cognizance of something and the other different theoretical acts, such as judging and the like, has furthered this principal misunderstanding of the nature of knowledge. For such acts, in contrast to taking cognizance of something, present us with an outspokenly active character. By showing the different character of the theoretical acts we can expose the nature of knowledge more sharply and clearly.

Consider an objective body of knowledge, represented, for example, by a science such as botany. All the statements which it has so far made about the known plant world are the result of a specific spiritual act, namely, assertion. An assertion is a very special kind of act in which, through the medium of a proposition, we claim that a state of facts exists. It bears an outspokenly active character and not only a spontaneous one. Its objects are actual states of facts. We cannot affirm a person, the color red, a statue, a value, and so forth, but only a state of facts, a "how-it-is," or a "that-it-is." Hence, we can affirm only that something exists or is formed in such and such a way. In the assertion, the state of facts is not given to us. Rather, we ourselves point meaningfully to the fact through the medium of concepts and words. We cannot affirm a state of facts to be so without simultaneously formulating a sentence and thereby positing a unique spiritual entity, the proposition, to which truth and falsity are primarily attributed. Here we in no way reach knowledge. Instead, we objectify knowledge which we already possess.

Affirmation or assertion, which Adolf Reinach in a masterful way distinguishes from conviction, is the real judgment in the full, strict sense of the word. Only in the realm of affirmation do we encounter the peculiar objective entity — the proposition.[1]

The affirmation, or judgment in the strict sense, forms in a certain way the classical end point and conclusion in the entire process of knowledge, an end point, however, which does not belong to the act of knowledge itself but which rather constitutes a new entity beyond it. In affirmation, one fundamental "intention," immanent to a specific and thematic knowledge,

---

[1] The proposition must be sharply distinguished both from the act of affirming or judging, and from the state of facts to which we refer in our affirmation. It is of the proposition that we predicate truth or falsity, depending on whether or not it corresponds to the state of facts in question.

finds fulfillment, namely, the "intention" to objectify the truth grasped, to make it a public affair, to fix it for other persons. Affirmation belongs to spiritual "acts" in the strict sense. These include questioning, promising, communicating, commanding, etc., all of which must be completely distinguished from responses and, even more, from every form of taking cognizance of something.

Taking cognizance, even in its broadest sense, must be distinguished from the judgment. They differ in the following respects:

1. In every act of taking cognizance, be it a simple perception of red or an insight into a state of facts, an object discloses itself to me, I *receive* a knowledge of it. The intention goes, as it were, from the object to me: I listen. With the judgment, on the other hand, no object is given to me; but I proclaim, so to speak, that a certain state of facts exists — that it *is* so. The intention clearly goes from me to the object. I speak and the knowledge of the existence of the "how-it-is" is presupposed.

2. The object of taking cognizance in the widest sense can be contents of all kinds, things as well as states of facts, qualities as well as events, spiritual persons as well as values. The object of judgments, on the contrary, can only be the "how-it-is," the state of facts.

The basic difference between the judgment and the act of taking cognizance of something remains the same even though both are closely knit together psychologically. Often taking cognizance of something is directly succeeded by a judgment. The various types of personal acts take place in a psychologically narrow neighborhood and so closely together in time that one is at first disposed and tempted to treat them as a single whole. Thus, for example, the conclusion which so rapidly appears in connection with some perceptions without any further thought on our part. For example, we hear the doorbell ring at a certain time and we conclude that the mail has arrived. Although an

KNOWLEDGE IN GENERAL 19

authentic conclusion is here present, which represents a different kind of act, in contrast to the perception of the sound, it takes place so quickly and so readily joins itself to everything else without a new start or beginning, that one is tempted to take these two very different experiences for a single whole. The inner meaningful conjunction of these two experiences, however, does not take away their essential difference. From the intelligence that my friend is coming, the response of joy not only presents itself directly and readily, but it is also profoundly and meaningfully linked to this intelligence. The consciousness of my friend's coming is the necessary presupposition of my joy, which builds itself organically and meaningfully upon it. But the difference between the knowledge of a communication on the one hand and the response of joy on the other is in no way diminished because of this.

Judging and taking cognizance of something, therefore, remain essentially different things, however closely linked together they are — however much the judging forms the classical end point of the theme of knowledge.

Taking cognizance of something must also be distinguished from yet another neighboring datum, namely, the theoretical response of *conviction*, which affirmation presupposes. Conviction belongs to the responses[2] of a person. In conviction the person gives an "answer," with specific content, to an object. As we see[3] in the case of veneration, esteem, enthusiasm, or love, the person directs himself with a specific content to an object, which represents an answer to the value of the object. It is, as it were, an inner "word" spoken to the object, a word meaningfully based upon the value of the object. Something analogous can be found in the case of conviction. Unlike an affirmation, it is not an act in the strict sense of the word; nor is it, like taking cognizance of something, a receptive taking in

---
[2] *Christian Ethics* (New York: McKay, 1954), Chap. 17.
[3] *Ibid.*

of something. It is rather a typical response. Only it is a *theoretical* response, like doubt and conjecture, in contrast to the affective responses, like joy, sorrow, enthusiasm, indignation, and love. In this case the answer does not refer to the positive or negative importance of an object, but rather to its existence. The inner "yes" of the conviction refers to the existence of a state of facts.

Conviction as well as affirmation must be sharply distinguished from taking cognizance of something. Conviction clearly differs from taking cognizance of something in the following ways:

1. Conviction possesses a spontaneous character, whereas taking cognizance of something, in the widest sense, is receptive. In the conviction, I speak, as it were, to the object. In taking cognizance of something, the object speaks to me. In conviction, the direction of the intention goes from me to the object. In taking cognizance, it is vice versa.

2. In conviction, an object does not disclose itself to me. Instead, I take a stand toward the object. Conviction is not a "having" of the content of an object, but an answer on my part to the existence of that content. It is not a "consciousness of" a content on the object side, whereby I am, as it were, void, but rather the accomplishment of some specific content in me, with which I give my answer to an existent.

3. The object of conviction can be only a "how-it-is," i.e., a state of facts. I cannot be "convinced" of a red color, a person, a value, or a material thing. I can only be convinced that something is, or that a thing is such and not otherwise. Taking cognizance, in the widest sense, is not restricted merely to the "how-it-is."

4. To be sure, conviction does not, like affirmation, aim at the "how-it-is," the state of facts, through the medium of propositions, but rather reaches it immediately. In conviction, however, we do not "discover" an object as we do in taking

cognizance of something. Instead, we give our answer to it. Consequently, conviction already presupposes knowledge of the "how-it-is." We can hardly think of a form of taking cognizance of something to which a conviction in the widest sense is not attached, either with reference to the existence or the character of the object in question. Nevertheless, taking cognizance of something and conviction are not identical. Indeed, conviction is necessarily a fruit of taking cognizance, but in its very nature it is completely different from taking cognizance itself, in which the "how-it-is" is grasped as existing. Conviction is essentially an epiphenomenon. It is therefore secondary with respect to taking cognizance. In taking cognizance, the object itself is the guarantee of its existence. It decides, and not I. In conviction, the decision rests with me, even though it is completely rooted in the known object and has in no way a voluntary character, much less a capricious one. Nevertheless, it is always the accomplishment of my response to the existence of an object.[4]

It is a matter of fundamental importance to distinguish taking cognizance itself from all those spiritual attitudes which, on the one hand, precede it as a preparation and, on the other, are organically rooted in it. The failure to distinguish clearly between taking cognizance of something on the one hand and conviction, thinking, and judging on the other, has led to a misunderstanding of the decisive feature of taking cognizance as being a "receiving." It leads to the fatal idealistic error of conceiving our knowledge of an object as a kind of "producing."

Yet even in the case of these other intellectual attitudes there can be no question of any bringing forth of the object. We need only consider a case in which we really produce a spiritual reality, in a promise, for example. With a promise we create an objective liability on our part to fulfill what we have

---
[4] Ibid.

promised, and an objective claim on the part of the other person that we fulfill our promise. This unique, objective, legal entity, liability, which is to be distinguished fully from any mere "feeling of being liable," is posited in the world through our act of promising. Whereas previously it did not exist, now we have brought it into being. In the case of the spontaneous intellectual acts there can be no question of a similar production. In conviction, for example, I respond to a "how-it-is," but the "how-it-is," the state of facts, is neither brought into being nor changed as a result of my conviction.

On the contrary, it belongs to the very meaning of conviction that it turns toward a "how-it-is" which in its existence is completely independent of the accomplishment of my conviction. With affirmation one can, it is true, speak at first of a "producing." But here too it is not the content of the object which is in question, not the known world of beings, but at the most the formulating and expressing of the proposition. The proposition constitutes itself through the affirmation. It is produced by it. But here the relation is quite different from that which exists between a promise and the liability it produces. Only by way of a broad analogy can we speak of the "production" of a proposition.

If we have learned to understand taking cognizance of something in the widest sense as that unique spiritual contact with being whereby the being in its own nature reveals itself to us and if we have understood taking cognizance to be a transcendent contact with being, which represents neither a real participation in the being of the known object nor any kind of production or creating, we must now realize a third essential feature of taking cognizance of something, in the widest sense of the word. Even though the thoroughly receptive character is the decisive feature of taking cognizance in the broadest sense, nevertheless it is not a purely passive affair. Every case of taking cognizance has also an active component, which we can refer to as a spiritual "going with" the object and its nature. I am thinking here not only of the preparatory acts, like attentiveness, that explicit turning of the mind toward the object which displays itself in so many gradations. This is rather a presupposition for taking cognizance of something, not an element of taking cognizance itself. It merely effects a contact with the object on the part of the knower. If a person sees a house, another person, or an event, without being attentive to it, his mind is "absent," and consequently it does not linger before the seen object. There is no real contact with the knower's mind. But by the active, spiritual "going with" which we have in mind here, we mean something which is an element in the process of taking cognizance itself. It is, as it were, the intentional echoing of the being of the object, the consummation of the "understanding" of the actual momentary object, the full, explicit, spiritual reception of the object.

This "going with" that belongs to taking cognizance of something, this spiritual penetration, plays quite different roles in the perception of the different kinds of objects. The higher and more complicated the object and the more meaningful it is, the more prominent becomes this "concerting" with the object and the more essential is its part in the whole process of taking cognizance. In the simple perception of a color it has not the same meaning and depth as in the perception of another person or even of an essence.

This active component in taking cognizance of something in no way implies a contradiction to the basically receptive character of knowing. The active component not only does not cancel the receptive character, it does not even imply a limitation of it, for it may not in any sense be understood as any kind of production of the object of knowledge. This "going with" is only an active co-operation with the self-disclosure of the object. It is not a production of the object. Neither is it a "copy" of the object, not even in the broadest sense in which we can call a formulation of a sentence a "copy" of the intended state of facts. It is, furthermore, a spiritual "infiltration" into the object, which does not produce a second spiritual object, but explicitly executes the intentional participation in the object or the spiritual possession of it.

This "going with" is a typical starting point for the idealistic misinterpretation of taking cognizance of something as a producing of the object. Taking cognizance of essences, above all else, is easily mistaken for a spiritual "creating" of these from the material of the perceived, concrete object. This mistake is all the easier in the case of taking cognizance of essences because the active element in taking cognizance plays a much more important role here than in taking cognizance of concrete existents. In truth, however, it is as little a creating of an object as are the other types of taking cognizance. Here, as anywhere, it is a receiving of an objective being. This receiving, when taking cognizance of essences is in question, only requires a much more active, spiritual "going with" and "concerting" with the object. The activity in taking cognizance of something is simply an active accomplishing of the receiving. In no way does it cancel out the basis of all taking cognizance as consisting in a self-revealing of the object.

We may speak in a twofold way, therefore, of the active elements in taking cognizance of something: (1) with respect to the preparatory turning of attention toward the object and the focusing upon it of a gaze corresponding to the depth and meaningfulness of the object; (2) with respect to the spiritual "going with" of the object. This "going with" is embedded in taking cognizance itself and is the alert and active taking-in of the object, which gains in importance with the increasing profundity and meaningfulness of the object. Neither the activity which precedes taking cognizance nor the activity involved in it has the character of creating or producing the object itself or a new spiritual structure, such as the proposition, which might be conceived of as the "copy" of the state of facts. The element of "going with," embedded in taking cognizance, is an activity in the passivity, an activity which is indispensable for full receiving.

To summarize briefly, then, taking cognizance of something represents first a unique spiritual contact with a being, in which the being displays itself to us in its specific nature. This transcendent spiritual contact represents an intentional participation in a being which must be sharply distinguished from a real or physical partaking. It is even more correct to call it a spiritual possession. St. Augustine calls it "*habere quoddam.*" Second, taking cognizance is in no way a production of the object known, but a receptive grasping of it. It does not even possess the spontaneity of conviction or, still less, of affirming, for it is to be distinguished sharply and altogether from the sphere of judging in the strict sense of the term. Third, the receiving, in which the object discloses itself, is even then not a purely passive thing. It contains as such an active component also, the spiritual "going with" the *ratio* or essential nature of the object known.

CHAPTER II

BASIC FORMS OF KNOWLEDGE

In its widest meaning knowledge includes all those acts in which directly or indirectly an object is disclosed to us in its nature and its existence. Obviously knowledge in this broad sense manifests itself in many different ways, for instance, in perception, inference, intellectual intuition, and learning from other persons, through the spoken or written word. In the previous chapter we used the expression "taking cognizance of something" as synonymous with "gaining knowledge of something." Here we intend to call attention to a distinction which will throw more precisely into relief the nature of "taking cognizance of something," and show how this act differs from simple "knowing."

When someone tells us of a train accident, we learn something new. Previously we did not know that this accident took place. Such learning is one of the many forms of taking cognizance of something, of appropriating something new to our mind. It has a dynamic character. It includes a process, becoming acquainted with something, a change.

If we then meet a second person who also tells us that this accident has occurred, we do not acquire any new knowledge, since we already know the fact he is relating. We will answer, "Yes, I know it already."

The type of knowledge to which we refer when we say "I know it," clearly differs from the type of knowledge which forms

BASIC FORMS OF KNOWLEDGE 27

the subject of taking cognizance. This knowing, in which, as it were, we possess the object, has a static, not a dynamic, character. It is not a process of appropriation involving a change, but a static possession.

This static knowing is the result of learning; learning aims at the establishment of knowing. Thus we may also reply to a man who tells us something that we know, "Yes, I have *learned* it already." In mentioning that it has been told to us, we imply that this information succeeded in creating a knowing, and thus, we can no longer learn it because we know it already.

These two types of knowledge, namely, taking cognizance and knowing, differ even in a more formal and fundamental way from each other than perception does from inference.

Yet in distinguishing taking cognizance from knowing, we in no way mean to deny their essential and most intimate connection. But in themselves they represent not only different stages of knowledge, but two definitely different acts of knowledge. The one is the dynamic process of learning, of acquiring knowledge; the other, the static possession of the object. This difference pervades the entire sphere of knowledge independently of the specific nature of taking cognizance. Suppose someone makes the acquaintance of another person and perceives his face for the first time. He grasps that he has blue eyes, blond hair, an aquiline nose, and so on. He learns many things through perception. Upon seeing him a second time, although he again perceives all these things, he does not learn them again, because he already knows them. What happened in perceiving him for the first time cannot be repeated, provided that he does not forget that the man has blue eyes, blond hair, and so on. Learning leads to knowing, but once knowing has been established, learning in the same respect cannot take place.

Here, as in the case of learning something through other persons, the learning, with its dynamic character, clearly differs from the act of knowing, with its static character.

The same applies if we reach a form of knowing through deduction or induction. Taking cognizance, or the acquiring of knowledge — the "learning" — is always definitely an act different from the knowing which results from it. Taking cognizance and knowing are distinguished by the following marks.

First: taking cognizance has, as we mentioned before, a dynamic character, whereas knowing is static.

Second: taking cognizance is an appropriation; knowing is a possession resulting from this appropriation.

Third: taking cognizance takes place in a certain moment of time, more or less limited, and it belongs to the type of attitudes which are essentially restricted, in their existence, to a concrete period of time; knowing, on the other hand, can also subsist superactually;[1] that is, it perdures in us in such a way that it can be immediately actualized within us.

Once we know something we continue to possess it superactually even if we are concerned with other things. This relation to the object which is implied in knowing, this spiritual possession, subsists even when we are focused on other objects.

The conserving power of man's intellect — present in all knowledge, and indispensable for every case of taking cognizance of something — as distinguished from the intellect's receptive and appropriating power, manifests itself in a special way in the superactual character of knowing.

The superactual existence of knowing discloses itself in the fact that the static possession, the awareness of the object, can always be actualized again. Only when the object has been forgotten does the knowing cease to exist. We shall understand better this third difference between taking cognizance and knowing after we make some distinctions in the realm of knowing itself.

---

[1] In *Christian Ethics*, Chapter 17, we called attention to the superactual character of many personal attitudes, faith and love, for example, and we noted the importance of superactual existence for the depth and continuity of personal life.

In the process of inferring, which is itself a form of taking cognizance, the premises are present to our mind as actualized. We must actualize our knowledge of the premises in order to make the inference. But there are many other cases in addition to inference when our "knowing" is fully actualized. If something preoccupies us, if we always think of an event which has great importance for us, we have present in our mind something which is already known and which is now actualized; in other words, there is a question here of actualized knowing. Yet our spiritual possession of the object is not restricted to those moments in which our mind is consciously focused on it.

The things we know in a superactual manner form a continuous basis for all the other things on which we concentrate at any particular moment. The implicit awareness of the realities we know superactually modifies those varying situations in which we focus our attention on this or that object.

Knowing implies a relation between us and an object, and this relation subsists superactually as long as we do not forget what we know. Many facts constitute the superactual basis of our life. Thus the Christian, no matter what he may actually be doing here and now, knows in a superactual way that Christ was born, that He died on the cross, that He is risen, that He is divine, and that He redeemed the world.

When we say that we know some facts superactually and that this superactual knowing subsists along with all other activities of our mind, we do not merely mean that the knowledge of something is, as it were, stored in our mind, and that we can draw it out of this reservoir of memory, or that it comes into our mind by some association or by our being reminded of it by others. By superactual subsistence we mean that we never lose some kind of implicit awareness of it. It lives as a basis in our mind in such a way that every concrete actual moment of our life would be radically changed if we did not know it.

This superactual knowing in the strict sense is possible only with respect to certain kinds of facts and objects.

The fact or object must be of decisive metaphysical importance. It must concern the most existential and fundamental questions, such as relate to all the basic elements of a *Weltanschauung*. Thus it is above all in the sphere of religion that we encounter superactual knowing.

The fact or object must at least have a high value, and thus be inserted into the world of goods in which our life displays itself. Knowledge of the existence and of the personalities of beloved persons certainly forms a continual existential basis of our life, even when we are concentrating on completely different objects. Just as our love subsists superactually, coloring and forming every situation, so does our "knowing" of the beloved subsist. Again, we may have superactual knowing of great works of art, the beauty of which we have fully grasped and which have become parts of the *caelum empyreum*. The same applies to beautiful countries. In brief, every good endowed with high values, a good which plays such an existential role in life that without a knowledge of it our life would be different, is an object of superactual knowing. Or, to put the matter in other words, any object is an object of superactual knowing if the knowledge of it radically affects life.

In an analogous fashion, the great evils connected with man's situation on earth are objects of superactual knowing.[2] We know superactually that we must die. We know that we are exposed to all kinds of dangers at every moment. Man's metaphysical situation, expressed by Pascal when he calls man a "thinking reed," is an object of superactual knowing. We also are always

---

[2] The superactual knowing of great evils is especially obvious in the case of a metaphysical pessimist. That this pessimism is at bottom false, since it rests on a misunderstanding of the sovereign position of values, does not prevent such knowledge from existing superactually and coloring the entire conscious life of the pessimist. The reader is referred to *Christian Ethics*, Chapters 5 and 6, for our discussion of a metaphysical optimism based on the autonomous character of all genuine values.

aware that every beloved person is surrounded by dangers which threaten his health, life, and earthly happiness. In short, the fact that this earth is a valley of tears is superactually known by man. The same applies to single great evils, which change the shape of our entire life, such as the death of the person most beloved.

It would be a great error to believe that the only beings present to the mind are those actually encountered in that small section of reality upon which the mind happens to be focused at the present moment. There is much more than this present to our minds at any given time. The world which, as it were, we carry with us, in which we live, the spiritual firmament under which we move and the sun of which illuminates our life, forms the implicit background against which the concrete content of our perceptions, thoughts, and activities appear.

Thus we see that one area of superactual knowing embraces those goods and evils which play a constitutive role in our lives, either because of their supreme metaphysical importance or because of their high value. But there are other goods and evils which can be the objects of superactual knowing, at least for a certain period of time, even though they do not play this constitutive role. I do not simply know the death of a dear friend and then push this knowledge aside. It lingers in my superactual consciousness, coloring my thoughts and activities for weeks, perhaps months. So, too, the expected arrival of a beloved person superactually preoccupies me although at any given time I am actually attending to some other object. Again, I know superactually that a war is going on just as long as the war lasts.

The realm of the superactual includes, finally, all those facts which have a structural function in the exterior frame of our life. Among such facts may be included the country we are in at a given moment, or, more important, the country in which we reside, as well as the town in which we live. If we were not implicitly aware of these facts, our lives would certainly be changed. These facts form a background for all the changing objects of our consciousness.

In contrast to all these beings and facts, there are many things which cannot be the object of superactual knowing. Thus, our knowledge of how a substantive is declined in Latin or in German has not the character of superactual knowing. Knowledge of such matters certainly remains a spiritual possession even when our mind is directed to other things. But it subsists merely potentially. It does not influence all the actual situations of our day. It does not form a background for our actual experiences. Rather, it is conserved in a reservoir, out of which it may be drawn. During the times it is not actualized, it is merely at our disposal so that it can be actualized whenever it becomes, for one or another reason, thematic. It is evident that the distinction made here between superactual knowing, on the one hand, and, on the other, potential knowing, whereby many facts are kept in the reservoir of our memory, points to a difference not only in the known objects in question but also in the very nature of the knowing itself.

Thus we see that there are three basic forms in which knowing can occur: first, in the actual form, when we actualize the spiritual possession of an object and when the known object is fully and consciously present to our mind; second, in the authentic superactual form, when the implicit awareness of certain facts and objects forms a continuous background for other experiences; third, in the form of memory, wherein the knowledge subsists merely potentially.[3]

We do not, of course, pretend that this brief analysis has said all there is to be said about the differences in knowing

---

[3] We prescind here from the profound difference which Bergson, in his *Matière et Mémoire*, has discovered between the technical memory, which deals with names and words, and intellectual memory, which deals with former experiences. Our third form of knowing refers to technical memory. The specific modifications of knowing implied in intellectual memory is not our topic here.

BASIC FORMS OF KNOWLEDGE

which result from the varying importance of objects — all the way from the supreme metaphysical importance of certain goods to the merely technical importance of certain others. Still, we have said enough to throw the three basic forms of knowledge into relief. We must now turn to distinctions of another kind within the sphere of knowing.

For example, there are two basically different types of knowing which in German are called *kennen* and *wissen*.

They are definitely two species of the genus of knowing. They are both static and both can occur in any of the three forms of knowing we have discussed thus far. They differ, first of all, in regard to their object, and, second, in their status as spiritual possessions of an object. The type of knowing designated by the German term *wissen* refers exclusively to states of facts. It is always expressed in sentences such as: "I know that the moon is round, that Caesar crossed the Rubicon in 49 B.C., or that 2 plus 2 is 4." Only facts or states of facts (the reality to which a proposition refers) are objects of this type of knowing.

On the other hand, that type of knowing which is called *kennen* in German refers to every type of being that is *not* a state of facts. We express this type of knowing when we say, for example, "I know this melody; I know this person, this country, this town, this color." In short, *kennen* refers to any object whatsoever, substance or accident, everything except states of facts.

Hereafter we shall use the English term *knowing* to signify what the German means by *wissen*, and the English phrase *having knowledge of* to represent the German *kennen*. We fully realize, of course, that in ordinary usage these English expressions in no way clearly indicate the difference in question. Hence, these terms are introduced artificially as pure *termini technici*, because there are no genuine terms in English to indicate this important difference.

Knowing in general, as introduced above, that is to say, static spiritual possession, in contrast to the dynamic taking cognizance of something, has thus two subdivisions. The first, in which the objects of knowing are states of facts, has been called *knowing* in a more limited sense. The second, wherein all types of being which are not states of facts are known, has been called *having knowledge of* something.

The difference between knowing and having knowledge of something is not restricted to the formal and structural difference of their respective objects. Both are characterized by a different act of knowing. Knowing in the narrower sense has a more linear character; that is, it is more direct and clear-cut. If we are asked, "Do you know that a war has broken out?" or "that a train has been derailed?" or "that the Queen of Siam had a child?" we answer with a clear "yes" or "no." If now we are asked whether we have knowledge of a person or of a work of art, for instance, *King Lear* or the *Fourth Symphony* of Beethoven, we may also answer with a simple, "no," to indicate the fact that we are totally unacquainted with the object in question.

But if we answer a question like this affirmatively, instead of a simple "yes," we may say, "only superficially," or "to a certain extent," or "well," or "through and through." In short, a large scale of a more or less intimate knowledge is possible here. There are many gradations.

Having knowledge of a person or of a book or of a work of art can, therefore, be more or less complete. It refers not to the existence of something, but to its "such-being," in all parts and elements.

If a primitive stage of having knowledge of something is reached by taking cognizance of it in a perception, new acts of taking cognizance of the same object will lead, step by step, to a more adequate and complete possession of it.

Suppose we perceive a house for the first time. We become acquainted with it and gain a superficial knowledge of it. When we see it several times more, our knowledge of it is increased in different directions. For example, we become aware of many details of its façade, and thereby our knowledge of the house is increased in the direction of a greater differentiation. When we also see the back of the house and its interior, our knowledge of the house is increased in a different direction, that of completeness, for we are now increasing our knowledge of the whole object by becoming acquainted with all its parts. And when we grasp more and more the artistic beauty of the house, our knowledge of it will be increased in the dimension of depth.

We can distinguish different stages of knowledge even with respect to objects simpler than a house. In the realm of knowledge there are degrees of *intimacy* as well as degrees of understanding. In the area of *knowing* in its limited sense, however, the objects of which are exclusively states of facts, we find no similar gradations. Yet here we can speak of degrees of *certitude*, whereas we cannot do so with regard to having knowledge of an object.

For instance, if someone is asked in a trial: "Did this man tell you what he has done?" he may answer: "It seems to me that he did, but I'm not certain." Again, someone in a process of research, after having discovered an important fact, but not yet having ascertained it fully, may say, "I do not yet know with certitude whether it is so or not."

The certitude of knowing may sometimes refer to my recollection, and then it is independent of the certitude of taking cognizance of something which led to the knowing. It refers simply to the perfection or imperfection of static possession. I may thus not know with certainty what I grasped before with full certitude. This certitude of recollection refers only to the act of knowing and thus is restricted to an individual person.

But the degree of certitude of knowing may also be an immediate result of the degree of certitude of taking cognizance. If someone simply told me a fact, I may say that I do not know it with the same certitude as if I had seen it with my own eyes. Here the degree of certitude is a consequence of the certitude of the taking cognizance of something, but it still may be restricted to my own person. Others may know it with certitude. Finally, the degree of certitude of knowing may refer not only to the way I took cognizance of it but also to the objective possibility of taking cognizance of it by any man. It refers, for instance, to the question of how well a given historical fact is ascertained or to the question whether the state of facts has an empirical or an apriori character.

Though we must distinguish these two types of knowing in the larger sense, they interpenetrate each other continually. With every stage of knowledge of an object, knowing (in the narrower sense) of a certain state of facts goes necessarily hand in hand.

The same applies *mutatis mutandis* to taking cognizance and knowing in the larger sense. We have already mentioned that taking cognizance and knowing in the larger sense, embracing the two above-mentioned species, though forming two definitely different acts which are distinguished by several marks, are nevertheless closely connected. Every case of taking cognizance necessarily gives birth to static knowing. Moreover, both the dynamic taking cognizance and the static knowing have the same theme. Taking cognizance answers the question "How is it?" Its theme is that something is so and so. This theme has a dramatic character corresponding to the dynamic structure of this act. In knowing, the theme of "it is so" no longer has the dramatic note, for it now assumes the character of peaceful fulfillment, according to the static structure of this act. Nevertheless the same theme is present. This theme, which both types have in common, we shall call the "notional" theme. It is concerned with the very core of knowledge, with the specific appropriation of something, with the unique relation to the object which knowledge embodies, with the penetration of the object by our intellect, with the understanding it. We stress that taking cognizance and knowing are both dominated by this "notional" theme, because there is still another theme in the sphere of knowledge, which we may call the contemplative theme.

Later on, in Chapter V, we shall elaborate the differences between these two themes and the implications connected with these differences.

CHAPTER III

THE NATURE OF PHILOSOPHICAL KNOWLEDGE IN CONTRAST TO PRESCIENTIFIC KNOWLEDGE

Thus far we have treated of knowledge in general and have distinguished the basic forms of knowledge from each other. Now we shall seek to show in some detail the difference between philosophical and prescientific knowledge.

The contact with things gained through prescientific knowledge falls into two basic types. First, there is the naïve contact with being, in which the world with its numerous regions of being simply discloses itself to a person's mind during the course of life. Second, there is the more or less theoretical knowledge of being, in which one uncritically and unsystematically, although reflectively and basing himself on some principle, strives to know certain strata of being.

1. Naïve prescientific knowledge

We turn first to the naïve type of prescientific knowledge, which has a very important function for philosophical knowledge. For the present, however, our concern is to show how this naïve form of taking cognizance of something differs from the philosophical.

Philosophical taking cognizance of something is always distinctly thematic. This means that contact with the object is decisively ruled by the theme of appropriating some knowledge about it. The mind is clearly directed to the object as to something-to-be-known. This form of taking cognizance possesses an inner dramatic character which is pregnant with the desire of appropriating knowledge about the object. If we look at naïve knowing we find, at first, cases in which taking cognizance is completely unthematic. This is always true, for example, when we perceive something casually, without clearly directing our attention to it. Thus, we are expecting a friend and we casually perceive the surroundings while our attention is wholly taken up by the expectation of his arrival. Such casual perceptions certainly lead us to a knowledge of different contents, but not only is there no explicit appropriation involved, there is not even present here the theme of taking cognizance. The essential theme of this situation is primarily not theoretical. An affective or practical theme dominates the situation, namely, the desire to meet a friend. A secondary theme also present here consists in a conscious wondering about the arrival of the friend. To this belongs the perception of all signs which could point to this arrival — of all that happens at the place where we believe he will come. Far beyond this theme, however, lies the casual perception of a house, a group of trees which I see standing somewhere, the song of a bird in the trees, and the like.

Needless to say, we do not have in mind here those cases in which we are so distracted that no act of taking cognizance occurs, even though our senses are affected by external stimuli. What we have in mind is a real grasping, but one which proceeds completely unthematically. In the situations which we have in mind here, casual impressions take place whereby we take cognizance of something, but in them neither the object known nor knowledge about the object is thematic.

This completely unthematic, naïve contact with being is very far removed from philosophical taking cognizance of something. It is so precisely because it lacks the thematic touch.

We might add that this naïve grasping it a fortiori completely uncritical. Whenever taking cognizance is in no way thematic we reach the climax of uncritical, naïve acceptance of the aspects of an object.

Another type of naïve taking cognizance is ordinary acquaintance with a content, as when one sees a color for the first time or meets another person for the first time. Here knowledge is tacitly thematic, but, in opposition to a philosophical contact with being, there is no explicit awareness that knowledge is thematic, there is no tension between the "how-is-it" and the "it-is-so." It is a simple naïve acquaintance with a content. Yet, in comparison to those situations wherein objects are only casually perceived, the content of knowledge is here a matter of conscious grasping.

When someone sees a landscape for the first time, it is usually not with the explicit intention to get acquainted with it, but rather with the attitude of a child whom we take for a walk. He grasps certain features of the landscape, acquiring a knowledge about it, but all this without the inner question: "How is it?" and likewise without the answer: "It is so." There is only the naïve taking in of the existence of an object together with its nature.

Such naïve knowledge is clearly different from philosophical knowledge. First, the explicit theme of knowledge is absent; second, there is no critical attitude which seeks to push forward an ascertained identification of a being in its true essence and which, consequently, questions the aspect given in perception.

There are, furthermore, far-reaching areas of naïve knowledge which differ from philosophical knowledge because of their pragmatic character. Very often our naïve grasp of something is closely linked with the accomplishment of practical purposes. As we search for ways and means to reach a practical goal, we frequently make various observations and perceive different aspects of an object. A prisoner, for example, discovers a window through which he hopes to escape. The window as such is not too interesting to him. It is only a means for his escape. The knowledge of the nature of the room is not in itself thematic for him. In a secondary way, however, it is, because an eminently practical feature, which as such lies completely beyond the theme of knowledge, coincides with a certain part of the nature of the room, inasmuch as the very possibility of escape depends upon the character of the room.

Again, a thirsty man is seeking water and suddenly perceives a well. The perception of the state of facts, namely, "Here is a well," is even accomplished with acute attention. It has a distinctly thematic quality, not, however, in itself, but only secondarily for the sake of quenching his thirst.

If a cook notices that "the water is now boiling," this fact is distinctly perceived. Nevertheless, it is not only completely imbedded in the accomplishment of a practical purpose, but the actuality of this state of affairs has interest and importance only insofar as it is a means for a practical end. The knowledge of this state of affairs has, therefore, only a secondary thematic character.

Philosophical taking cognizance of something differs in a twofold way from all naïve knowledge that bears a pragmatic character. First, in the latter, the knowledge in question is only secondarily thematic. The question: "How is it?" is not thematic as such, but only insofar as it is an indispensable prerequisite for the accomplishment of a practical end. This implies an essentially different attitude toward the object than is found in a philosophical approach to it. The object in itself is not taken with full seriousness. It is purely secondary to my interest. Second, and more important, pragmatic taking cognizance of something is necessarily one-sided. It favors the knowledge of those characteristics of the object in question which are important for a practical purpose. One perceives only what is important from the standpoint of practical application.

The cook does not ask what kind of process is involved in boiling water. He is interested only in finding out when the water will boil, how he can make it boil, what he can do with it in the preparation of foods, and so forth. The thirsty man perceives only that "there is water which is drinkable." Many other aspects of the object are unconsciously or, perhaps, even consciously passed over. If, before going outside, we observe the weather in order to dress properly, only so much of the situation discloses itself to our spiritual glance as is required for us to determine what clothes to wear. The beautiful lighting of the sky, the special formation of the clouds — these are very easily overlooked at this moment.

The pragmatic attitude is, on the one hand, a classical stimulus which leads to certain discoveries; on the other hand, however, it necessarily leads to a prejudiced limitation of our knowledge, in that it limits our perception to only one small section of a being. It lets us see only so much of the object as is necessary for a specific practical end. This one-sidedness, moreover, is dictated chiefly by relatively subjective points of view, and the preference of certain elements is by no means determined by that which constitutes the main theme of the object as such. This pragmatic deformation is particularly opposed to philosophical cognizance, which seeks to understand the object in its own, deepest sense. Furthermore, philosophy aims to understand the object in its objective relation to other objects. Hence, it is not limited by subjective practical intentions. The prerequisite for all philosophical taking cognizance of something is a full interest in the object as such and in the knowing contact with it. Pragmatic naïve perception does indeed possess a certain explicit thematicity, in contrast to the two forms of naïve perception mentioned previously. Nonetheless, it is equally distant from philosophical taking cognizance of something, perhaps even more so.

When we speak of the thematicity of knowledge we have

to distinguish, furthermore, between two different aspects, namely, the thematicity of the object itself, and the thematicity of knowledge itself. The latter, which makes the process of knowledge to be thematic, implies that our interest is focused on the acquiring of knowledge as such, that we aim for a most complete, most certain, and most accurate knowledge. This thematicity of knowledge may display itself in different ways. Not only may it embrace the perfection of the knowledge, it may also look in the direction of a sound and lasting knowledge. Consider, for example, those learning experiences in which we intend to acquire knowledge of a language, of a history, or of any science. In these cases, the gaining of knowledge as such is the theme, and the theme goes in the direction of a sound and lasting possession of the object through knowledge.

It is evident, of course, that no knowledge can exist unless the object also exercises a certain thematic role. By its very nature knowledge is directed toward the object and is concerned with the object. The very character of an intentional partaking of the nature of the object, of a spiritual possession of it, excludes the possibility of a knowledge in which the object is in no way thematic.

Nevertheless, this object-thematicity covers a wide range. In some cases it is all but subdued and, in others, it is all important. When we want to know whether or not a person whom we love is sick, the object of our knowledge is dramatically thematic, far surpassing the thematic character of the knowledge itself. But, in contrast to a situation like this, the thematic nature of the object is relatively small compared with that of knowledge in the case of a philologist when he examines minutely the authenticity of a passage which has little interest in itself.

Later on we shall return to this distinction between object-thematicity and knowledge-thematicity. We have mentioned this distinction here, although briefly, because of the important role it plays in distinguishing naïve knowledge from scientific knowledge.

In the naïve type of cognizance which is purely inattentive and nonexplicit, neither the object itself nor knowledge of the object is thematic. In the second form of naïve knowledge, that exemplified by the simple acquaintance with an object, there is no explicit thematicity either of the object or the knowledge. At most we can speak of a tacit thematicity. In pragmatic, naïve perception, the object, as we have seen, is not itself thematic, but is so only secondarily, that is, as a means for achieving some purpose which is more or less explicitly thematic. To an even greater degree is knowledge of the object only secondarily thematic in such pragmatic perceptions. It is secondary not merely in the sense of being knowledge which serves as a handmaid for something else, but it is also secondary in the sense that such knowledge is merely a prerequisite for an extratheoretical theme, namely, the purpose we have in mind. Everything is subordinated to the practical goal which is of primary importance.

There is, however, another form of naïve perception in which the object about which knowledge is sought is independently thematic, although there is no independent knowledge-thematicity. This is always the case when we deal with the perception of a fact which, because it possesses either an importance in itself or an importance for me, implies an active intervention on my part.

For example, we see a man whose life is in danger. As soon as we have grasped this fact we rush to help him. In taking cognizance of such a fact, however, there is no thematicity of knowledge, and thus such cognizance is very different from scientific and, even more so, philosophical knowledge. But the perceived state of facts is highly thematic in itself. It dominates the whole situation. Its existence is grasped, therefore, with the highest emphasis, and it interests us entirely as such. It is taken completely seriously and plays a role very different from that of a mere means. To be sure, there is also a question of means here. We are also concerned with the distance between the man and ourselves and with the availability of life preservers, ropes, and the like, which we might throw out to him — in short, with the different means to help him. Taking cognizance of these possible means is specifically pragmatic and clearly differs from the original grasping of the fact that the man's life is in danger.

In cases of pragmatic knowledge, there is no independent thematicity either of object or of knowledge. In taking cognizance of a fact such as that exemplified by the man whose life is in danger, however, only the knowledge has no independent thematicity. The object, on the other hand, possesses a full and dramatic thematicity. This difference has far-reaching consequences for the completeness of the disclosure of the object. Here, in the case of the drowning man, there is no pragmatic deformation of the knowledge of the object. Likewise, there is no artificial limitation of those elements within the object to include only those features which are significant for my special purpose. It is true that in the case of the drowning man, the object is perceived only to the extent that its decisive importance is understood in its full actuality. After this, the mind is entirely absorbed in taking active measures to help the man. Nevertheless, the decisive importance of the object is the meaningful center of the whole situation. Here the thematicity of the object prejudices the completeness but not the depth of the cognition. Furthermore, this limit on completeness is rooted in the objective meaning of the thing and is not subjectively imposed as it was in the case of purely pragmatic knowledge. On the other hand, we must sharply distinguish philosophical knowledge even from this form of naïve perception, which, although not imbedded in the basically practical attitude, engenders it and transforms us from one who simply takes cognizance of something to one who acts. For here there is no thematicity of knowledge itself. In other words, we are not here primarily concerned with acquiring knowledge; knowledge as such is not of principal importance.

In this example, it is true, we discuss an extraordinary case. Even so, this type of a nonpragmatic, but practical, attitude, which is engendered by taking cognizance of the matter involved, plays a great role in our naïve contact with objects. For it need not always be a situation of such gravity and such intense actuality. In principle the same type of taking cognizance exists when I grasp any fact endowed with a value or a disvalue, which suggests, according to its meaning, an action on my part.

All of these forms of naïve taking cognizance of something differ from philosophical knowing in many respects, although the difference is not everywhere the same.

They differ in that, first, they lack the explicit thematicity of taking cognizance; second, they are uncritical; and, third, they are unsystematic.

Another form of naïve taking cognizance is present when we want to gain an explicit acquaintance with something, perhaps to enjoy it or to enter into any relation with it having a contemplative character not rooted in knowledge.

Suppose we are traveling to a country in order to get acquainted with it. Unlike the explorer, we do not consider the country primarily as an object of *knowledge* for us. For the explorer, taking cognizance as such is thematic. For us, however, the object and the contemplative possession of it are primarily the themes. Again, we are happy to make the acquaintance of a man about whom we have heard much. We finally get the chance to meet him. We get acquainted with him and gaze into his face with interest. We note his behavior, his whole personality. Taking cognizance of him is clearly intended and is to a certain extent explicit. Nor is it pragmatic, as when

THE NATURE OF PHILOSOPHICAL KNOWLEDGE

a judge or detective seeks to get acquainted with a man, in order to "see through" him. Furthermore, it is not limited to grasping a certain important content which at once tends toward a practical intervention. Finally, it is not a matter-of-course knowing, but a grasping born out of a man's interest. At times it entails a wondering awareness of the other man's personality. Even if the thematicity of the object prevails, there is not lacking here a certain thematicity of knowledge. And yet this form of naïve taking cognizance is also quite different from that proper to philosophical knowledge.

The difference should be apparent. This form of naïve taking cognizance already differs from the merely historical investigation into a personality since it is marked by a lesser thematicity of knowledge and the lack of a systematic and critical method. But when we contrast it to philosophical knowledge there is the added difference that it lacks both the depth-dimension and the focal direction of philosophy. Philosophy looks toward the general and essential. Philosophy is different because of its completely different object of knowledge and because its starting position has emerged from the whirl of actual life. As we shall see later on, this emerging from the whirl of actual life in no way prejudices or contradicts the existential contact with being which philosophy presupposes.

There is, however, in naïve knowledge, a still higher form of taking cognizance. We refer to those rare cases in which, at a special moment, the essence of something becomes crystal-clear to us. Thus, in a certain situation we may behold with marvelous clarity the very character of a personality, or the genius of a nation or of a work of art, or an ethical value like fidelity and veracity, or the essence of love, or an essential fact like the transient character of all things earthly. Such rare moments occur when there is a fertile contact of our mind with being, when being speaks to us as from its very depth, when we touch reality in the liveliest and most organic manner. Obviously these moments are not given to every man in his lifetime. They occur only in the life of a spiritually awake and deep personality. In addition, these moments in naïve experience refer exclusively to important objects, possessing a high content of meaning and value. They may be found in the lives of great artists and ethical personalities and likewise in the prephilosophical contact of genuine philosophers with being. This superior form of naïve taking cognizance is by far the nearest thing to philosophical taking cognizance. It is even more related to it than all strictly scientific knowledge. These moments we might call the philosophical moments in life. In the case of this kind of taking cognizance there is a high thematicity of the object as well as of knowledge itself. The latter is here completely unpragmatic. Indeed, it is even lifted above the actuality of fleeting, temporal existence. In it we momentarily gain, as it were, the contemplative place of pure philosophical knowledge, a place related to eternity. The insight given in this rare moment might bear the character of an essential truth. In any case it always takes a direction toward depth. Despite these similarities, however, it still differs from philosophical knowledge because it is uncritical and unsystematic.

We may summarize our results thus far. We have seen how philosophical knowledge is distinguished from prescientific, naïve knowledge in all its forms. The first type of naïve knowledge is completely casual and unthematic, whereas philosophical cognition is always thematic. The second type of naïve cognition, the ordinary acquaintance with an object, is only implicitly thematic, whereas philosophical knowledge is always explicitly so. In the third type of naïve taking cognizance of something, the goal is always some pragmatic end, which completely dominates and rules the situation, with the result that the knowledge gained is always partial and one-sided, whereas philosophical knowledge is completely unpragmatic and is concerned with the totality of the object. A fourth type of naïve

THE NATURE OF PHILOSOPHICAL KNOWLEDGE   49

knowledge entails a situation of practical and immediate importance; in it the object to be known is of immense value, either in itself or to us, and hence there is present here a thematicity of the object, but there is no explicit or independent thematicity of knowledge itself; philosophy, on the other hand, entails the highest thematicity both of the object and of the knowledge itself. Besides this, philosophical knowledge differs from all these forms by reason of its critical and systematic character. The fifth type of naïve taking cognizance of something entails the thematicity of the object and also a certain thematicity of knowledge, but the latter is imbedded only in a concrete, existential situation and it thereby lacks the direction toward the general and the typical,[1] and also the direction toward depth. Philosophical knowledge, on the contrary, always implies a certain spiritual distance from the concrete, existential objects of experience. It is directed always toward the general and the typical, and it aims at delving into the depth of the object. Moreover, contrary to naïve knowledge, it is always critical and systematic.[2] Finally, it may be that a form of naïve taking cognizance of something has the full thematicity both of the object and of knowledge, and aims also at the depth-dimension and the position of distance from the actuality of life, and can even be directed toward the general and the typical, but it is still uncritical and unsystematic. By way of contrast, philosophical knowledge not only has the highest thematicity both of the object and of knowledge, not only is completely unpragmatic, not only aims in the direction of depth

---

[1] The term *typical* is used here to translate the German *principiell*. Thus, to know something *principiell* is to know it in principle — to know its "type" or "logos."

[2] In claiming that philosophical knowledge is essentially systematical, we do not mean to imply that the philosopher must aim at building up a system. On the contrary, in the Prolegomena to *Christian Ethics*, we stressed the danger of premature systematization. We mean by systematical knowledge a knowledge which displays itself not in aphorisms, in the formulation of an occasional and special truth, but one which proceeds step by step in the exploration of a topic, in a conscious, ordered manner, confronting every new insight with the former.

and toward the general and typical, not only possesses the perfection of a standpoint related to eternity, and not only is more distant from the existential situations of actual living, but it is also always critical and always systematic.

2. Theoretical prescientific knowledge

Prescientific and prephilosophical knowledge is, however, as we have already seen, not limited to a naïve existential contact with an object. It includes also a reflective and cognitive relation to an object, and this we can no longer call naïve in the full sense of the word. If we think about a saying or a phrase of a wise man or a poet, or about a conviction concerning the validity of certain rules of life, or about the conscious views of the average man and his theoretical sayings about the world, we find that the genesis of these convictions and judgments is completely different from a naïve taking cognizance of an object. Here we have not only knowledge which is directed exclusively to a state of facts but which has also grown out of thinking and inferences, instead of perceptions. In addition, we deliberately leave out of consideration here the appropriation of views from authoritative or hypnotizing influential personalities, from tradition and from public opinion. Despite the great role of such appropriation in the accomplishment of this prescientific and prephilosophical world-picture, there is in it no real knowledge and least of all philosophical knowledge.

Within the framework of prescientific and prephilosophical knowledge are, therefore, two world-views, the one naïve and the other theoretical. If we now limit ourselves to the knowledge which gives rise to a theoretical world-view, we can appreciate that the position it takes toward being is completely different from that of a naïve contact. One here remains no longer within the sphere of a natural contact that comes as a matter of course. Rather, one approaches reality with a theoretical attitude. One does not allow the object itself to speak. Instead, one tries to

THE NATURE OF PHILOSOPHICAL KNOWLEDGE

acquire a quasi-systematical knowledge of it by observations, reflections, and inferences.

If we think of such a proverb as, "Pride goeth before a fall," or of the words of Ovid, "*Donec eris felix, multos numerabis amicos,*" or of what people formulate as their views about life and morality, or of what men say theoretically about women, we can easily see the difference between such sayings and theories and the various naïve forms of taking cognizance. Such statements are, first, of a general and typical nature, and, second, they spring from an attitude of theoretical knowledge. Man presses upon a new spiritual key, as it were, a key radically different from that of naïve taking cognizance of something. He steps toward the object with an intention to gain theoretical knowledge. Finally, there is the natural concomitant to this attitude which gives rise to a third difference: an explicit thematicity of knowledge dominates the situation.

In this respect, therefore, theoretical prescientific knowledge is more similar than naïve knowledge to philosophical knowledge. We will see, however, that in another respect it is more different from philosophical knowledge than are certain forms of naïve cognition.

It differs most of all from philosophical knowledge by its lack of systematic and critical characteristics. It always bears the character of a mere aphorism, despite its direction toward the general and typical. Such general sentences are "scattered around," and they stand without being embedded in a systematic sequence of objects and proofs. It is uncritical, inasmuch as one proceeds neither from evident insights nor from a careful, critical selection of facts. The inferences are not made sharply and critically. The lack of being critical is far more serious here than in the case of naïve knowledge. The reason why this is true is that here a claim is made that the knowledge is theoretical and typical. This demands a more critical caution than does naïve knowledge. Moreover, without such a critical attitude here the results are far more dubious, because they are more distant from the thing in question, because the process of knowledge is much more complicated, and because the language of being undergoes greater refraction before it at length becomes formulated.

Within the framework of this theoretical prescientific knowledge, however, we must distinguish between two essentially different kinds: organic and inorganic knowledge. In proverbs and sayings of wise men and poets we find the organic theoretical prephilosophical knowledge. There is a relatively organic path here which leads from naïve taking cognizance of something to a more general and theoretical awareness. Perhaps these sayings and inductive conclusions stem from an incisive and important experience of one's own life, or they may be the results of what one often observes here and there. In any event, they are always an organic outgrowth of a naïve taking cognizance of something. The reflections are consequent upon it. They are, as it were, the theoretical awareness of impressions condensed from a naïve knowledge.

As long as a person, during times of misfortunes, merely endures many disappointments at the hands of his fellow men, he simply perceives the fact that one is left alone in misfortune. He may even infer, on a nontheoretical level, that this fact is true in general, but still his knowledge remains on the plane of a naïve living contact. As soon, however, as he wishes to emphasize the general truth, as soon as this fact takes on the character of a proverb, with its outspoken thematicity of knowledge, he quits the level of naïve knowledge. A completely new consciousness begins, which goes far beyond a naïve knowledge-contact with an object. Nevertheless, this prominent conscious awareness of the general fact is linked in an organic way to the naïve cognizance of it.

If a man "reasons" about life, moral values, art, and so forth, without relating his mind to the language of the objects he has

THE NATURE OF PHILOSOPHICAL KNOWLEDGE

perceived in a naïve cognizance, then we are presented with another, an *inorganic*, type of prescientific knowledge — or, to speak more correctly, with what we should call extrascientific and extraphilosophical knowledge.

Let us think of a man who, in his naïve living contact with reality, grasps clearly the majestic and absolute character of moral values, and who responds with enthusiasm to positive values and with indignation to negative ones, with complete seriousness and decision; who, however, as soon as he speaks theoretically about the sphere of morality, affirms in sincere conviction that moral values are relative to time and persons, or that they are mere projections of subjective feelings. He is not aware of any contradiction between his naïve cognizance and his theoretical convictions. This shows not only that we have here different spiritual keys in naïve and theoretical cognitions, but also that the theoretical key has lost all organic contact with the naïve knowledge and that, consequently, it draws from sources quite different from those given in the naïve contact.

The wells from which these theoretical views flow are many. We prescind now from those cases in which we simply repeat what we have somewhere read or heard about this or that object, that is to say, what was unconsciously taken over as public opinion or the common knowledge of an epoch. For this does not deserve the name of knowledge. We limit ourselves to those cases in which we actually think about an object, in which we, on the basis of certain premises, infer this or that about an object, or else have recourse to certain arguments which we learned from someone else and which seem obvious. In fine, we limit ourselves to those cases wherein we still have knowledge in the broadest sense of the word. This kind of theoretical knowledge comes either from a certain scientific or philosophical thesis which has percolated down into the general common culture and has been taken over unconsciously, or from prejudices of the public mind, or, again, from so-called personal experiences which here, however, have a completely different function than in the case of the organic form of theoretical knowledge. In the organic form, it is true, a single experience may lead to a generalization. Thus, if a person is seriously disappointed in one of his fellow men he may develop an unjustified general mistrust of all men. Because his single experience had such an incisive emotional importance, he may cry with full conviction: "Every man is a liar!" But in the case of the inorganic form of theorizing, a single experience is simply the starting point for the theoretical key's coming into play. The experience is made into a generalization, not because of the weight it has in naïve living contact, but because of the generalizing tendency of the theoretical attitude.

"Oh! I know these people!" someone may say of another nation. "They are superficial." If you ask why, he will answer: "I once knew a man from this nation and he was very superficial." Men who tend toward this type of reasoning allow certain facts, which they know from naïve cognition, to fall right into their theoretical attitude, and they proceed to employ these facts merely as examples for their uncritical induction.

It is obvious that the link to naïve cognition is of an essentially different nature here than in the organic type of theoretical knowledge. The language of being, heard in naïve cognizance, is not found at all in the results of theoretical reasoning of the inorganic kind, even when it proceeds to a generalization from a so-called fact which has been experienced. For facts like these are employed completely "from without" in the theory. They are used in a way similar to that in which an experiment is employed to verify a theory, but uncritically. The close contact with the things themselves, which is an integral part of naïve cognizance, is absent here. We grasp here only so much of the object as can satisfy the capacity of this theoretical key.

THE NATURE OF PHILOSOPHICAL KNOWLEDGE 55

All statements, even those made in the presence of the object, have an analogous character. They are already at a theoretical distance from the object. They are laid down by a "reason" starting from an arrogantly superior, and at the same time, very uncritical position. It is apparent that this theoretical knowledge is inorganic. Not linked to the original naïve cognition, it sovereignly disregards it. This inorganic knowledge approaches the object only "from without" and with no direct contact with the object. In the case of this kind of extrascientific and extraphilosophical theoretical knowledge, either the naïve contact is consciously omitted — and this is falsely believed by some people to be especially critical — or the naïve contact is unconsciously ignored, and this is characteristic of the man who always proceeds from general, apparently evident, facts and deduces everything from them.

Someone might argue as follows: "All ethical values are relative, for different people and different epochs have often held wholly opposite views on the goodness and badness of one and the same moral datum." Here, ignoring completely the aspect of value present in the naïve contact with the object, one reasons in a wholly uncritical way from a premise that is taken over from another person with no profound understanding of the real meaning of the statement. For, in truth, the differences over what is good and bad do not as such prejudge anything about the relativity of value. Again, someone may argue: "All values are relative, for we cannot know more than what appears to be so. But insofar as we know anything it is always relative to our subjective ability of knowing." Here an allegedly self-evident proposition, born of a false philosophy, is accepted as a premise without any spirit of criticism by one who thinks he is especially critical in that he has lifted himself above the aspect present in the naïve contact with the object. In one moment he might be indignant about the moral actions of a man, and, by being indignant, he actually deals with moral values as something objective. In the very next moment, however, he either does not consider his former indignation or, if he does, he believes it to be of little consequence. This type of man is essentially committed to the belief that his theoretical knowledge, concluded from loose reasoning and unexamined premises, is much more worthy of trust than is his naïve cognizance of something.

This inorganic, theoretical prescientific knowledge is the home of all dilettantism, all *apparently* self-evident propositions, all "short cuts" to knowledge, all shabby rationalistic theorizing. The lack of being critical has here an essentially more disastrous effect than in the case of naïve cognition and even than in the case of organic theoretical knowledge. For we actualize here an intellectual key, the importance of which stands or falls with the degree of genuine criticism attached to it. The naïve cognizance of something possesses the classic note of a real contact with being, and as such retains a certain interest even when it includes a delusion or error. It still reflects something of the nature of the object, even though in a form that needs mending and refining. The organic type of theoretical knowledge has, of course, a much better opportunity to reach a truth than does the inorganic type. But even apart from this important superiority, we must notice that the organic type possesses, as such, a real interest in that it is not only knowledge but it is also a reflection of a genuine personality. For in it still lives something of the naïve contact with the object, something of its classic note, even though in a much more refracted form than in the naïve cognizance of the object. The uprooted form, however, of the knowing contact with the object, in which the mind emancipates itself from all naïve existential contacts and relies completely upon its theoretical ability of knowing, becomes a caricature of genuine knowledge because it lacks genuine criticism and system. It commands no interest at all.

THE NATURE OF PHILOSOPHICAL KNOWLEDGE 57

As long as someone really gives back what he grasps in his naïve cognition or, if he at least utters general convictions which are linked organically to a naïve form of knowledge, then what he says is of interest and may be taken seriously. As soon, however, as someone starts to reason theoretically about the world and about different spheres of being with complete elimination of the naïve, lived contact with reality, and, furthermore, proceeds uncritically and unsystematically, his utterances lose every objective interest. The actual lack of criticism convicts this "knowledge" in a damaging way because of its inner pretension to be critical. In naïve cognition also this "reasoning" often creeps in suddenly. For example, someone may try to prove or substantiate his naïve impression of a thing. By his intention to prove or substantiate he initiates an attitude which cuts off the naïve contact with being and which switches him, as it were, to the theorizing key. He reverts to simply known general facts and from these he sweepingly draws conclusions over the voice that speaks to him in the naïve contact with being. This vain attempt to ground or prove a theoretical truth destroys all real contact with the object and plunges the mind down to the unfertile level of reasoning without criticism.

The difference separating both these forms of extraphilosophical theoretical knowledge from philosophy is apparent. They lack all criticism and system. But the lack of criticism is of a different kind in each case and it differs according to the form of the extrascientific and extraphilosophical knowledge.

a) In the organic form, the uncritical note lies in that one fails to test the theoretical generalization against the naïve contact with being, and thereby fails to reach the unequivocal concrete "givenness" of the object, as is done in real philosophical knowledge. Instead, what is given in the naïve living contact, with all its subjective and pragmatic limitations and its accidental one-sidedness, is simply raised to the plane of the theoretical and typical. In the case of philosophical knowledge, the thing experienced itself, brought to a pure and fertile intuition, is the decisive factor determining all the aspects which flow from the naïve cognizance of that thing. In this way, by joining such an attitude to the highest form of naïve cognition, we accomplish an essential, luminous contact with the object and we allow only the unequivocally self-identical object to decide upon the true state of facts.

Philosophical knowledge points to an evident "given" in reality. The critical character of philosophical knowledge is decisively marked by its clear distinction between evidence and non-evidence and its clarity about the respective stages of "givenness." The deciding point lies here. Certainty is granted to the extent that knowledge of a respective state of facts coincides either with the degree to which this state is "given" or with the strictness of its indirect disclosure — its deduction.

When it is a question of the organic form of prescientific theoretical knowledge, on the other hand, the activity of the theoretical key does not involve a fresh draught from the thing itself, purified and luminous, but only a higher stage of generality of the aspect which crystallizes out of the naïve cognition. The validity of such knowledge is, moreover, always something of an accident. The premises are not evident nor are the conclusions drawn strictly. Even if the conclusion derived in a particular case is objectively strict, this strictness is not the result of a methodical principle of this knowledge. The transition from a naïve cognition to a theoretical insight is completely unmethodical and uncritical. Philosophical knowledge, however, explicitly includes the methodological principle that we proceed only from well-founded and, if possible, evident premises, and that we infer only strict conclusions. The awareness of this method need not, however, imply that in every concrete case a philosopher is fully conscious of the specific process of knowledge which he uses.

Thus, in the opinions of the great philosophers, we often

THE NATURE OF PHILOSOPHICAL KNOWLEDGE

find that they claim to have deduced something when in truth they have grasped it directly and intuitively. This is certainly an imperfection — not, however, one which takes away from the knowledge its philosophical character.

In the case of genuine philosophical knowledge there must always be a methodical consciousness; that is the questions of the degree of givenness and of the strictness of conclusion must be explicitly posed. Moreover, one must be fully conscious of the degree he has reached.

The examination of the givenness of a state of facts and the strictness of a conclusion is an outspoken methodical principle of any scientific and, even more so, of any philosophical knowledge.

b) Lack of criticism in the inorganic form of extrascientific theoretical knowledge goes much further. It is first represented by the completely vague basis from which the hoped-for knowledge is to be gained. This already signifies a lack of criticism of the worst sort. In place of a naïve living contact with the object are more or less undigested general philosophical and scientific propositions, or even arbitrary generalizations of single observations. For the most part here we are dealing with the unperceived influences of certain philosophical or scientific theses, which impregnate, as it were, the intellectual atmosphere and pervade the *Zeitgeist* and which now, because they have been taken over unconsciously, are confused with the indisputable, self-evident, ultimate points of departure, that is, with principles in the strict sense of the word.

The allegedly self-evident fund on which we draw does not derive from the language of the object afforded by naïve knowledge, however inadequate, nor even from an object that is pragmatically deformed for the most part. It is rather a maze of theoretical theses which in their structure appeal to a conscious critical understanding in a totally different way. Their acceptance as indisputable, self-evident, and settled points of departure, therefore, represents a lack of criticism of a completely new and even more fateful kind.

Even when general propositions are taken over consciously, without, however, an examination of the object, because of a certain *apparent* self-evidence, there is a complete lack of criticism displayed. They are consciously declared to be axioms, and the pretension is that these general propositions are self-evident. The lack of criticism here is unpardonable because one is here deliberately theoretical and yet takes over, as self-evident, propositions which are snatched from their context and which are definitely not self-evident. One intends to begin with no presuppositions and, at the same time, one actually presupposes an entire philosophical theory, in addition to many scientific theses which are wrongly relegated to the metaphysical plane as absolutely certain axioms. One fails to see that these so-called axioms are not evident facts, but are rather the complicated results of a certain theory. The utter lack of criticism is particularly manifest in the perfect self-delusion represented by this knowledge.

Philosophical knowledge, which does not take over as self-evident even those aspects of the object which present themselves to us in naïve cognition, never tacitly relies on such general propositions, which can say nothing more for their validity than that they seem to be familiar and also that, because of custom, they seem to be too self-evident to be examined critically. True philosophy intends to tolerate neither conscious nor unconscious presuppositions which do not place their credentials before the tribunal of knowledge. It is linked, moreover, in an entirely different way to a naïve contact with the object. Unlike inorganic theoretical knowledge, philosophy does not eliminate naïve contact with the object. On the contrary, it deepens and purifies it. Philosophy, therefore, is linked to the highest form of naïve cognition insofar as it seeks to penetrate to an even deeper and more unequivocal givenness of the object than is present in naïve cognizance of it. Extra philosophical reasoning, on the other hand, either consciously or unconsciously gives up all contact with the object.

The difference, then, between philosophical knowledge and both forms of theoretical prescientific knowledge, the organic and the inorganic, is apparent. The former is a critical, methodical, and systematic knowledge proceeding from the full but purified nonpragmatic contact with the object.

In passing we might mention, as a supplement to our criticism of inorganic extrascientific knowledge, that it lacks a real link to genuine tradition. The seriousness of this will appear later on when we discuss the nature of the link to tradition.

Certain general theses of dubious philosophies percolate into the world-view of the unphilosophical average man. These doubtful theses often figure as points of departure for that inorganic reasoning about life and the world which we discussed above. To be sharply distinguished from this, however, is the classical penetration by philosophical elements into a naïve world-view. For this indeed belongs to the very meaning and task of philosophy. The infiltrations differ in the kind of influence they exert on world-views and likewise in the organ with which the unphilosophical man accepts the results. Only the relatively unconscious process of accepting these views is common, for in each case there is a marked absence of autonomous, critical knowledge. Yet, even if we prescind from the content-character of what is passed along, we perceive a thoroughgoing formal difference between the diffusion of the genuine tradition of philosophical results into the public mind and the illegitimate infiltration of pseudo-philosophical theories. And this difference is manifest as much in the type of transfer of the thing taken over as in the kind of accepting it on the part of the unphilosophical man.

Philosophical knowledge, then, is sharply distinguished from each form of prescientific and extrascientific knowledge. We are now faced with the difficult problem of separating philosophical knowledge from the knowledge embodied in all the other true sciences. Before we turn to this theme, however, we must delve further into the question concerning the object of philosophy. For the nature of philosophical inquiry and knowledge is understandable only in the light of the nature of the object of philosophy. In what follows we have the twofold task of pointing out the object of philosophy and of pointing out the nature of philosophizing, in contrast to all other forms of scientific knowledge.

CHAPTER IV

THE OBJECT OF PHILOSOPHICAL KNOWLEDGE

The object of philosophy is primarily of an apriori nature. A specific characteristic of philosophical knowledge is its principal aim, namely, to discover apriori and not empirical states of facts. This brings us face to face with a very decisive point, forcing us to give a detailed account of two classical conceptions, namely, the apriori and the empirical. For in truth, each of these concepts is ambiguous.

Even if all the meanings of apriori and empirical rest on some common note, since both are used to refer to a point of departure, still they ordinarily include other elements. In general, the meaning of the apriori and the empirical is not only equivocal but confused. It often happens that certain elements usually associated with these terms are considered to be necessarily connected with them, although in reality they are completely independent. We must, therefore, attach a clear meaning to each of these concepts.

1. *The characteristics of apriori knowledge*

Classical examples of apriori knowledge are taken mostly from the sphere of Euclidean mathematics or else from logic. Apriori knowledge in the genuine sense, however, is by no means limited to mathematics and logic. We shall not, therefore, restrict ourselves to these spheres in our examples of apriori truths, but from the very start we shall introduce the most striking types taken from other areas. Propositions such as "Justice cannot be attributed to impersonal beings" or "One and the same thing cannot exist and not exist simultaneously" are set apart by three unmistakable marks: (1) their strict intrinsic necessity, (2) their incomparable intelligibility, and (3) their absolute certainty. For these reasons, they possess a special dignity in knowledge. The note of strict necessity is related to the very nature of the state of facts. The note of high intelligibility also characterizes the state of facts, yet it also includes a relation to a possible knowledge. The note of absolute certainty, however, is related to the way in which the state of facts is given, to the manner in which the object presents its credentials to our mind. All three characteristics, the necessity of the state of facts, its intelligibility, and the absolute certainty of its existence, point to a knowledge of the highest dignity. Facts which can be seen with absolute certainty in their necessity and intelligibility are an ideal case for knowledge. Herein lies the decisive point of departure for the deep abyss which separates apriori from empirical knowledge.

The great achievement of Plato in his *Meno* was the discovery that within the sphere of knowledge there are cases in which we grasp with absolute certainty a necessary and highly intelligible state of facts. He saw how these cases differed profoundly from all other kinds of knowledge, and he appreciated the decisive importance of this distinction within the total sphere of knowledge.

A. Strict Necessity

In order to separate apriori from empirical knowledge, we shall examine the first characteristic of the former, i.e., its strict necessity. We shall try to point out, first, the necessity as such and, second, the strict intrinsic necessity as rooted in essences.

THE OBJECT OF PHILOSOPHICAL KNOWLEDGE 65

a) As such, necessity transcends the accidental, merely factual sphere. Although not identical with the notion of the general, it possesses a kind of generality. It can mean either a formal or a structural moment. If we are confronted with two such propositions as "Caesar crossed the Rubicon in 49 B.C." and "Moral values cannot be embodied in impersonal beings," we realize that the state of facts in the first proposition is accidental; in the second, however, it is necessary. One difference between these two states of facts is that one represents an individual event and the other, a general state of facts. But besides this difference we must note a further one. In the fact, "Caesar crossed the Rubicon," the link between "Caesar" and "crossing the Rubicon" is a factual one; in the fact that "Moral values can be embodied only in persons," the link between "Moral values" and "persons" is a necessary one. This moment of necessity is an ultimate datum. It cannot be deduced from something else and, therefore, it cannot be "explained." We can only point unequivocally to it, isolating it from all neighboring moments in order to see it in itself. When there is question of a necessary state of facts, such as "Moral values can be embodied only in persons" or "Something cannot exist and not exist at the same time," the relation between the two elements within the state of facts is of a completely different nature than the merely factual, accidental relation in such facts as "Caesar crossed the Rubicon" or "The sun is shining here today." There is an inner necessity joining the elements of the former state of facts together. In instances of merely contingent states of facts this is not so. This necessity, which cannot be overlooked by any unbiased person, is, of course, essentially bound up with the *generality* of the state of facts, but it is not identical with it. The accidental state of facts is a single, individual matter. The necessary state of facts, on the other hand, is always of a general nature. It is rooted in the ideal sphere of essences and not in the concrete sphere of individuals, although it is naturally found in all concrete individuals insofar as they partake of a certain essence. Every concrete willing, for example, necessarily presupposes a consciousness of the intended state of facts, but this is simply an individual concretization of the general fact that *Nil volitum quin praecognitum* (No willing without thinking). This truth exists in the sphere of essences and, specifically, in the essences of willing and of "consciousness of" something.

As we said above, even though every necessary state of facts bears a general character, the moment of necessity is not identical with that of generality. Its meaning, its content is uniquely different from that of generality. Above all, necessity must not be confused with the formal dominion of the general over the individual and single cases which are subordinated to it. Let us illustrate this. We might say, for example, that the truth, "The table in my dining room is round," is merely factual or accidental, whereas the proposition, "No willing without thinking," is necessary. And we might assign the following reasons for our statement; the proposition about the table is merely factual, for there are other tables which are eight-cornered or square; the proposition about willing, however, is necessary because *every* concrete act of willing must be based upon some knowledge about the intended state of facts. This is true enough, but still this analysis of the two different propositions combines two different moments without distinguishing between them. There is, first of all, the necessity which is rooted in the formal dominion of a type or universal over the individual cases subsumed under it, and second, there is the other and different necessity which establishes the necessary character of a certain state of facts and which signifies necessity both in the state of facts considered universally and in the particular, individual instances of this state of facts.

These two kinds of necessity must be sharply distinguished. The *formal* necessity grounded in the relation between a genus or species and the individual is, as it were, the basis for the spiritual step which is accomplished in any deduction. This formal necessity is completely limited to the relation between the genus or species and the individuals falling under that genus or species. On the other hand, the much richer and far more profound necessity to which we refer here characterizes the *general* state of facts as such, prior to any consideration relating the general truth to an individual, concrete case exemplifying it. The truth, "No willing without thinking," is necessary in itself before we think about the fact that this is necessarily true in every concrete instance of willing.

Here, when we say, "It is necessarily so," we do not simply mean that it must be so in an individual case because it is true in general. Here we are referring to the entirely unique structure of a general state of facts as such. Naturally this necessary structure can be found equally in every individual concretization of the general state of facts. This structural inner necessity, which is characteristic of the apriori, is much more primal and fundamental than the formal necessity, which is found in the dominion of the general over the individual case. It is, moreover, the foundation of this formal necessity. For only when there is a structural, inner necessity in a general state of facts is the individual case strictly subordinated to it.

b) After this analysis of "necessity" as such, we shall now consider in detail the intrinsic, stringent necessity that is rooted in essences. We shall find how important are the differences between the stringent necessity rooted in essences and the necessity of what may be termed "laws of nature."

We have said that such states of facts as "Moral values presuppose a person" or "The color orange lies between red and yellow" or "Seven plus five equal twelve" are necessarily distinguished from such merely accidental, factual, individual states of facts as "Mont Blanc is fifteen thousand, seven hundred eighty-two feet high" or "The weather is fine today." We must add now that the necessary states of facts are likewise distinguished from the facts treated in physics and chemistry, even though the latter possess a kind of necessity.[1] The fact, "Heat causes a body to expand," is not a merely individual, concrete fact, but a general one. With respect to its "members," moreover, it differs profoundly from such a fact as, "Caesar crossed the Rubicon." For there is here a quality of necessity which goes well beyond a factual togetherness. The causal link between heating and expansion is not merely a factual bond but it has, moreover, its general and necessary foundation in the nature of heat and expansion. Such necessity, however, is manifestly different from that found in such facts as "Moral values presuppose a person" or "Seven plus five equal twelve." First of all, its necessity is not absolute, and, second, it is not intelligibly grounded in the essence[2] of the objects in question. Thus, for example, it would not be nonsensical to conceive of them as being suspended and made inoperative by an act of God — as indeed is the case with a miracle. But it would be nonsensical to conceive this of a state of facts which is necessary by its very essence. The suspension of a state of facts necessarily rooted in the essence of a being lies absolutely and essentially beyond the scope of the notion of a miracle. We may, therefore, contrast these essential states of facts to the "laws of nature."

This difference between the two is rooted in the realities themselves. It exists between the necessity of essence and the necessity of natural laws, which we may term the necessity of

---

[1] In this epistemological analysis, we prescind from the question of whether in reality these facts have the character of laws in the Newtonian sense or have a mere statistical character, as modern physics claims, because the difference between a mere statistical statement and an apriori necessary truth is obvious. The statistic interpretation of laws of physics denies precisely their character of necessity.

It would thus be of no interest to oppose our characteristic of the necessity proper to apriori truths to this statistical interpretation. And, on the other hand, whatever may be the true character of these laws of science, the comparison between apriori truths and the Newtonian conception of scientific laws retains its significance in our elaboration of the character of absolute necessity.

[2] Later on, we shall see that a specific type of intelligible essence is required as basis of these strictly necessary facts.

nature. The necessity of essence is absolute. It has its strict foundation in the essence of the thing as such. On the other hand, the necessity of nature is somehow relative to the contingency of the world. It is not impossible to assume that a body is not expanded even though it has been heated. To assume, however, that an impersonal being such as a stone could be endowed with a moral value, justice or humility for example, is — though not contradictory — intrinsically impossible.

B. Incomparable Intelligibility

The second principal character of apriori facts, namely, their incomparable intelligibility, is closely linked to their intrinsic necessity. When compared to any empirical facts, whether purely individual or a general "law of nature," an intrinsically necessary fact is seen to possess an incomparable intelligibility. We "understand" that these necessary facts are such as they are. We grasp not only *that* something is such, but also *why* it is. It is only with respect to these facts that we can speak of having an "insight" in the full sense.

Compared to this full intellectual penetration into a necessary state, the grasp of any individual fact, for instance, "Today the sun is shining" or "This table is brown," is merely a blunt observation.

There is an analogous difference between the "insight" into a necessary fact and the grasp of a law of nature which is the result of an inductive inference. We can, to be sure, reach the knowledge of the fact that "heat expands bodies," but a fact of this kind does not possess the luminous intelligibility proper to a truth such as "Moral values presuppose persons" which enables me to "understand" it to accomplish a real *intelligere*.

This *intelligere*, this understanding from within, is possible only when the knowledge of an essentially necessary fact is at stake. This "intelligibility," which allows us to grasp the fact in its inner *logos*, necessarily presupposes the essential necessity of the fact; it is even deeply rooted in it.[3]

This feature of intelligibility is, of course, related to the question of knowability, and is not purely a characteristic of the state of facts alone, as is the necessity. Nevertheless, as we said above, this intelligibility is deeply rooted in the absolute and essential necessity.

If we compare a state of facts such as "heat expands bodies" with an essentially necessary one, we see that the former lacks entirely the inner rationality and inherent meaningfulness and, consequently, the intelligibility of the latter. The naturally necessary fact is, therefore, simply what our minds can grasp "from without." We are unable to penetrate it "from within." Our minds are not able to have an insight in the full sense of the word. In contrast to the essentially necessary facts, with their inner meaningfulness and their luminous character, the laws of nature possess something of the bluntness of the merely contingent, accidental facts.

C. Absolute Certainty

A third characteristic of apriori knowledge is its absolute certainty.

Absolute certainty, as we saw, is not a mark of the state of facts as such, but rather of the relation between the state of facts and the knowledge about it. Again let us compare the propositions, "Moral values presuppose a person" and "A color presupposes extension for its existence," with the proposition, "Heat expands a body." We have absolute certainty that the first two propositions are true, whereas we regard the truth of the last one as, at best, very highly probable. Although it is improbable to the highest degree, it is nonetheless possible that one might someday discover that no causal connection really

---

[3] This does not imply, however, that every absolutely necessary fact is intelligible for us.

exists between heat and the expansion of a body, and that in all the observed cases, in which bodies do actually expand after being heated, another, so far hidden, cause can truly account for the expansion. The high degree of nonprobability that this should be the case must not blind us to the fact that it is, in principle, possible. Thus, in propositions involving a "law of nature" we do not have absolute and indubitable certainty. Matters are quite different with apriori propositions such as "Moral values presuppose a person" and "A color can never be present without extension." It is nonsense to assume that someday we may discover that these propositions are not true. Here the state of facts is unequivocally and absolutely intelligible. Here there remains no gap concerning the credentials of its reality; its reality is undoubtedly and absolutely certain. There is no possibility of any eventual "disappointment" or refutation, for the state of facts in its necessity is laid completely and absolutely bare before our mind.

This decisive difference between apriori and empirical states of facts, and the apriori and empirical propositions corresponding to them, is, of course, intimately tied up with the manner in which these types of facts can become known. Apriori knowledge is achieved by way of immediate insight into essential states of facts. This very important statement must be further proved, for it calls attention to a special characteristic which defines apriori knowledge and distinguishes it from every other type of knowledge. In addition, it shows in a special way the difference between the knowledge of the existence of an object and the knowledge of the "such-being" or essence of an object. Above all, it clarifies the difference between insight into essences and the mere observation of the existence of something.

The causal nexus between heat and the expansion of a body is not in itself "given." Only the two facts, namely, heat and the expansion of a body, which follow each other in time, are given as such. The causal connection, the "through" between both, the dependence of the expansion on the heat, is only inferred. We make this inference because we observe that, under various conditions, under artificial and controlled variations of all pertinent factors, expansion regularly follows the application of heat. The step we make in inferring this causal bond between heat and expansion is, however, not absolutely strict and without a gap. There is still room, in principle, for the possibility of error — for a hitherto unsuspected addition. We affirm that the truth of the inferred conclusion is only probable, although, in ideal cases, we regard it with the highest probability.

This is the fate of all inductive conclusions in the precise sense of the word. There may be cases involving no hidden states of facts, but still the generality and necessity of such states is simply not given. In these cases, we base our conclusion on the observation of a great many, perhaps all, factual instances, casting our conclusion in a general and "necessary" proposition. But still our conclusion is not absolutely strict, and the precise connection between the observed facts remains unknown. This is true, for example, in the case of the proposition: "No man is taller than ten feet." Although the height of any individual man is, as such, an apparently given fact, the generality of such a proposition and, above all, its dependence on the nature of man, are not given. Our conclusion, although it has been made only after a great many observations, possesses at best only a very high probability. Knowledge of these empirical, general states of facts, having the character of a contingent necessity, lacks absolute strictness; because it is attained by induction, it is not without a gap.

The knowledge of simple individual facts, such as "This table is brown" and "Today the sun is shining," does not result from induction and consequently is exempt from the gap inevitable in any induction. Yet even this type of knowledge does not possess the absolute certitude which is proper to an insight into an apriori truth. When an individual fact is grasped in isolation from the rest of experience, there is always the possibility that we may be prey of an hallucination or of a dream. This possibility of deception exists, however, only so long as a concrete fact is grasped either for the first time or as it occurs here and now.

There is no possibility of deception with respect to a fact confirmed by the continuous stream of experience. As soon as an individual fact, such as the existence of a friend or brother or of the house in which we live, is inserted into the totality of our experience of reality, and confirmed time after time, it no longer makes any sense to say that we may be deceived about it, that we meet it only in a dream or an hallucination.

Our knowledge of such reality possesses, not a mere high probability, but full certainty, if it is confirmed by and integrated with the full network of our experience of reality. The famous Cartesian doubt applies only to the isolated experience of a single concrete fact.

Yet it remains true that such confirmation is required to reach absolute certainty about contingent facts. This illustrates the difference in certainty between apriori knowledge and all empirical knowledge of individual concrete facts.

Essentially necessary and incomparably intelligible states of facts, such as "Moral values can be embodied only in a person," can be grasped with absolute certitude without recourse to confirmation by the stream of experience. Even when we consider them by themselves, isolating them from the rest of our experience, even when we restrict ourselves completely to an insight into them, we still attain an absolute certitude, a truth beyond any possible doubt.

The incomparable intelligibility of these essentially necessary facts is intimately bound up with the absolute certainty we have regarding them. They disclose themselves to our minds in their meaningful intrinsic necessity, thereby enabling us to penetrate them with our intellect. This provides an absolute certainty, an intelligible certitude, which no other knowledge possesses.

In our appreciation of the absolute certitude of apriori facts, we must also realize that these absolute, certain facts have a *general* character. Consequently, our certitude concerning them differs profoundly from the certitude we have with respect to any individual concrete fact. Only in one unique case, in the frame of concrete individual facts or of real individual existence, can we reach a similar absolute certitude. It is the case of the Augustinian "*Si fallor, sum*" or the Cartesian "*Cogito ergo sum.*" Here alone our knowledge of a concrete individual possesses the same absolute certainty as does our apriori knowledge, even without the confirmation of the total network of experiences.

Knowledge of apriori facts proceeds in a direction differing basically from empirical knowledge of contingent facts. Some apriori propositions are seen intuitively as rooted in the essence; for example, the proposition "Being and not-being exclude each other" or "Moral values cannot be embodied by a nonpersonal being." Others are deductive conclusions, like most of the geometric and arithmetical propositions. It is not necessary to prove here that such deductive conclusions are not weakened by the incompleteness which is proper and essential to conclusions gained through inductive reasoning. A deduction can lead with absolute strictness to a conclusion and afford us absolute certainty. The conclusion derived through deductive reasoning possesses the same certainty proper to the premises. The deductive process as such does not lessen certitude. The certitude of its conclusion depends upon the certitude of the premises. The insight into intelligible and necessary facts, in which immediately grasped states of facts are given, is the primary reason for the absolute certainty of apriori propositions, both deductive conclusions and, afortiori, facts immediately grasped. Of course, the "givenness" referred

THE OBJECT OF PHILOSOPHICAL KNOWLEDGE   75

to here must be free from all the imperfections which are proper to the observation of merely contingent facts. Only a "givenness" completely different from that of observation and induction can support and truly give absolute certainty.

If there is an insight into an essentially necessary and absolutely certain state of facts, there is no question of observation of actual being. Whether or not I am the victim of fantasy or hallucination or whether I am dreaming or truly perceiving, is strictly irrelevant to the reality of a necessary state of facts. Let us assume, for example, that I perceive the color orange on the fruit of the same name. In this perception I realize that this color lies, according to the order of similarity, between red and yellow. The reality of this fact is in no way jeopardized by the realization that I may later on discover that my "perception" was not a genuine perception of an actual object, but rather an hallucination. For the question, whether or not the orange color is here and now present in reality, is irrelevant to the reality of the state of facts that "Orange lies between red and yellow." To grasp the truth of the state of facts, the "such-being," the essence of the color orange must be given to me. The real, actual *existence* of the color orange, however, need not be given to me. The fact in question is grounded exclusively in the such-being of red, orange, and yellow. Its reality, therefore, is independent of the validity of my grasping real beings endowed with these three colors. This does away with the possibility of disappointment, to which all mere observations are open. It also erases any question as to the incapacity of beings to grant us absolute certainty. Here the perception has only the function of affording me the opportunity, by the unfolding of a certain such-being before my spiritual eye, to gain an insight into the truth of the state of facts. But the perception, insofar as it is an observation of an actually existing being, does not act as a proof for the knowledge of the existence of this essential state of facts. In the case of the necessity of natural laws, that is, of the merely though highly probable propositions of chemistry and physics, perception actually does take on this role of proving the truth and reality of states of facts.

If the observation that "Hydrogen and oxygen in a specific compound yield water" should be an hallucination, then the general state of facts concerning the chemical make-up of water would hang in the air. Again, if a physicist should find that the observations reporting that a body expanded when heated were all made in a dream, then the inductive conclusion affirming a causal relation between heat and the expansion of a body would not be verified. He could not then lay it down as a law of nature that "Heat expands a body."

On the other hand, the truth of an essentially necessary state of facts in no way depends on mere observations. For example, take the proposition, "An object cannot be willed unless I am conscious of it." The truth of this proposition does not depend on whether my grasp and clarification of willing concerned a real willing or simply an imagined one. It does not matter whether I realized this truth in a dream or while I was awake. If in a dream I clearly and distinctly grasp willing in its such-being, so that I grasp as evident this state of facts to be essentially rooted in the such-being, then my knowledge is as valid and as certain as it would have been if I had been awake all the time. For, whether awake or sleeping, I have grasped a necessary fact which I understand to be rooted in the essence of willing and not in the actual, here-and-now existence of this or that act of willing.

States of facts which are essentially necessary and immediately understood are in reality completely independent of actual existence here and now. An essence is given to me. In it are grounded necessary states of facts, and in it, in the "givenness" of the essence, I understand these necessary facts. In other words, facts of this kind require only the "givenness" of a

THE OBJECT OF PHILOSOPHICAL KNOWLEDGE 77

such-being, and not an existential status to be grasped. And for precisely this reason, they are knowable with absolute certainty, for they transcend the essential possibility of deception and disappointment which attaches to existentially situated objects. At the same time, moreover, we also know, when we have perceived such essentially necessary states of facts, that they are binding for each instance in which a real, concrete object of this type may be found in reality; that is, we know that each case will verify the general truth. A single example, perhaps even a merely imagined example, can afford us certain insight into the truth of an essentially necessary state of facts. This single example is enough to give us the absolutely certain knowledge that in all possible cases wherein we are confronted by a real fact of this kind, this state of facts will inevitably and unfailingly be found.

The existence, within the total sphere of knowledge, of this fundamental difference between absolutely certain and essentially necessary propositions on the one hand and, on the other, merely probable and nonessentially necessary propositions, is one of the most decisive insights of genuine philosophy. As we have previously mentioned, it may be found in all truly great philosophers. Empiricisms of various kinds have attempted to deny the apriori, to deny the reality of absolutely certain and essentially necessary propositions. This attempt, as we shall presently see, necessarily leads to an absolute contradiction.

One of the main attempts to deny apriori knowledge proceeds from confusing propositions which are certain with merely tautological statements. It was Kant's great merit to elaborate for the first time an essential and most important difference in the realm of propositions, namely that between tautological and nontautological propositions. He termed the tautological propositions *analytical,* and the nontautological *synthetic.*

When we say, "Every son descends from parents," the predicate of this proposition merely repeats what was already and explicitly present in the concept of the subject. For, by definition, the concept "son" already includes a relation to parents. The proposition, therefore, is purely tautological. If, however, we say, "Every man has had parents," we affirm something new, since the concept "man" does not explicitly contain the note of a relation to parents.

This distinction of Kant has meaning and importance independently of his theory of knowledge. One need not accept any other element of Kant's doctrine, and especially not his idealism, in order to see that this distinction between analytical and synthetic propositions is of the utmost importance. It is a classic example of a first philosophical *prise de conscience* of an elementary difference which is, in itself, obvious. All propositions in which the predicate repeats that which has been included, by definition, in the concept of the subject, are tautological, void, empty, without any interest. Kant has also proved convincingly that the propositions of Euclidean geometry and of arithmetic possess, not an analytical, but a synthetic nature. The proposition, "Seven plus five equals twelve," is not tautological, for neither in the concept of "twelve" nor in the concept of "7" and "5" is there to be found an explicit relation to the state of facts which is expressed by this proposition. This synthetic character obtains not only in the example given by Kant, but in all propositions stating absolutely necessary, intelligible, and certain facts. In saying, for example, that "an impersonal being cannot embody a moral value, e.g., humility," we in no way imply by the very definition of the concept of humility that it can be found *only* in persons. We certainly grasp humility in persons, but we also grasp aesthetic values in persons. Yet we cannot therefore say that only persons embody aesthetic values. Thus we see that the proposition, "Moral values essentially presuppose a person," is in no way tautological, but rather expresses a new and important insight into the nature of moral value.

THE OBJECT OF PHILOSOPHICAL KNOWLEDGE 79

Again, the proposition, "Orange lies between red and yellow," is completely synthetic in the above-mentioned sense. For "orange" is a definitely specific type of color, the essence of which is not primarily derived from the fact that it lies midway between red and yellow. What we learn in this proposition is something completely new and full of content. It goes beyond what we already know when we simply think of "orange."

We must, therefore, keep ourselves completely free from the misunderstanding which would regard absolutely certain and essentially necessary propositions as merely analytical or tautological. This error strips such propositions of their epistemological dignity. In truth, they are so far removed from tautology that in a certain sense they represent the prototype of fullness of content within the sphere of knowledge, and surpass all empirical propositions in their expression of worthwhile and new content.

It is, above all, necessary to understand that what makes a proposition analytical and tautological is decidedly not the objectively necessary relation between the *being* referred to by the subject of the proposition and the *being* referred to by the predicate. In any true proposition, the fact that it *is* true implies that there is a real connection between the predicate and the subject. This relation also underlies every purely empirical proposition. But even when the relation between the two beings referred to as subject and predicate is necessary, for instance, such as that between moral values and a personal being, when the very nature of moral values requires a personal being as the only possible bearer, even then the proposition "Moral values necessarily presuppose a personal being" is in no way analytical. The necessary relation between two objects, the fact that something is necessarily rooted in the essence of another, does not make the proposition stating such a relation tautological. On the contrary, only when the subject by its very definition implies the relation to the predicate can we speak of a tautology. The analytical character of a proposition implies that the reference to the predicate is already included in the concept of the subject. But the concept of the subject is emphatically not the same thing as the essence to which the subject refers. Concept and essence must, therefore, be sharply distinguished. Although the state of facts in question is necessarily rooted in the essence of the being to which the subject refers, this in no way indicates that the proposition is analytical; it indicates rather that the proposition is true. A tautology exists only when the concept, as opposed to the essence of the subject, explicitly includes the predicate. The statement, "Every effect presupposes a cause," is an analytical proposition. In the very concept of "effect," the relation to a cause is included. But if we say, "Every becoming or every change presupposes a cause," the proposition is in no way analytical or tautological, because the concept "becoming" or "change" includes by definition no reference to a cause. It has a full meaning even if we prescind from its relation to cause. The fact that the objective relation between becoming and a cause is an essential and necessary one in no way renders the proposition tautological. We must, moreover, realize that the notion, "by definition," can be understood in different senses. In traditional philosophy, "by definition" is sometimes used as equivalent to "belonging to" the essence, or "being rooted in" the essence of a being. For instance, one may say that the character of "rational animal" belongs by definition to a human being. But it is evident that the concept of man does not explicitly include the notion of a rational animal. The proposition, "Man is a rational animal," is far from being tautological. We learn something new when Aristotle "defines" man as a rational animal. His statement is an answer to the question: What are the very characteristics of the being which we call man, the being which we know by experience in our own person as well as in other persons? Whether or not this answer is adequate or satisfactory is not our problem here. We are interested only in the fact that the proposition, "Man is a rational animal," is not tautological.

Thus, "by definition" here means exclusively that something belongs, in reality, essentially and constitutively, to the essence of a being. We, on the contrary, intend a very different meaning when we say, "by definition." Thus, we would say that in the statement, "Every rational animal possesses reason," the predicate is contained by definition in the subject. Here not only does the real being essentially include what is said in the predicate, but the concept which forms the subject in this proposition explicitly includes the predicate.

It is the explicit inclusion of the predicate in the concept of the subject which makes a proposition tautological. In short, when knowledge of the state of facts which the proposition affirms is already used to build up the very concept which functions as subject, the proposition is then a mere repetition of what has been already explicitly said by the subject. Such a proposition is, of course, analytical, that is, a tautological proposition.

The proposition, "Moral values can be embodied only in a person," is not tautological. In saying, "moral values," we refer to a certain type of values, such as justice, generosity, purity. What underlies our concept, "moral values," is the specific quality of these values, and not their exclusively personal character. Obviously, we cannot form the concept of moral values unless we have already perceived them. And in our perception, of course, they were grasped as qualities of human acts. But even if a reference to a human person is included in the notion of moral values, this in no way implies that moral values are *exclusively* found in personal beings. To discover that they are in fact exclusively found in personal beings is a genuine insight, and to state it is far from being tautological.

When we use the term, "moral values," we are indeed thinking of values which we witnessed in human beings. Yet this in no way indicates the impossibility of impersonal things (such as a stone or a tree) being the bearers of moral values. Neither does it in any way indicate that moral values may be embodied in all personal beings and not just in human persons.

We can, thus, clearly see that the role which the reference to human beings plays in the concept of moral values does not give the slightest ground to call the proposition, "Moral values are embodied exclusively in persons," tautological. The state of facts expressed in this proposition is something completely new, adding something important and decisive to our knowledge of moral values. It is emphatically not a mere repetition of something which had to be known already in order to form the notion of moral values.

The same applies to propositions such as, "Moral guilt presupposes responsibility" or "A color presupposes spatial extension." All these propositions are antithetically opposed to merely tautological ones.

To grasp an apriori state of facts, it suffices to delve into the nature of the being to which the subject refers; and to draw out, as it were, the state of facts in question. This process must be clearly distinguished from what takes place in the formation of analytical propositions. In the latter, the predicate is explicitly included, by definition, in the concept of the subject and can be "drawn out" of it by attending to the concept of the subject alone. In the apriori proposition, on the other hand, what we "draw out" is completely new in comparison to the concept of the subject. It is something which has been found by contemplating the nature of the being to which the concept of the subject refers. An unbridgeable gap lies between these two types of proposition. In order to formulate an analytical proposition I need only attend to the meaning of the concept. For synthetic apriori propositions, on the contrary, I must contemplate the *being* in question. I cannot remain within the immanent framework of the proposition, but must transcend mere "logical" correctness to draw out from being some of its fertile plenitude.

There is, however, still another confusion which must be eliminated. As I pointed out in the Prolegomena of *Christian Ethics*, all philosophical discoveries differ radically from discoveries in science. They consist, not in making us acquainted with beings, nor in showing us beings which were completely unknown in prescientific experience, but in a *prise de conscience* of facts which are in some way familiar to us and which in great part are constantly presupposed by us in our life. Aristotle's discovery of the nature and rules of the syllogism does not imply that the rules of the syllogism were totally unfamiliar to man and that they were never used in drawing conclusions until Aristotle's works were published. On the contrary, these rules were in some way known by all men, at least implicitly.

This characteristic of philosophy, which applies precisely to apriori knowledge, i.e., knowledge of absolute, necessary, intelligible, and certain facts, may also be confused at times with the character of tautology.

The fact that the apriori proposition is a *prise de conscience* of something which was in some way already familiar to us, does in no way render it tautological. In reaching an insight into such a state of facts as, "Love includes a desire for union," we have the consciousness: "yes, that is it; that is the true nature of love." Still the fact that we confront it with the voice of the being of love given in our prephilosophical, lived experience, in no way denies the synthetic character of this proposition.

Kant committed a fundamental error in overlooking the synthetic character of metaphysics, and in restricting synthetic apriori propositions to the sphere of arithmetic and geometry. It is difficult to understand how the very man who discovered the difference between analytic and synthetic propositions is the same man who overlooked the synthetic apriori character of propositions in ethics, metaphysics, and the other fields of philosophy. It becomes understandable, however, when we consider that Kant approached these problems from his theory of knowledge, which denies intellectual intuition any role apart from the two forms of intuition, time and space. Nevertheless it must be emphasized that the distinction between analytic and synthetic propositions retains its meaning and significance independently of Kant's entire theory of knowledge.

Closely linked to this fundamental error is Kant's opinion that the propositions of general logic and, therefore, the principle of noncontradiction, are analytic. In reality, the principle of noncontradiction is anything but analytic. It is true that analytic propositions have no content other than their being grounded on the principle of noncontradiction (since they are nourished by nothing else than by the truth of this principle). This does not, however, imply that the principle itself is analytic. In brief, if the principle of noncontradiction itself were analytic, a mere repetition which says nothing about the realities to which it refers, it would be impossible to determine whether any proposition is tautological. For instance, let us take the proposition, "All rational animals are rational." The analytic character of this and all tautologies depends precisely on the fact that the principle of noncontradiction is not analytic, but rather a basic, meaningful truth really applicable to beings, and really stating an important fact about them.

There is yet one more point to consider. The principle of noncontradiction is of such an elementary nature that it is not only silently presupposed in every grasp of a state of facts, but it is also luminous with elementary self-evidence. In the case of an explicit contemplation of being as such, this principle is perceived to be true without reference to anything else. Now this elementary self-evidence of a state of facts must not be confused with the formal, explicit containment of the predicate in the subject of tautological propositions.

That being and not-being exclude each other, that something cannot simultaneously exist and not exist is a prototype for all synthetic propositions. It owns an immense, decisive fullness of meaning and content. What we grasp here is the polar opposite to the spiritual idling which is represented in the tautological proposition. To call the foundation of all the things in the world tautological and contentless is, in effect, to erect the gigantic edifice of being and truth on air.

From all that we have said above, the following may be ascertained. Within the total sphere of knowledge, there are propositions which specify themselves as essentially necessary, highly intelligible, and absolutely certain, in contrast to all other kinds of propositions. At the same time, these necessary propositions have a distinctly synthetic character in our sense, i.e., non-tautological. There are, then, states of facts which are full of content, that is to say, not at all tautological, and which can be understood simultaneously as absolutely certain and necessary. It is these which we distinguish as apriori in contrast to the empirical, be this the mere "accidental" single state of facts or, instead, the general and "necessary" laws of nature, which at best can be understood only as highly probable and never as absolutely certain. We saw, moreover, that all states of facts which are grasped through observation and induction are of an empirical nature. The path leading us to the apriori is essentially different. It lies beyond the world of single observations and inductions. The knowledge gained from it is well out of reach of the essential and inevitable faults affecting the certitude of induction. We grasp an apriori truth in focusing on the essence or "such-being" of the object. Hence, there is no possible room for the question whether or not the object, brought to a state of "givenness," really exists here and now.

The knowledge that there are absolutely certain and essentially necessary truths which are not tautological is indeed a common possession shared by all the truly great philosophers. No such common accord exists in answer to the question: "What are the grounds that explain why apriori knowledge is possible?" On the contrary, a wide diversity of answers exists with regard to this question. What is even more important, very diversified elements, having nothing to do with each other, are dragged into the consideration of the apriori problem. That is to say, the question of the existence of apriori knowledge has been loaded with many elements completely foreign to it. This is easily perceived when we examine closely in what sense apriori knowledge is said to be "independent of experience." Apriori propositions are characterized as being independent of experience — as is implied by the very term, "apriori." We have seen that they are indeed independent, in the sense that they do not require blunt observations or inductions. For the most part, however, the term "experience" has a much broader meaning. Independence of experience, in this broader meaning, has also been demanded as a characteristic of apriori knowledge. In what follows we shall attempt to expose this equivocation of the term experience — an equivocation which must be resolved if we are to gain a right understanding of the apriori.

2. The many meanings of the concepts: apriori and experience

A. The Meanings of Experience

The term "experience" has at least two meanings. If someone says, "I cannot talk about love. I do not know what it is because I have never experienced it," the sense of "experience" here is evidently quite different from mere blunt observation. Here it means that something has never disclosed itself in its essence to my mind, that it was never given to me in a concrete moment which would have enabled me to grasp it in its essence. Failure to "experience" in this sense means, to be sure, that there has never been an observation of the existence of a

THE OBJECT OF PHILOSOPHICAL KNOWLEDGE   87

definite type of reality, but above all it here signifies the complete lack of knowledge of the such-being in question. We may call this experience the "experience of such-being," in opposition to blunt, empirical observation.

Perception is the starting point for each of these two kinds of experience. Still this should not make us unaware of the essential difference between them. It is true that, when an object is given to us, when it stands in its self-presence before our minds, it gives us an original knowledge of its such-being and also a knowledge of its real existence. Both go hand in hand in perception. Nevertheless, these two kinds of taking cognizance of something are different one from the other. We have already seen the proof of this, for we have seen that even when an observation is invalidated because the "perception" later on turns out to be an hallucination, still taking cognizance of the such-being remains untouched. Thus if someone becomes acquainted with the color red through an hallucination, the result is that he had no experience of an actually existing red thing, but he most certainly had a genuine experience of its such-being.

At this point it is legitimate to ask: Are there contents which need never be given to us in their such-being at least once? Are there contents which we know independently of every concrete perception of such-being? A blind person does not know what colors look like. Not only can he not grasp the real existence of a color, he also does not know the such-being of the colors red, yellow, blue, and so forth. These singular qualities have not disclosed themselves to his mind in their essence. Evidently, in the case of colors we are dealing with contents which, before they can be known, must have been presented to the human mind in their such-being at least once in a concrete instance. But is this true of contents like "unity," or of the basic ethical values, "good" and "bad"? Is it necessary that unity, which plays such a fundamental role in the knowledge of every some-thing, should have disclosed itself to us in a concrete perception, in a concrete meeting of our mind with the object? Or do we, as spiritual persons, receive its essence in some other way? Do we perhaps know unity "innately"? Is knowledge of it given to us in the same way as the capability of thinking or of loving is given?

In brief, are there any contents which we know independently of every experience, in the broadest sense of the word — experience of such-being as well as of existence? Are there contents which need not be grasped by us even once in a concrete and somewhat qualitative perception in order to be known by us? This is a classic problem of philosophy. We meet it in Plato's teaching of *reminiscence*, of Descartes's *innate ideas*, and in Kant's *categories* and *forms* of intuition. This problem also can be termed "the problem of the apriori." That is to say, one can choose to call apriori only those contents which are said to be independent of every experience, including the experience of such-being. But at the same time one must clearly understand that this question is entirely different from the question: "How is the absolutely certain knowledge of necessary states of facts possible?"

There are two completely different concepts of experience. The one refers to observation of actual singular beings and to induction. The other refers to every concrete disclosure of a such-being. Corresponding to these two different meanings of experience there are two equally different meanings of what is signified by the thesis, "the apriori is independent of experience." Apriori means something different in each case. As far as knowledge of an absolutely certain and essentially necessary state of facts is concerned, all that is necessary is independence from experience in the sense of observation and induction. It is by no means necessary that such knowledge be independent of experience in the sense of the experience of such-being. Two different questions can be raised. One asks: Is there an abso-

THE OBJECT OF PHILOSOPHICAL KNOWLEDGE 89

lutely certain knowledge of essentially necessary states of facts: if so, how is it possible? The other asks: Are there contents which we know (innately or otherwise) independently of any acquaintance with a such-being, even once? Whether the second question is answered yes or *no*, nothing is decided thereby with respect to the first. These are two completely distinct problems, although both may be appropriately called "the problem of the apriori." But apriori has a different meaning in each of the two questions. We are not, of course, interested in the question of terminology. We are simply concerned with the fact that we are dealing here with two entirely different and independent classical problems of philosophy. Unfortunately, very often in the history of philosophy these two distinct questions have been confused and treated as a single problem about the possibility of apriori knowledge.

Only the first apriori problem, which asks about the existence and possibility of absolutely certain knowledge of highly intelligible and essentially necessary states of facts, will occupy us here. Although both problems may fittingly be called classical, the first is incomparably more important than the second, which asks whether there are contents which we can know independently of every possible experience.

We go so far as to say that the question which asks whether apriori knowledge exists, in the sense of an absolutely certain knowledge of highly intelligible and essentially necessary facts, is the epistemological question. It is the cardinal question, whose answer decides the stage of dignity which our knowledge can attain. It is such a fundamental question that its decisive import reaches even to the most detailed and remote philosophical problems.

It is not difficult to understand how much the confusion of this question with the other question concerning apriori knowledge has stood in the way of an answer to it. This confusion makes the unequivocal givenness of absolutely certain and essentially necessary facts dependent upon the answer to the relatively obscure question: whether there is knowledge independent of all such-being experience.

There is the tacit presupposition that knowledge of absolutely certain and essentially necessary propositions is possible only if it is possible to know, anterior to every concrete perception, the essence or such-being of certain states of facts. This presupposition is not only false, but it also results in artificially limiting apriori propositions to those few contents which can meaningfully support the question of whether we can have an innate knowledge of their such-beings without having even made their acquaintance in a concrete perception.

Moreover, no form of innatism can in any way explain the possibility of apriori knowledge. Why should the essence of a being, by the fact that it is known without any experience of its such-being, render this essence more intelligible? Why should it enable us to grasp with an absolute certainty necessary facts rooted in this essence? This independence of any experience of essence is not required for apriori knowledge. Furthermore, even if we had such innate knowledge, its innate character would in no way increase the possibility of apriori knowledge. It is impossible to see why innate knowledge should possess this intelligibility and enable us to gain insight into necessary absolute facts with an absolute certainty. Why should our knowledge of a state of facts rooted in a being possess the character of absolute certainty by reason of our being born with this knowledge? Certainly such a knowledge would be independent of observation and induction, and thus would not be corroded by the imperfections concerning certainty which, as we saw, empirical knowledge inevitably carries with it. But this independence as such is not equivalent to the intelligibility of apriori facts. Nor, again, does innate knowledge imply any guarantee of the truth of a proposition. The innate character could also be linked to a human insufficiency and thus be invalid.

THE OBJECT OF PHILOSOPHICAL KNOWLEDGE

In truth, apriori knowledge is independent of observation and induction because of its incomparable intelligibility. The converse statement, that it possesses its intelligibility thanks to its independence of observation and induction, is false. The self-evident truth of these facts, the truth which elevates us above observation and induction, would not be guaranteed if the independence of observation and induction were the result of innatism. Compared with the theory of innate ideas, Plato's theory of reminiscence would, relatively speaking, serve as a better explanation for the absolute certitude and intelligibility of apriori knowledge. In presuming that a perfect intuition into the ideas was granted to us in a preexistence, Plato at least tries to trace this intelligible knowledge to a previous higher experience.

His explanation is superior to innatism in that it traces the source of apriori knowledge back to a perfect experience, and includes the disclosure to our mind in a most perfect intuition of the being in question. The contact with reality, as well as the intelligible character of this reality, is here implied. To this extent, therefore, Plato's theory does justice to the facts.

But apart from the erroneous assumption of a previous existence, his explanation has other great weaknesses. It does not at all explain why an apriori knowledge is possible with respect to certain objects and impossible with respect to others. Why does such a reminiscence occur in the case of geometrical figures and not in the case of a dog or of an oak?

Moreover, though an experience of such-being is here admitted, why deny that an experience of this kind could take place in our present life? Why not see that an experience of such-being in our present life may grant us an intelligible insight and that dependence upon an experience of this kind is in no way incompatible with apriori knowledge?

In order for propositions to have the highest dignity of knowledge, that is, for them to be absolutely certain, incomparably intelligible, and essentially necessary, they need be independent of experience only in the sense of the observation of actual singular beings and of induction. This does not mean that such knowledge must be independent of experience in the sense of a such-being experience. It is apparent that we cannot know colors without becoming acquainted with them at least once through a perception. Does this dependence on the experience of such-being impair and frustrate the possibility of an apriori knowledge about colors? Not at all. The proposition, "Orange lies between red and yellow," is a classic example of a valid apriori proposition, for it is absolutely certain and essentially necessary. The apriori character of this proposition demands only that, for an insight into this state of facts, there is no need for observations about actually existing colors and no need for induction. This condition, when fulfilled, gains for the apriori an immunity from the inevitable possibility of deception which is characteristic of observations about existents and of induction. Hence it is necessary to keep the concept of the apriori free from every pretention toward an independence of experience in the widest sense of the term, that is, including the experience of such-beings. For this experience in no way excludes absolute certainty, intelligibility, and essential necessity.

B. The Apriori vs. Presuppositions

The apriori in our sense, furthermore, must be kept free from yet another element which has played a great role in the history of the problem of the apriori, especially in Kant. This is the confusion of the problem of the apriori with that of presuppositions, in which the problem is to see how certain states of facts serve as the basis for further knowledge.

This latter is another classic philosophical problem, namely, to examine what are the most general and most basic principles which are presupposed for all further states of facts. This involves an examination of the architectonic structure of being to find out which elements are formal prerequisites for others. It is a problem that plays a decisive role in the meaning of the two concepts: *formal* and *material*.

For example, the propositions of logic are a formal prerequisite for arithmetic; and the proposition of mathematics are a formal prerequisite for physics. This pair of opposing concepts, formal and material, has a relative, and not an absolute, nature. Thus, formal refers to a function of one state of facts or one object in its relation to another proposition. The principle of noncontradiction is in itself a material truth. In both logic and ontology, the incompatibility of truth with falsity and being with nonbeing is a material principle. But in all the other areas of knowledge, like mathematics, physical science, ethics, aesthetics, ontology of the person, and so forth, the principle of noncontradiction possesses a formal character, inasmuch as it is grounded not in the specific nature of the objects which make up the respective themes of these areas, but rather in the content of being which is already tacitly presupposed by all these objects. This is true in an analogous way of many less general principles. Although they are material in themselves, they exercise a formal function for a certain field of knowledge.

Sometimes, the term apriori is used to signify a formal presupposition for experience. In this sense of the term, apriori facts are those which are presupposed for any experience.

Kant, of course, was especially preoccupied with this structural problem. When he asks, "What makes experience possible at all?" he does so with a view to discovering the apriori elements of knowledge. In Kant, to be independent from experience assumes the meaning to be presupposed for experience. For him, the apriori character of space and time is given by the fact that we, as he alleges, presuppose space for all our external perceptions and time for all our internal ones. In other words, he thought that they were apriori forms because they play a formal and foundational role for the objects of both internal and external experience. The same is true with respect to the categories which, according to Kant, are already presupposed in every perception.

This formal, foundational role which certain contents and states of facts play in relation to other objects, however, has no necessary connection with the apriori character in the sense in which the apriori refers to absolutely certain, intelligible, and essentially necessary truths. Absolute and essential necessity is a characteristic which certain states of facts possess of themselves, without regard to their relations to other states of facts. Likewise their intelligibility and their absolute certainty characterize them in relation to their knowability, and not in regard to their structural relation to other objects.

A state of facts may be structurally constituted in such a way that it is a formal presupposition for other objects without being absolutely certain, intelligible, and essentially necessary. The one is not a consequence of the other. So long as I merely notice that a state of facts is necessarily presupposed in all the remaining areas of knowledge, I have not yet proved its essential necessity. The fact that it is so widespread a presupposition argues only that I have gained a concept of relation. The fact, moreover, that it is an indispensable presupposition simply attests to its functional importance for other states of facts. But it says nothing about its own inner essential necessity, its intelligibility, and its absolute certainty. Suppose that the only thing we could say about the propositions "A is not non-A" and "Being and not-being exclude each other," is that they are indispensable presuppositions for all other states of facts. Then we should not have established their apriori character in our sense. We can and we do term these propositions apriori in our sense only because we can understand them with absolute certainty and intelligibility as essentially necessary *in themselves*. Indeed, the mere fact that a proposition is an

THE OBJECT OF PHILOSOPHICAL KNOWLEDGE 95

indispensable presupposition for other facts is not even a proof for its truth, and much less a proof, therefore, for its apriori character in the sense of absolutely necessary, highly intelligible facts. And, on the other hand, there are genuinely apriori states of facts which possess only a slight formal function with respect to other facts, for example, "Orange lies between red and yellow" or "Willing presupposes knowledge." The first proposition is of such a concrete nature that we cannot say it is the formal presupposition for much further knowledge, much less for experience in general. A self-evident consequence of its absolute certainty, intelligibility, and essential necessity is that it must be found confirmed in every single case of orange. But this is only a consequence and not the proper content of being absolutely certain and essentially necessary. But even this "consequence" of the apriori character is distinctly different from the "formal" character which is included as an essential characteristic of the Kantian apriori.

Here we can also see how an element is included within the concept of the apriori which does not belong there. In other words, the problem: "Which states of facts function as the formal presuppositions for all remaining objects or for broad areas of knowledge?" is confused with the genuine problem of the apriori, the question about absolutely certain and essentially necessary states of facts. This confusion exists despite the fact that the problems not only are different but also are completely independent of each other. Much closer to the "formal-presupposition" problem is that classical structure-problem, discussed above, which asks whether there are contents which can be known independently of experience in the broad sense. It is, however, completely independent of the apriori problem which, from the standpoint of absolutely certainty, intelligibility, and essential necessity, inquires into the extent to which certain states of facts can, as knowledge, possess varying degrees of dignity.

C. The Apriori and Experience

A final mark of an apriori state of facts in our sense of the term is that it is *not* essential that it be knowable for every man. Universally available knowledge is not, therefore, as Kant believes, inseparably connected or even identical with the apriori. As noted previously, apriori knowledge in our sense must be independent only of experience in the sense of blunt observation and induction, but not of every experience in the broad sense that includes the experience of such-being. Since this is so, a truth can be apriori and still the possibility remains that a person cannot understand it so long as he lacks an experience of the such-being in question. A blind man, therefore, can not be expected to understand the apriori proposition about the order of similarity of orange, red, and yellow. There is, of course, the possibility of asking whether a certain content is such that it must unfailingly and without difficulty be known somehow to every man. This would apply to contents like time, personal being, or, indeed, being in general. The question might be asked whether there are insights which demand a more specific perception in order to be understood. But these questions are not decisive for the problem of determining whether or not we can understand this content as an essentially necessary, highly intelligible, and absolutely certain state of facts.

Thus far we have seen that apriori knowledge is in no way incompatible with such-being experience. We have seen, furthermore, that knowledge is *empirical*, if it is rooted in experience as taken to signify blunt observation and induction, not in experience in the larger sense of the term in which it embraces as well the experience of such-being. With even greater force, then, the question arises: Why is it possible to have knowledge of essentially necessary and absolutely certain states of facts in some areas, whereas it is not possible to have such knowledge in others? The experience of such-being is present in the case of all objects. Why, then, is this experience sufficient in some cases to give us an absolutely certain understanding of a state of facts, whereas in other cases it is valueless unless supported by empirical observation? In brief, if it is enough to appeal to an experience of such-being in order to attain insight into an apriori state of facts, why is not apriori knowledge possible with respect to all objects? To answer this problem, we must now examine what it is that affords the possibility of knowledge of such dignity on the mere basis of a such-being experience. Our attention now turns to the central problem having to do with the radical difference between apriori and empirical knowledge.

3. *Genuine essences are capable of being grasped intuitively*

To discover the radical difference between apriori and empirical knowledge, it is first necessary to see how apriori knowledge depends upon a certain kind of essence structure. In the case of absolutely certain and essentially necessary states of facts, as we have seen already, our attention is centered on the such-being of the object, not its actual existence.

For example, when we understand that moral values necessarily presuppose a person, we contemplate the such-being of moral values and persons. There is no need to ask whether the moral value which we focus upon, in order to make clear to ourselves the essential characteristics of moral values, is actually present in reality or whether it is only something which we have imagined or dreamt.

On the other hand, when we are interested in knowing the nature of a metal, gold, for example, its actual existence is profoundly important. We cannot possibly eliminate the question whether the perceived thing actually exists or is the product of dreams and hallucinations. If here we should look only to the such-being of gold and put, as it were, its existence into brackets, a number of awkward consequences would result.

First of all, there would be no genuine interest in knowing

an object such as gold if it did not actually exist. Any interest we might have in the specific essence of gold is entirely dependent on the fact that, in a perception of this kind, we are dealing with the perception of a real, actually existing object.

Second, a such-being of this kind would resist all attempts of our intellect to discover any truths necessarily grounded in it, as is the case when we contemplate the such-being of moral values. We may, indeed, in the contemplation of gold as such, grasp a much more general fact, such as "This thing cannot exist and not exist at one and the same time." But this fact is rooted, not in the specific essence of gold, but in the nature of being as such. Again, it is possible for us to understand, as we contemplate the such-being of gold, certain essential facts, such as spatial extension, which are valid for material things in general. But this does not in any way affect our thesis that we cannot derive any essentially necessary, luminously intelligible, and absolutely certain states of facts from the bare contemplation of an object such as gold. For these apriori propositions are rooted, not in the being of gold as such, but in the being of gold only insofar as it is at the same time a material thing. By perceiving merely these general necessary states of facts we do not grasp the specific content of gold as distinguished from silver or lead.

Even more, we must not confuse certain essential unities which lie in the aesthetic appearance of gold, its beauty for example, with the constitutive essence of the metal, gold. When we delve into the such-being of willing and obtain the insight that there is no willing unless there is knowledge, we deal throughout with a constitutive state of facts for the willing as such, and not merely for the aesthetic appearance of willing. But all possible focusing upon the such-being of gold can never lead us to a state of facts grounded in the constitutive essence of gold. Gold does not turn its constitutive such-being, its essence, toward us. Willing, on the other hand, does. We learn something about the such-being of gold only "from with-

THE OBJECT OF PHILOSOPHICAL KNOWLEDGE 99

out," in a roundabout way, only in a detour, only through "observations." We refer to single observations, such as the measurement of its specific gravity, melting point, and the like. This way (i.e., induction), according to its very nature, ends in only empirical states of facts. It is apparent, moreover, that everything we learn about the directly perceivable properties of gold must be stripped of all knowledge interest as soon as we suspend the actual reality of the perceived object, that is, as soon as we prescind from the actually existing gold. For the knowledge interest in this such-being is entirely dependent upon the fact that, in this kind of perception from which the knowledge proceeds, we deal with a real object, that we deal with the perception of a real, actually existing thing and not with an hallucination. We should be accused of simply playing around if we claimed that we were examining descriptively an imagined kind of metal or an imagined type of beetle. It is, therefore, clearly up to the kind of such-being of an object whether or not a delving into it, putting aside any consideration of its real existence, possesses any knowledge interest at all, and whether it yields the knowledge of absolutely certain and essentially necessary states of facts.

To sum up: The possibility of apriori knowledge depends upon the kind of object known. To gain an absolutely certain and essentially necessary insight, it is not enough that we have an experience of such-being and that we prescind from the question of actual existence and induction.[4] We must have also a very special kind of such-being and a givenness which is possi-

---

[4] Husserl stressed this prescinding from existence in his term: "putting existence into brackets." He erroneously believed that this would suffice to guarantee apriori knowledge independently of the nature of the object. It is the basic weakness of Father Lauer's critique of Husserl (cf. his *Triumph of Subjectivity* [New York, 1958]) that he never singles out the main error in Husserl's "bracketing theory," namely, the failure to see that, except for necessary essences, all objects of knowledge lose their interest as soon as we prescind from their concrete, real existence, and that they yield no apriori knowledge, no matter how much we bracket them. It is this failure which led Husserl to *transcendent idealism*, a position radically opposed to the one set down here.

ble only with this type of such-being. The ability of objects to become known exists in a variety of basically different ways. In order to understand this variety within the sphere of the such-beings of objects, we must discuss different basic types of such-beings.

Thus, in order to shed additional light on apriori and empirical knowledge, we shall inquire into the stages of meaningfulness which are found in the realm of such-being. A tremendous gradation of meaningfulness is at once apparent when we look at reality in its broad outlines. Every existing thing is a unity, and its such-being must in some way be characterized as a unity. This unity is flanked by two opposite poles: the first is intrinsic impossibility, and the second is the chaotic, amorphous object devoid of all content. The intrinsic impossibility, which is the antithesis to unity, is either something contradictory in itself, such as a wooden iron, or a square circle, or some nonsensical thing such as a blue number, or a square joy, and the like. Since such things contain incompatible elements, they thereby militate against unity. Such pseudo notions are radically opposed to, and are the complete negation of, unity.

Advancing from the lower to the higher, we shall present the various stages of unity. We shall begin with what is chaotic and possesses only accidental unity, advance to genuine unity, and proceed thence to the necessary unity which represents the genuine essence, the Idea.

A. Chaotic and Accidental Unities

The lowest stage of unity is chaotic and accidental.

A completely amorphous and chaotic mass is the opposite of a real unity, not with respect to the inner connection of elements, but rather with respect to its failure to be a "something" that is thrown into relief as distinct from surrounding beings. It is in conflict, as it were, with the "external side" of unity, whereas what is intrinsically impossible opposes the "inner side" of unity. The more shapeless and the more formless something is, the more it approaches the "non-being" of chaos, until at last it reaches a point where it ceases to be a "something." Thus, concerning the antithesis to the chaotic, there is an enormous gradation in the realm of possible things. No such gradation is to be found in the sphere of possible things with respect to the impossible. There is rather only the decisive alternative of possible or not-possible.

Within the realm of the possible, however, there are many levels or gradations, beginning with the chaotic and merely accidental unity and proceeding to intrinsically necessary unities. As long as we say of a unity only that it is possible, nothing is stated about its stage of positive meaning. If a unity is understood simply as possible in principle, this merely means that there are no self-contradictory elements within it and that it is, therefore, not excluded from reality. But this knowledge does not give us the slightest hint how far this unity is opposed to chaos, or how organically meaningful and, it may be, even necessary, the inner connection of the elements of this unity is. There are unities which are indeed possible, but which, with respect to the connection of their elements, are impoverished in meaning — purely accidental, like a heap of stones or a group of random tones which do not make up a melody. From the point of view of meaning, this is the lowest stage of unity. There is no inner coherence of elements, but merely a factual coherence. Unity is maintained only because it is found in something really existing or, in the case of an imagined unity, only because we happen to be considering it here and now. As a such-being, it does not stand on its own feet at all. We are not able to attach any objective meaningfulness to this unity; it has no real *eidos*, no genuine form. Only an external element keeps it from falling apart and dissolving into the world of the chaotic. It lives only by reason of a blunt facticity, which may come about because it happens to be thought of, or represented, or imagined by someone, or occurring in reality.

Let us take an example. We are able to draw geometric figures which lack every principle of form yet constitute a unity, although a unity that is arbitrary, accidental, and almost senseless, in contrast to the unity of a triangle, quadrangle, trapezoid, and the like; nothing objective is struck with this unity. It has no such-being which stands autonomously. It is kept together as a unity only by our arbitrary act of construction. Intrinsic consistency is even less in the case of a heap of heterogenous objects, such as a pile of junk or rubble. The unity present here is purely factual, born only out of the contingent time-space environment. The single elements which happen to be parts of this purely factual unity might, if taken separately, have a meaningful unity. But their togetherness forms no meaningful unity. Instead of being intrinsically united, they are kept together only externally. A unity of this kind lacks any real inner consistency. What unity there is is due only to a factual grouping.[5]

This is the lowest stage of unity from the standpoint of meaningfulness. Since the such-being of a unity of this kind is so poor in meaning, it is turned in the direction of the chaotic. Furthermore, by contemplating the nature of a unity of this kind we cannot rise to the knowledge of anything authentically generic in the sense of a "type."

B. Unities of a Genuine Type

A higher stage of meaningfulness, basically different from that discovered in the impoverished unity just discussed, is found in those beings whose unity stands for a genuine type. We encounter this higher level of unity in the such-being of objects such as gold, metal, stone, or water. These objects have a meaningful nature, a quiddity which justifies our speaking

---

[5] Of course, this implies that the parts have a quite general ontological affinity, e.g., that each of these parts is a corporeal thing.

THE OBJECT OF PHILOSOPHICAL KNOWLEDGE 103

of them as real types. Their unity forms the basis for a true universality. Here there is not a generic character which implies exclusively an opposition to the single existing individual. Rather a certain stage of generality is to be found here which allows many possible future differentiations (from species to sub-species).

Moreover, the stage of generality is not an arbitrary one, but is grounded in the meaningful unity of the such-being. The "suchness" of a scribbled geometric figure or of a heap of junk is completely arbitrary in its generality. We cannot, furthermore, form a concept of this unity but we must content ourselves with a description of the such-being as a whole.

The such-being present in a genuine type evidently has an inner consistency that is quite different. It is something objectively meaningful, standing in sharp contrast to what is purely accidental and factual. It is not simply held together from "without," but rather possesses a unity from the "center," and its elements are combined, not accidentally, but intrinsically and meaningfully.

Compared with beings possessing an impoverished, radically contingent unity, genuine types have a further dignity. They are, in a completely new sense, serious "somethings." Whatever has only a meaningless, impoverished such-being is not a species nor can it ever be a serious object for science. In addition, whatever is held together exclusively by *de facto* accidental existence has, from the point of view of existence, a nonserious character.

We must, however, distinguish two strata in those beings whose such-being has the character of a true type. In the one stratum we find the such-being of appearances, e.g., the appearance of gold, of metal, of water. This "type," which the appearance offers to us, and which is the starting point for naïve concepts, we may call its "face," its outer or "appearance" unity. We must distinguish it from the second stratum, which is the nature of the type of matter possessing this "face." If science deals with these objects, it does not limit itself to describing the appearance or the "face" of these beings. Rather, science seeks a nature more fundamental than the one situated in the stratum of appearance. It wants to know the constitutive marks of this kind of being possessing this appearance. To be sure, if we seek to know the nature of gold, for example, its distinctive color is one characteristic. But its specific gravity, its chemical composition, and so on, are more decisive for determining its constitutive nature. The scientific question, "What is gold?" clearly leads us beyond those characteristics of gold which play a role in our life, such as its unique attractiveness which determines its role as adornment, and its use as money; in short, this question leads us beyond the "face" of gold.

The constitutive nature, which is what science is chiefly interested in, is not accessible to our mind in the same way as is the outer nature, the face. In order to investigate the former we need a more complicated research. In many cases it is not disclosed by a merely descriptive observation, but requires instruments of all kinds.

Sometimes scientific research may prove that the constitutive nature of two or more objects is the same, even though their appearances exhibit great differences. In short, there is the possibility here of showing that beings which, because of their different appearances, claim to belong to two different species, have in fact the same constitutive nature. A familiar example of this reduction is the scientific discovery that coal has at bottom the same constitutive nature as a diamond.

Let us first consider the such-being unity of appearances. The unity of gold or of water, though definitely the unity of a genuine type, is contingent in character. If we prescind from the real existence of such objects, they lose their interest as serious objects of knowledge. If I dream of a new type of metal and state upon awakening that this type of metal was only

THE OBJECT OF PHILOSOPHICAL KNOWLEDGE 105

the product of a dream, then this type would be of no interest to science, even though the non-existing metal offered me a typical appearance unity.

Moreover, in contemplating the unity displayed by appearances, we cannot grasp any necessary states of facts essentially rooted in it. A unity of this kind is not so luminously intelligible as to allow us, by delving into it, to grasp various facts with absolute certainty. A mere contemplation would lead us no further in our knowledge. Unity of this kind calls for description. To enrich our knowledge we must proceed by describing the appearance — a procedure which clearly and typically differs from intuitive insight.[6] Description goes around the object and accumulates all the observations concerning it. Description is a typically empirical way of knowledge.

Afortiori, new observations are required to answer our questions about such contingent realities as water and gold. What is water's effect on other beings? What use can we make of it? The answers to these questions can never be drawn out of its outer, "appearance" unity, but demand fresh observations. What is the freezing point of water? What is the degree at which water begins to boil? The correct answers to these questions cannot be grasped by delving into the "appearance" unity of water. Nor can I, from the contemplation of water, know the laws of hydraulics. A being of this kind lacks the full intelligibility of apriori states of facts and receives the character of a serious object of our knowledge only when the being having this appearance unity really exists. Though we can grasp here, as mentioned above, that certain features are unessential, still we can never absolutely know whether an observed feature is essential or not. Consequently, our concept of these beings is either artificially closed or else is open to eventual correction.

The same applies with even greater force to the constitutive

---
[6] We shall see later on that certain "appearance such-beings," that is, the outer faces presented to us by some realities, are open to other types of knowledge than description, though never to an apriori knowledge.

structure, the inner such-being. The unity of the species, the structure which science aims to elaborate, is not only not intuitively given, but it is also in some way hidden. In contrast to the "face" of these beings, the inner constitutive unity can be reached only through complicated experiments, such as we find in chemistry, and through the use of instruments like the microscope. Thus this "unity" is so far from being accessible to an intuitive contact that we rather "compose" it, as it were, out of the single elements that we grasp experimentally. Here, the states of facts which we want to learn are not disclosed by intuiting the such-being of the respective object; for, on the contrary, we can only reach a notion of the constitutive such-being by grasping, through experiments, several states of facts concerning this being. The knowledge of these beings with regard to what concerns their constitutive nature is typically a knowledge "from without." A such-being hidden in this way lacks real intelligibility, though it is certainly a true type, a genuine species. It lacks the character of intrinsic necessity and presupposes the real existence of the being in order to be a serious object of our knowledge. Thus we see that neither the "face" of water or of gold, nor their constitutive such-being unity can be a basis for apriori knowledge.

An analogous situation obtains for beings like an oak tree, a pine tree, a lion, a dog, and so on. It must, however, be stressed that the relationship between a being's apparent unity, its "face," and its constitutive such-being varies very much according to the nature of the being in question. The gap between the chemical formula of water and water itself, such as it presents itself to our immediate experience, is quite different from that between the appearance of a tree or an animal and the scientific notion of the respective species. In the case of inanimate, corporeal bodies, the difference between appearance unity and constitutive such-being entitles us to speak of two completely different levels, not to say different worlds. In the case of an animal or a plant, on the contrary, outer unity is closely linked to constitutive unity. Although they do not coincide to such an extent that the naïve concept of these beings as grasped through their "appearance" unity in prescientific observations must not be corrected, they never lose their significance for the constitutive being. Even in stating that the dolphin is not a fish, but a mammal, it remains an essential feature of this animal that it lives in water, looks like a fish, and so on.

All these important differences cannot be discussed here, as our interest is exclusively focused on the difference between apriori and empirical knowledge. We only want to state that the difference between "appearance" unity and the constitutive such-being is analogous, not univocal.

The "face," or the appearance unity, plays a greater role for the species of these beings and is in general a characteristic manifestation of their essence. In many other epistemological respects, moreover, the unity of essential structure involved here differs from that discovered in water and gold. Nonetheless, it shares the same contingent character.

The outer, appearance unity of a lion or of a horse, which is at the basis of our naïve concept of them, is also the result of several observations. It is not intuitively given, as is the such-being of love or of justice. It has not the intelligibility which would enable us to draw out of it states of facts. Here, too, we can proceed only by observation. Moreover, the outer unity never informs us strictly about those features which belong necessarily to these species and those which are more or less accidental. It may be that in one case a color is typical for a species, for instance lions; and in another case, for instance cats, no specific color is typical. Although we find that a certain color is typical for the species *lion*, it is always possible, in principle, that we may discover a lion which is black or white. Only experience, in the sense of observation, can decide whether or not a lion of another color *de facto* exists. And even if experience should never show us an existing lion which has a white color, we should not be entitled to say that a white lion is strictly impossible. For this type of such-being unity is neither intelligible nor necessary. When we ask what essentially belongs to this species — what characterizes it, we never aim at elements rooted with absolute necessity in the essence. The contingent character of this such-being clearly discloses itself when we realize that "essential" here means what is de facto constitutive for a species, and not what is intrinsically necessary and what is absolutely to be included in the essence in question. That a quality or property is "essential" to a such-being of this type ultimately rests on whether or not the individuals of the type exist in this manner, whether or not the property is supported by real concrete existence. All this applies equally to the constitutive such-being of the species, including those elements of a physiological and anatomical nature, which are accessible only through experiments and by the help of instruments. Afortiori, these elements are knowable only through empirical observation. The physiological and anatomical aspects of a species have the contingent character of an outer, appearance unity and lack the full intelligibility of apriori states of facts.

Certain outer unities, however, may offer a still more meaningful essence than that of being simply the valid "face" of hidden constitutive such-beings. Let us consider the appearances of gold, water, and lions from a different standpoint. We can say of a man that he is "like a lion." What we really do here is to focus on a certain appearance, which we may call "lion-ness." In the same way we can speak of "water-ness" and of "gold-ness." In speaking in this way, we call attention to a kind of aesthetic essence which has meaning independently of the real beings possessing the character in question. We thus deal with a purely qualitative "essence." In the case of lion-ness, we refer to such aesthetic features as majestic strength, dignity, ferociousness. In the case of gold-ness, we point to radiant beauty, preciousness, and splendor. In the case of water-ness, we refer to fleeting flexibility, to the refreshing character of water, to the purifying character of ablution, and so on. This aesthetic essence is indeed to be found in the appearances of water, gold, lions, and no doubt other beings. But in no way can we say that all contingent types possess this aesthetic essence. When it is found, however, it has a more intuitive character and a higher intelligibility than does the "face" of other objects.[7]

But this aesthetic essence, which plays a predominant role in poetry, and is often at the basis of *epitheta ornantia* and comparisons in poetry, is in no way an object for science. As significant as it is in poetry, as precious as it is for characterizing the nature of certain things by an analogical use of these "aesthetic essences," it offers no key to an exploration of the real beings possessing this note.

In order to belong in reality to the species "lion," an animal need not possess this "aesthetic" quality of lion-ness. As a matter of fact, the female lion possesses it much less than the male.

Ice, though the same species as water, does not possess the aesthetic essence of "water-ness"; in fact, its aesthetic character is outspokenly different. These aesthetic essences, which play a great role in the beauty of nature, have an important and significant role in the real world. They do not, however, have the kind of intelligibility which would enable us to reach insights into necessary facts by contemplating them. We can, to be sure, draw characteristic features out of the aesthetic essence simply by focusing on it without any need for establishing empirical observations. Nevertheless, these aesthetic essences have a con-

---

[7] Only those "faces" which have an aesthetic essence lend themselves to a kind of understanding which transcends mere description. But even this understanding is in no way an apriori knowledge.

tingency which bars them from providing a basis for apriori knowledge. Our knowledge of the aesthetic essence has a "descriptive" character which, to some extent, is intelligible. Still it is a description, and not an "insight" into necessary states of facts.

Thus we see that the constitutive such-being of these genuine types as well as both their "face" and their aesthetic essences, though meaningful and typical, bear the character of contingencies, of "inventions." Though certainly beyond the power of man, they are, as it were, inventions of God. Because of this contingency, they in no way lend themselves to an apriori knowledge.

C. Necessary Essential Unity

When, on the other hand, we deal with objects like a triangle, a person, will, love, and so forth, we are confronted with a totally new and different type of unity. These objects bring us to the stage of necessary unity. It is sharply distinguished from the impoverished type of unity and also from the very meaningful but nevertheless contingent unity just discussed. It can be grasped clearly through a series of characteristics.

Here the high point of inner consistency is reached. Here is the polar opposite to a unity held together merely from "without." The essential, constitutive unity found here is not hidden, but is intuitively accessible. Yet it is not the such-being unity of an appearance, the mere outer appearance unity. It is the very constitutive essence of the object itself.

For example, the unity intuitively given to me when I contemplate the essence of red is not only the characteristic of the "face" of this being, or even a mere "aesthetic" essence. It is the constitutive essence of the quality red. The duality of "appearance-unity" and "constitutive unity" is canceled here. This cancellation is due, not to the fact that we deal here with a mere quality, but to the fact that red has a necessary unity.

THE OBJECT OF PHILOSOPHICAL KNOWLEDGE 111

This duality is also canceled when we contemplate the such-being of a spiritual person. We can grasp that the being of a spiritual person is not extended in space and that the spiritual person alone can be the bearer of moral values. What we have before us when we understand these facts is the constitutive essence of the person itself. This is directly and intuitively accessible to us and we grasp it as a necessary unity.

In cases like these, it would be completely senseless to invoke the above-mentioned distinction between appearance-unity and constitutive such-being and to pretend that a constitutive structure, hidden up to now, could be discovered which might contradict these truths. Here the constitutive such-being itself is not only not withdrawn from our immediate experience but is also intuitively given.

An authentic genus or species is given in a unity of this kind. Not only is there no arbitrariness, but also the limits of the genus and species are unequivocally given. The essence of red is clearly given in opposition to all the nuances of red. The same is true of the essence of the triangle in opposition to all types of triangles, or of the living being in opposition to animals and plants.

When we think of the constitutive nature of a lion, the line which defines one specific kind from all the others is not unambiguous. It is unambiguous, however, in the case of the triangle or the color red.

When we deal with a necessary, such-being unity, we find that the difference between merely accidental elements and elements which are constitutive for the genus is unambiguously given. Whether the brown color and the mane are merely accidental elements, or whether, instead, they are typical characteristics of a lion, can be apprehended only by experience, in the sense of a blunt observation and induction. Nor can the contemplation of the "appearance" unity of the lion teach me anything about it. But in the case of a single triangle, I can at once understand that the size of the triangle is not constitutive for the essence, triangle. The size of a triangle is intuitively seen to be an accidental element standing outside its necessary such-being unity.

Moreover, the authentic generic such-being offers itself to our minds completely by itself. We need only glance at an individual concrete example. We can "read the such-being" right off the object. In the case of meaningful but nonnecessary unities, we obtain the species by an abstraction and we gain a knowledge of the constitutive such-being through the observation of many single cases. On the other hand, with respect to the necessary unities, the species stands out on its own. Far from being the result of combining several experiences, far from being something "built up" by them, a generic feature of a necessary unity imposes itself as such upon our minds. The object alone is totally responsible for the generic character of the species which we perceive. In short, we are given the species concretely in the single thing.

We must emphasize the fact that the necessary essence is given in its generic character when we perceive a concrete individual being possessing that essence. When we see a triangle for the first time, we grasp not only this concrete triangle, but also the genus "triangle." The necessary such-being in its generic character discloses itself intuitively in the concrete individual triangle which we perceive. This genus or species is not reached by abstraction, as in the case of morphic unities. No specific intellectual process on our part, comparable to the building up of a concept, is required to reach the generic. But thanks to the very nature of the necessary essence, the generic imposes itself on our mind when we perceive the concrete individual. The genus or species is given in the perception of the concrete being.

That the genus is given does not, of course, imply a philosophical *prise de conscience* of the nature of the genus. Nor does the awareness of it resulting from the perception suffice for grasping apriori facts which are rooted in it.[8] But even when a philosophical *prise de conscience* is present, it does not imply any abstraction, unless, of course, abstraction is defined to mean a focusing on the necessary essence and on the genus and species and a prescinding from all accidental features of the concrete example. Only when abstraction is so defined can we speak of abstraction here.

This disclosure of the species and genus in the concrete being belonging to the species is a specific mark of necessary essences. The intelligibility of the species and genus implies here its manifestation in the concrete individual being. Yet we must again stress that this apprehension of the essence of the species and the genus is decidedly not equivalent to a philosophical *prise de conscience* of it and still less to a complete knowledge of it.

The disclosure of the species or genus in the perception of an individual concrete being possessing a necessary unity is not only fully possible, but it is in fact the only possible way for us to be acquainted with the such-being of the species. We do not make the acquaintance of a species by perceiving it independently of a perception of a concrete individual example. It is true that in the case of a philosophical intellectual intuition, which patently presupposes that we are already acquainted with a species through the perception of an individual example belonging to this species, we can delve directly into the species without considering the concrete individual. In this case the focusing on a concrete example has a different, rather auxiliary role.

Plato, who in his *Meno* discovered the difference between apriori and empirical knowledge, did not grasp this fact. He takes it for granted that the species of a triangle does not dis-

---

[8] This does not apply to the most general states of facts, such as "Something cannot be and not be simultaneously." In these cases, the naïve experience of a being allows us to grasp these general truths, albeit not philosophically.

close itself when we focus on a concrete individual triangle. He therefore postulated an immediate intuition of the species in a previous existence, an intuition in which no individual example of this species intervenes.

Instead of seeing that in the case of these necessary essences, the species intuitively discloses itself in the perception of the individual example, Plato reduces the role of the perception of the concrete individual to that of merely evoking in us a memory of the previous, pure intuition. This error, of course, goes hand in hand with Plato's failure to grasp that the difference between apriori and empirical knowledge is rooted in the such-being of the object.

We must now consider another feature of these necessary essential unities and establish the following thesis: It is essential for this kind of unity that we deal with a "potent" such-being, that with respect to its content it stands completely on its own feet, and that it does not cease to remain a thoroughly serious object for our knowledge even on the assumption that there exists no actual object of this kind. As a matter of fact, these classical necessary unities are so potent that in a certain sense they are, even if no examples of their kind happen to exist. We cannot banish a genuine *eidos* into the kingdom of fantasy, fiction, hallucination, or dreams. In whatever way these unities disclose themselves to our mind, they stand to such an extent on their own feet, thanks to an inner potency and the plenitude of their necessary meaningfulness, that the complete autonomy of their being is untouchable. For their full validity, they require the support neither of presence in an existing object nor of being thought of by us. They alone possess an *ideal* existence in the full sense, a kind of existence which they possess by reason of the solidity and necessity of their such-being. They cannot be touched by any relativity in the act in which they become present to us.

These "necessary" intelligible unities are so filled with *ratio*

THE OBJECT OF PHILOSOPHICAL KNOWLEDGE 115

and with intelligibility that their objective validity no longer depends upon the act in which we grasp them. We saw before that if in a dream the such-being of a triangle, of red, or of willing were clearly and unequivocally given to me, the essence itself would not be merely dreamed. Although an essence, a such-being, comes in a dream, it has meaning of itself and thus in no way would it be discredited. On the other hand, if we should dream of a certain metal unknown to perception, or of a new kind of beetle, the dream index would touch not only the existence of these contents but also their such-being. The such-being also would be simply a dreamed-of content. For this reason it would forfeit all serious knowledge interest. But in the case of such-beings possessing a necessary unity, the dream index is completely external to them and can not rob them of their validity and meaningfulness.

We must now advance still further. With respect to the evident states of fact, which are necessarily rooted in these essences, any possibility of an invalidation through a distortion, or insufficiency of our mind, is excluded. Here it would be senseless to say, "Perhaps all these states of facts are not valid, perhaps the insight that moral values presuppose a personal being as bearer is only due to a distortion of our intellect, such as craziness or idiocy."

Nor would it make any sense to apply the Cartesian doubt to the insight into the fact that "Something cannot be and not be simultaneously," or "Responsibility presupposes freedom." For the luminous intelligibility and rationality of such insights precisely proves that we are neither crazy nor idiots. Indeed the extreme form of insanity would be to affirm that dogs are just, or that stones are charitable, or that Mars both exists and does not exist.

We do not mean, of course, that the capacity to have these insights into necessary facts excludes any kind of distortion of mind, or guarantees mental sanity. We mean only that in the accomplishing of these insights, any distortion of a person's mind cannot manifest itself. He may be affected by a distortion of mind with respect to other things. But when he accomplishes these insights, to this extent at least is he sane, for the very lucidity and rationality of these facts exclude any negative influence of a distorted mind on them.

We are playing with words if we assume that the insight into the fact that "Something cannot be and not be simultaneously," or that "Moral values presuppose a person," could be the result of a distortion of our mind. When we prescind from the luminous intelligibility of these apriori truths, as we do in the fiction that they might be the results of a distorted mind, then the very notion of "distortion of mind" loses all sense.

The unities in which these necessary states of facts are grounded stand entirely on their own feet. All attempts to make these insights relative are dashed to pieces by the meaningfulness and power of the such-being in which they are rooted. If they are unequivocally and clearly given, they do not need any criterion for the integrity of the act that grasps them, but, on the contrary, they themselves justify the grasping act as not contaminated by error.

These necessary unities are the only genuine "essences." They are the "Ideas" toward which Plato primarily aimed in his discovery of the world of Ideas. They are the original source of all *ratio*, the highpoint of intelligibility. With respect to them our mind is in a unique position.

We saw that these necessary and highly intelligible essences exclude any assumption that they are mere fictions or illusions. Even if we suspend the question as to whether any just man truly exists, the essence of justice clearly excludes the possibility that it is a mere fiction or illusion. It could never be the mere product of a human mind.

It is in any case something objective, possessing an autonomy of being. It *is*. We have only to compare it with the such-being of a horse or a mountain in order to grasp the "ideal existence" which justice as such possesses, independently of its concrete realization in a man, an ideal existence which the such-being of a subspecies of beetles, for example, in no way possesses.

The very fact of this "ideal existence" reveals itself especially when we consider that all the states of facts rooted necessarily in these essences are an eminent object of synthetic propositions, full of plenitude and importance. The most classical domain of truth comprises the propositions referring to these necessary states of facts, to these eternal verities.

As we shall see later on, these eternal verities apply to all possible reality and thus contain a fundamental insight into reality. When we grasp the full validity of these states of facts, their intrinsic impact and import, then we understand that it is impossible to deny the "ideal existence" of these beings.

The fact that we have not yet a metaphysical place at hand in which to locate these necessary such-beings does not permit us to deny the ideal existence which justice, love, the number 3, color, etc., clearly reveal as their property. By screaming in horror "That is Platonism!" instead of admitting, free from any prejudice, an unambiguously given feature, we act like Procrustes who cut off the feet of men because they did not fit into the bed he had made.

Instead of accepting a fact such as it is, independently of all questions concerning the difficult problems which may arise from this fact, one feels entitled to discard the fact.

We, on the contrary, must accept the difficult problem imposed by this undeniable feature of beings which possess a necessary and highly intelligible essence, the feature, namely, of "ideal" existence. And starting with this very feature which is given to us as an undeniable reality, we must analyze its metaphysical implications. A serious analysis of these necessary essences may bring us to the knowledge that they exist in God in a way different from the divine "inventions," as we called the morphic unities, the meaningful yet contingent types. Without broaching metaphysical problems in this epistemological context, we may still hint at the fact that this "existence" in God obviously can have many different meanings, according to the necessary essence in question.

In the case of being, truth, justice, charity (love), we can say that God embodies these "essences" in the sense that He Himself is absolute Being, Truth, Justice, Infinite Charity; whereas in the case of necessary essences like the number 3, or the color red, existence in God has a completely different meaning.

In speaking of "ideal existence" we must, however, make still another fundamental distinction. We find necessary intelligible unities not only among beings which have a real individual existence, or which could really exist, but also among those entities which by their very nature cannot form a part of the real world in the full sense of the word. I am thinking of entities like the proposition and the concept, entities which have been called *entia rationis,* "beings of the mind." A proposition definitely has a true necessary essence, and all states of facts rooted in the nature of propositions are necessary and intelligible, and can be grasped with absolute certainty. Logic deals with the nature of propositions, and the kind of knowledge in question is indubitably apriori.

On the other hand, the entity, "proposition," is of such a nature that we can never predicate real existence of it in the full sense. Concerning this entity we can never raise the question which we can raise concerning a person, a house, an animal, love, justice, and so on, the question, namely: "Can it be found in the real world?" "Does there exist a real person?" "Does a just act ever take place?" "Can we find true love in existing men?" A similar question would make no sense in the case of a concept or a proposition. We can only ask: "Are the concepts adequate or the propositions true?" We cannot ask whether they are to be found in reality or not. But, on the other hand, they are certainly something. They are a serious object of knowledge and clearly differ from fictions like a centaur or a nymph. Patently we are here thinking of the entity, "proposition," which consists of a subject, a predicate, and a copula, and not of acts of judging, in which these propositions are formulated and uttered. The acts of judging are, of course, beings which claim a full individual real existence. Yet, judgments, in the sense of propositions, must be radically distinguished from these acts of judging. Again, with respect to propositions, we encounter the attempt to escape from the problem concerning the kind of being of these entities. Either they are confused with acts of judging, or they are reduced to a mere combination of words, whereby again words are interpreted in a completely nominalistic manner. In either case, the problem of the kind of existence these things have has been evaded.

We prescind of course from the "escapism" accomplished by the famous "nothing but" formula. We are interested in the real nature of entities like propositions and concepts. They have a "necessary" intelligible essence and are serious objects for our apriori knowledge; they are excluded, however, from individual existence in the real world. In attributing "ideal" existence to them, we may refer either to their character of intrinsic necessity which separates them from all mere fictions or illusions, or to the fact that such beings are excluded from reality, and are incompatible with full, real existence.

Clearly the two meanings of ideal existence are different. In one sense it refers to a special kind of perfection and, in the other sense, to an imperfection, an ontological "thinness." We want to retain the first meaning in our analysis. Thus, when we study the relation between ideal existence and real existence, we mean to use "ideal existence" in the sense of a specific perfection of a being possessing a necessary unity, and not in the privative sense of essentially not-real entities.

It would, however, be a complete misunderstanding to believe that, by admitting the ideal existence of these necessary and highly intelligible essences, one is led to posit a kind of "two-world" system, one of real individual existents, and the other of "ideal" existents. The link between individual, real existents and these realities which possess, thanks to their necessary essence, an "ideal existence," is a very deep and close one.

We do not intend to broach the entire problem of the relation between this "ideal existence" and "concrete individual existence." Still less do we intend here to offer a solution to this extremely difficult and mysterious problem. We only want to add some hints which may insure a more precise formulation of this problem and a sharper appreciation of its complexity.

First, we have to realize that any question about the real existence of a being involves, on our part, an understanding of the kind of existence which the essence in question "calls for."

We have already mentioned entities, such as propositions or concepts, which by their very nature can never become real in the full sense. These important entities, of which we predicate truth and falsity, have exclusively an "ideal existence" in the privative sense of this term. We thus can prescind from them in this context because the question of real existence does not even pose itself.

In the case of numbers, however, such as two or three, we are confronted with entities which are in no way excluded from the real world. Certainly we do not find them as we do substances such as a piece of matter, or a plant, or an animal, or certain accidents, such as a movement of a corporeal body or a quality pertaining to it. Nevertheless, when I state that two and not three persons are in my room, I refer to a concrete real fact. Without attempting to analyze the kind of reality numbers have, we can state that they enter in a specific way into the real world, although they do not have the kind of reality possessed by substances and by many accidents.

Colors present us with still another and different type of real existence. First of all, they can assume a full individual existence as qualities of corporeal things. Whether or not the things possess the quality of being colored independently of our mind is not decisive here. In any case, the colors assume an individual concrete existence as real aspects of these things.[9] If, however, the object having a red color exists only in an hallucination of which we are victims, evidently the color red would not have the same real existence as it has in objectively existent things.

However, even the hallucinated color would not sink to the same level of nonexistence as that of a merely hallucinated house. For the house claims to have a fuller existence in the exterior world than does the color, and thus the gap between the real house and the merely hallucinated one is much greater than in the case of the color. But on the other hand, the color red, because of its "ideal existence," retains still a higher reality even if it is merely hallucinated. Because of the necessary intelligible unity of red, the "being-perceived" means here another degree of reality than in the case of the house. For the "reality" of an hallucinated house is the void and minimal existence of something merely "perceived." Closely linked to this feature of ideal existence possessed by colors is the fact that there are many gradations between the two extremes of the existence of the color as a property of a corporeal thing and as an hallucinated color. We need only think of the fact that a green mountain seen from afar presents us with a blue color. Again, objects assume different colors in a certain light, e.g., the rosy color of a cloud at sunset. Or again under the influence of certain drugs, we might "see" yellow. In every case the color itself is something serious, something definitely "there," although in each case it has a different kind of foothold in reality.

---

[9] In our next chapter, we shall deal in detail with the reality of this aspect.

There is again another existence in question when we inquire about the reality of moral values. Here the "ideal existence" already implies a full reality. The truth of the statement, "There is an objective moral good and evil," is fully verified by the "ideal existence" of moral values. The ideal existence of moral values is certainly of an incomparably greater weight and impact than that of colors. The validity of moral values already guarantees their full metaphysical impact. They are for that reason the true and real norm for judging personal attitudes. We have already mentioned that this "ideal existence" entitles us to speak of a real existence in God.

The "ideal existence" of moral values implies also that they belong to certain attitudes to such an extent that, with the reality of these attitudes, they too will become realized in an individual concrete case. Their "ideal existence" provides, as it were, for their place in the concrete individual existing world, as values embodied in certain acts.

When a morally good act takes place in this world, something new takes place with respect to all those kinds of "reaching down" into reality credited to things having an ideal existence. The real existence of a moral value is obviously a completely new stage, for it implies that a moral good has been concretely realized. But it is nonetheless secondary when compared with the reality which the moral values already possess thanks to their ideal existence. The metaphysical role and fathomless reality of moral values are not increased by this concrete realization, as important and decisive as this realization may be from other points of view. The "oughtness" proper to moral values reveals their deep significance for reality. The fact that human attitudes *should* be morally good shows that the reality of moral values is guaranteed by their "ideal existence."

We are confronted with still another situation concerning real existence when we think of entities possessing a necessary

THE OBJECT OF PHILOSOPHICAL KNOWLEDGE 123

essence like person, willing, love, or contrition. The real existence of person implies that a concrete individual person exists, or has once existed. Here the fullest type of existence is in question and the difference between "ideal existence" and real individual existence is the most outspoken and far reaching.

The same applies analogously to personal acts such as love, will, knowledge, contrition. Real individual existence implies that these acts have really taken place in individual persons. A clearly marked gap separates their ideal from their real existence. After this brief sketch of the different types of real existences which are at stake according to the nature of the being in question, we want briefly to indicate how the respective real existences manifest themselves from a philosophical point of view.

In the case of numbers, no special manifestation of their role for the real world is needed. They intervene everywhere: two perceptions, two trees, two headaches, two paintings, and so on. The thought of any real world in which numbers would have no place, or to which they would not apply, is obviously an impossible fiction.

Color manifests its real existence in every perception of the colored world surrounding us. Colors have a different kind of real existence than do numbers, so that we are here in another situation. For the ideal existence of colors does not guarantee their role in the real existing world, as it does for numbers.

But, as we saw above, the very fact that the exterior world presents itself to us as colored guarantees the real existence of colors. Whether or not the color is a property of corporeal things, independent of our minds, does not affect its real existence, as long as it is the real aspect of the exterior world.[10] We saw above that even the mere "being-perceived" assumes in color another dignity and objectivity, because of its ideal existence.

---

[10] We shall discuss the objectivity of aspects in the next chapter.

We have already mentioned the way in which moral values manifest their reality, how their ideal existence as norms for the validity of moral actions implies a certain real existence.

The specific realization of a moral value in a concrete act of an individual person manifests itself only empirically in the concrete perception of such an act. My certainty that a moral value has been realized depends upon my certainty of the reality of the act as an act and its specific nature. Thus, the question here no longer concerns the manifestation of the realization of a moral value, but the manifestation of a human act in its specific nature, an act of love or contrition. In short, that contrition is morally good is absolutely certain. But that I have here and now witnessed a genuine act of contrition — this alone is open to question and doubt in any concrete case.

When we turn to the real existence of persons, an incomparably fuller and more authentic existence, the problem of reality receives unique support from another source. We said before that here the gap between "ideal existence" and real existence is most outspoken and far-reaching. For this reason we may know that the essence of a person is so potent that it rules out the possibility that this essence is a mere illusion or fiction, such as a centaur or a nymph. But this knowledge does not offer us any guarantee of the concrete existence of an individual person.

Nevertheless, in the case of the reality of a person, we are in a unique epistemological position because of the fundamental fact referred to by both the Augustinian "*Si fallor, sum*" and the Cartesian "*Cogito, ergo sum.*"

The absolute certainty with which we grasp here the real existence of our own person, the fact that every possible error and deception necessarily presuppose this real existence and affirm it as indubitably certain, gives a unique position to the knowledge of the existence of a person, a knowledge of a full, metaphysical, objective existence.

Thus in this unique case of the person, the intrinsic necessity and intelligibility of the essence, which is the basis for all apriori knowledge concerning the person, converges with an absolute certainty about the real individual existence.

After these hints concerning the relation between ideal existence and real existence, we must emphasize the fact that these essences, so powerful that they do not need the support of existence in order to distinguish them from mere inventions of fantasy, have a unique reign over existing things. Their relation to existing things exceeds by far that of the merely "possible" thing. When its such-being is not nonsensical or self-contradictory, when, therefore, it is not essentially excluded from the world of real things, then an object is said to be possible. A such-being of this kind, insofar as it simply grants a possibility for existing, need not be necessary. It can, in fact, be even impoverished in meaning and even purely accidental. Its relation to existing things, moreover, is only negatively defined. It implies that a possible instance of this such-being is not excluded from the world of real things. Necessary and essential unities, on the other hand, not only are not excluded from the existing world but also stand in a more positive relation to it. We might say that they are basic classic components of the existing world. Nothing arbitrary, nothing accidental is found in the concrete existence of their respective objects insofar as the essence-kernel is concerned. They are, as it were, in a classical way, destined to become real.

On the one hand, it is totally inadequate, as we saw above, to classify as mere "possibles" those beings possessing a necessary intelligible such-being; on the other hand, this inadequate term, "possible," undoubtedly hints at an important fact. It expresses, though insufficiently, the classical meaningful relation which these beings have to real existence, independently of whether or not they actually have been realized. The import of "ideal existence" and its deep link to real existence are hidden in this term. This dawns on us when we realize that metaphysics is defined as the philosophy of real being, both possible and actually existing. The term "possible" obviously does not refer here to beings which simply are not excluded from being. No, the possible which is here taken as part of reality, and as such a topic of metaphysics, obviously includes something deeper than flying oxen or golden mountains. Whether or not an object possesses dignity enough to be a topic for metaphysics depends, not on its being a "possible thing" in the sense of the not-impossible in principle, but on the deep inner direction toward real existence. Only this notion of possible justifies our calling possible things a part of reality, together with individually existing things.

It must, however, be emphasized that on no account may we construe this to mean that the real existence of these objects is itself grounded in a necessary such-being. There is no essentially necessary real existence present in these cases. Their real existence remains contingent in contrast to their ideal existence. A necessary real existence is present only in the case of the absolute being, namely, God. Even here, however, we are unable to know the real existence from the essence of God alone.

Let us now summarize the different stages of such-being unity and inquire into the consequences these stages have for the knowledge of the difference between apriori and empirical knowledge.

In the world of objects known to us we find a large gradation in the meaning of various such-beings, beginning with the purely accidental and impoverished, then those unities which, although meaningful, are yet contingent, all the way to the necessary and essential unities. Not every object has a necessary and highly intelligible unity, and even some objects which do have a necessary unity are not immediately and intuitively accessible to us. Here lies the decisive line dividing apriori from empirical knowledge. Insofar as we deal with impoverished objects, an essential and general knowledge is impossible. At most they form the object of a purely empirical description. Insofar as we deal with objects having a meaningful but not a necessary unity, especially those whose constitutive such-being unity is partly hidden, as in the case of different kinds of material things or single species of animals and plants, these objects are accessible only through empirical knowledge, in the sense of observation and induction. On the other hand, insofar as we deal with objects having a necessary and concretely and intuitively revealed unity of essence, we deal with objects that are accessible through apriori knowledge. That is to say, we are able to understand apriori truths as being necessarily grounded in them. By this we do not mean to say that whatever is knowable in them is of an apriori nature. In short, we do not say that whatever is characteristic of them can be understood as necessarily grounded in their essence. Above all, the knowledge of the real existence of these objects is very definitely empirical. But also of an empirical character are those various laws which deal with the genesis and "natural history" of an object endowed with a true essence. In short, everything which can be rightly predicated of such an object without being rooted in its essence is of an empirical nature. Such empirical knowledge includes, for example, all the psychophysical laws of human beings. It is true, of course, that in being a spiritual person, man possesses a necessary essence which can be intuitively grasped and in which we can understand apriori essence-relations as necessarily grounded in the essence. The proposition, "No willing without understanding," is an example of such a necessary essence-relation.

Thus we see that the possibility of apriori knowledge, that is, absolutely certain knowledge of essentially necessary states of facts, is grounded in the type of such-beings of certain objects. It is grounded in an object's constitutive unity which has been intuitively revealed to our mind. We understand that apriori knowledge cannot be adequately or correctly conceived, as Husserl believed, by saying that it results simply from looking at the such-being of any object and bracketing its real existence. Husserl's method leads to an insight into absolutely necessary and intelligible facts only when we deal with certain kinds of objects, namely, those which intuitively reveal to us an essential unity that is necessary and possesses high intelligibility. That which irrevocably divides apriori from empirical knowledge is dependent upon the essentially profound difference in the objects themselves, the difference, namely, between objects which possess an intuitively revealed, intelligibly necessary unity, and others possessing either a contingent but meaningful unity or even a merely accidental such-being unity that is impoverished in meaning. For essentially necessary states of facts are grounded only in the necessary and highly intelligible unities. The necessity of the such-being is presupposed whenever the members of a state of facts are joined by a necessary link. When we deal with objects having meaningful but contingent unities, the states of facts grounded in these unities can bear at most the character of contingent necessity. Moreover, only in the case of intuitively revealed, necessary, and highly intelligible unities is the necessary grounding of states of facts in the essence given to our minds. When, however, we deal with unities that can be known only "from without," by a detour, when we deal with meaningful but partly hidden and contingent constitutive unities, we can never grasp the grounding of laws of nature in the such-being unity. Only in our knowledge of objects, whose highly intelligible, necessary essence can be seized intuitively, are we independent of experience in the narrower sense, that is, of blunt observation and induction. With regard to these objects we are in the unique position of being able to understand with absolute certitude, without recourse to observation and induction, the states of facts which are necessarily grounded in their essence. Each essence, furthermore, can be grasped as the necessary ground of other states of facts which belong to the necessary unity.

Thus independence of experience in the broad sense, that is, in the sense of an experience of such-being, is by no means required, as we will now see even more clearly, for the knowledge of the apriori. Nor is it required that there be apriori knowledge only of objects which are presuppositions for the possibility of experience, whether in a broad or narrow sense.

Apriori knowledge bears upon states of facts which possess two characteristics. First, they are necessarily grounded in a necessary such-being unity; second, they can be understood by us with absolute certainty, either through the intuitive givenness of the necessary such-being unity or through a deductive inference from a directly understood necessary state of facts.

The possibility of apriori knowledge, therefore, is provided by objects having a necessary essence which can be intuitively seized. Hence, it follows that the circumference of apriori knowledge is much larger than it is often thought to be. Apriori knowledge is not only possible, it is also the only possible and suitable knowledge, not simply in the fields of mathematics and logic but also in metaphysics, especially the ontology of the person, in ethics, aesthetics, and many other areas of human knowledge. Here the facts, propositions, and relations which are thematic are all of an apriori nature.

It follows, from what we have said above, that the attempt to explain the difference between apriori and empirical knowledge by the degree of abstraction reached cannot be accepted as satisfactory.

It is true that in ascending to a much higher genus, we can reach an intelligible and necessary essence which offers us the possibility of an apriori knowledge. When facing a mouse, we prescind from the species "mouse," as well as from the genus "mammal," and focus only on its being a living substance;

we certainly reach a necessary and intelligible such-being then. The same applies to every individual substance when we abstract from its species, as an oak, or as a silver fox, etc., and focus exclusively on its character as a "substance" or even only as a "being."

But it would nevertheless be wrong to believe that the intelligible, necessary character is only to be found in the most general genera or even transcendentals. We saw above that not only has color such a necessary such-being, but even that the different species of color, such as red, blue, yellow, have this. We also saw that not only values in general have a necessary, highly intelligible such-being, but also moral values as such and even also justice, humility, generosity. We saw that not only the person has such a necessary such-being unity, not only the genus, personal act, but also something much more concrete, such as the species of willing, love, contrition, and so on.

This fact clearly proves that the necessity and intelligibility of the objects which enable us to attain an apriori knowledge are not dependent upon the degree of generality of a genus. Nor are they the result of the degree of generality of a genus.

It is not thanks to the degree of abstraction that we reach a necessary and highly intelligible object. Rather, the difference between a merely morphic unity and a necessary, highly intelligible unity is rooted in the very nature of a being. The difference between apriori and empirical knowledge depends upon the intrinsic nature of an essence, a such-being, be it species, genus, or a transcendental, and not upon the degree of generality or abstraction, for example, the third degree of abstraction.

The question might arise: with regard to the limits of apriori knowledge, how can we know whether or not we are dealing with an object having a necessary such-being capable of being grasped intuitively? What criterion is present? We answer that the criterion presents itself when we contemplate the such-being of an object. We do not need here a specific mark prior to and external to the object. If an object's essential and necessary unity can be seen intuitively, we can, by focusing on its such-being, understand essentially and with complete certainty that we are dealing with a being of supreme intelligibility and unity. This is an elementary characteristic of this kind of object. Errors here are possible, to be sure, but to be safe from these errors, we do not require an external criterion. The character of a necessary, intelligible unity is its own criterion, and is unambiguously given to the degree that we fully grasp the such-being of the object. Our understanding of it goes hand in hand with our fully focusing on this such-being.

4. *Epistemological characteristics of genuine essences which can be grasped intuitively*

There is thus a great division among objects, a division ultimately based upon the fact that some objects have an essentially necessary and highly intelligible unity which can be intuitively grasped. This division is completely *sui generis*. It must not be confused with other criteria affecting ontological dignity. It has, for instance, no relation to the difference between substance and accident.

There are both substances and accidents whose such-being is necessary, highly intelligible, and open to intuitive insights, whereas other substances and accidents do not possess such unity. For example, the substance *human person* has a necessary, such-being unity, whereas the substance *dog* does not. In short, the ontological difference between substance and accident is not only distinct from our difference between necessary unity and contingent unity, but it is also independent of it.

What is more, we may not take the difference in question here and rank it with a region of being. The vital world is a higher region of being than the world of mere material things, and the personal world is higher than the merely vital world. These ontological differences in rank or dignity of being are independent of the question that asks whether or not we are dealing with objects having a highly intelligible, necessary essence capable of being grasped intuitively.

Thus, the such-beings of triangle and the color red, which belong to the material world in the broad sense, are necessary and intelligible unities. Weariness and blood circulation, although they belong to a higher region of being, possess meaningful unity, to be sure, but a unity that is merely contingent, not necessary.

This great division between the apriori and the empirical is a result of the totally unique element in the condition of objects. This classical reality of the *eidos*, this inner power of certain such-beings, which is significant for necessary and essential unities, crosses other fundamentally important differences among objects. Whether or not a certain object has a genuine essence, an *eidos*, cannot, therefore, be deduced from the presence or absence of other fundamental perfections of being. Nor should we be puzzled when we find that some objects contain an intuitively intelligible and necessary unity despite the fact that in other respects they stand ontologically on a lower stage than objects which do not reveal any *eidos* to our minds. The perfection embodied in the necessary essence is ontologically only one among several decisively important ones. In relation to our knowledge, however, and especially to the degree of certainty of our knowledge, it is a very decisive one. Necessary essences possess a meaningfulness which makes them the source of all *ratio* and elevates them to being a unique counterpart to the grasping mind. With these necessary essences we reach the most privileged situation for our mind. The intuitive and absolutely certain insight into necessary and highly intelligible facts is indeed a priceless "banquet" for our intellect.

It is especially important that we do not confuse the intelligibility of these intuitively revealed necessary unities with the "transparency" that lies in the possibility of a concept to be defined.

When, for example, we answer the question "What is four?" with "Four is one plus one plus one plus one," we break down this essence into its components in a peculiar manner. We must fully distinguish the intelligibility proper to the necessary essences as such from this singular transparency possessed by certain such-beings, which allows them to be broken down and reduced to other known things and, conversely, to be synthesized again from the components. The distinction becomes still clearer when we think of cases wherein the definition does not even touch the nerve of the such-being but simply picks out essential characteristics of the object, as when we say, "Man is a rational living being." This definition, although it is only of essential characteristics, yet seems to claim to give a breakdown of man's authentic such-being, his innermost essence.

If an object can be broken down and if its real essence can be represented by a formula, then the object possesses a special rational clarity. But this is not at all identical with the intelligibility of essences. It represents only one form of an intellectual penetration. Many necessary essences, however, because they are strictly original data, are not reducible to other known components. Hence, with respect to them, the form of intellectual penetration present in objects of rational clarity is not even possible. What is more, this particular form in no way represents the climax of intellectual penetration.

Above all, this transparency is not at all required to make apriori knowledge possible. Many necessary essences stand in their fullness before our minds and are grasped as things which cannot be broken down or reduced in any way. Such, for example, are the color red, the essences of love, space, time, and so forth. Here intelligibility means a unique "meaning-fullness" which renders it possible for our minds to grasp the object "from within." Here there is a case of *intelligere*, in the strict sense of *intus legere intima rei*.[11] When we put these necessary essences before our mental eye so that they are able to unfold themselves in an intuitive plenitude, then we are certainly far removed from the thin transparency which is broken down in a definition.

This is likewise true when it is essentially possible to break down an essence into a definition. For to be able to say that four is one plus one plus one plus one, we must have had the essence of four intuitively accessible to us. It is indeed the original givenness of the essence of four which makes possible the insight into the fact that four is one plus one plus one plus one. This intuitive accessibility of the essence and its special intelligibility, both of them necessary presuppositions for apriori knowledge, are distinctly different from the transparency of the definition inasmuch as the possibility of obtaining a genuine essential definition, in contrast to a mere descriptive definition, already presupposes on its part the givenness of the essence.

This accessibility of necessary essences, as opposed to the hiddenness of the constitutive such-being unities, or the mere descriptive givenness of the appearance unities, does not mean that we "know" these essences without further exploration. Focusing, for example, on the essence of *person* enables us to understand with absolute certainty a state of facts necessarily grounded in it even though the essence of person has a mysterious depth and is anything but transparent.

The path to the more profound and inner penetration into the essence goes beyond the insight into the state of facts necessarily grounded in it. The further we come, the more the essence discloses itself to us. Here we must pay attention to two things. First, in the givenness present in the fruitful, intuitive contact with the object, which forms the starting point

---

[11] Even if this etymology of St. Thomas Aquinas is questionable with respect to the language, the word yet represents a grasping of the object in a classically basic and decisive sense.

for all further insights into the essential facts related to the essence, the essence is revealed in a way which differs completely from the "transparency" of an essence that makes it possible for us to define the object. We should fall into a vicious circle, and, indeed, put the cart before the horse, if we first demanded the kind of knowledge of an essence which can be projected into a definition in order to acquire insights into the state of facts in question. This, of course, is what actually happens in the case of tautological propositions. Here an essence is circumscribed in the sense of breaking it down by a definition. Then the predicate simply repeats the state of facts which was the ground of the definition in the first place. Second, if we should know every state of fact pertinent to an essence, the disclosure of the essence itself would be completely different from the transparency which provided the basis for definition. To appreciate this fact we must understand that most essences are basic and primal data. This means that we must perceive each essence if we are to know it. We cannot deduce it from other data. All essences which are indeed primal in this sense are, therefore, something more than a "sum of properties." For this reason they can never be dissolved into a mere sum of characteristics, into a unity made up of transparent and definable parts. Out of the knowledge of all necessary states of facts grounded in an essence, a light flows and illumines the essence itself and reveals it to our minds. But this light does not dissolve the necessary and essential unity into components in such a way that a definition cast from these components could replace the intuitive grasp of the essence.

There is yet another possible misunderstanding which we must eliminate. In our elaboration of the specific character of apriori insights, we have always chosen as examples self-evident and readily acknowledged facts, such as, "Something cannot be and not be simultaneously"; "Moral values presuppose a person as bearer"; "Colors presuppose extension"; and so on. We must now insist, however, that apriori knowledge is not at all restricted to facts like these, which are so self-evident that the very first glance suffices to allow us to grasp their truth. We have chosen such facts as examples because they make it easier for us to grasp the character of apriori knowledge in contrast to empirical knowledge. But to say that knowledge is apriori is not to say that it is obvious at first sight. These two expressions are by no means synonymous. Philosophy, especially, must not be restricted to those facts which are self-evident at first sight.

We have already mentioned the difference between philosophical and scientific discoveries. Philosophical discovery often consists in a *prise de conscience*, an acute and fully conscious awareness of facts which are presupposed and thus in some way known in our lived contact with being. Such is the principle of noncontradiction, the principles of efficient and final causality, the laws of the syllogism, and many others.

The way in which certain things are presupposed and in some way known varies greatly according to the nature of the being and fact in question. We presuppose, though in a way different from our presupposing efficient causality, the fact that moral values cannot be attributed to impersonal beings. We would be shocked if someone were to speak of an innocent stone, a just tree, or a generous cat. Again in a different way, the difference between generosity and purity is familiar to us. We would, for instance, not attribute purity to someone because he readily gives part of his income to help a friend, but we would attribute generosity to him.

But a great abyss yawns between naïve awareness, even in its most conscious form, such as in the case of the principle of noncontradiction, and the philosophical *prise de conscience* of these facts.

It would be a naïve, not to say a silly error, to believe that

THE OBJECT OF PHILOSOPHICAL KNOWLEDGE 137

philosophical statements of the kind, for instance, found in Aristotle's *Organon*, are not real discoveries. It was a great philosophical deed to accomplish this philosophical *prise de conscience* and to place, as it were, these facts on a pedestal where they shine forth in their self-evidence. The fact that now, after such a philosophical deed has been accomplished, after the principles of logic have been drawn up into the region of full light, they are self-evident at first sight must not let us minimize the philosophical accomplishment. Aristotle's discoveries in logic are no minor conquests. A *prise de conscience* with respect to things we take most for granted in our life experience is often especially difficult. The "distance" from objects, which is indispensable for a philosophical *prise de conscience*, is difficult to achieve in these cases. The objects are literally too near to us to be seen clearly.

But what has to be stressed is that in most cases the apriori state of facts can only be reached by delving deeply into the being in question, after a long and difficult philosophical analysis. We shall examine the nature of this philosophical delving later on when we deal with the method of philosophy. Here it is sufficient to stress that many necessary and intelligible facts which philosophy lays bare through an apriori knowledge do not necessarily have this character of self-evidence. The fact that love is a value response, essentially implying an *intentio unionis* and an *intentio benevolentiae*, and the fact that there is a difference between the *imago Dei* and the *similitudo Dei* are all apriori facts and typical topics of philosophy. They have not, however, the obvious character of "Two plus two equals four" or "Moral values presuppose a person." Certainly a philosopher should lay bare his results in such a way that they become either evident or strictly proved by deduction. But this evidence, which makes it possible for an intellectual intuition to grasp apriori facts with absolute certainty, often presupposes, on the part of the reader or learner in philosophy, another philosophical gift and another degree of co-operation than does the understanding of specifically obvious facts such as: "Moral values presuppose a person."

The very problem we are dealing with here, the nature of apriori knowledge, is an example of those philosophical topics which, although ultimately evident, are by no means easy to explore and obvious at first sight.

Finally, we may not equate the formal rationality of the deductive conclusion with the unique and lucid intelligibility of the necessary essences, although the latter causes the intuitive insight into these essences to be a primal source of *ratio*.

The kind of knowledge wherein we understand that, because of such and such a reason, something else has to be, in short, the "concluding" of something from certain premises, appeals to many people as the climax of intelligibility and rationality. As soon as they come to a state of facts which cannot be deduced from others, they are convinced that this is less luminous and intelligible. This is a great error.

Here, one form of intelligibility and rationality is confused with intelligibility and rationality as such. This one form is thought to be the only contrasting alternative to blunt observation, to the impoverished intelligibility of the mere fact. Completely overlooked is the essentially deeper well of intelligibility and rationality. With respect to intelligibility and rationality, the deepest and most decisive difference exists between a directly understandable state of facts that cannot be deduced from anything else and the mere observation of an actual fact. Examples of the first are: "Moral values cannot be attributed to an impersonal being"; "Being and not-being exclude each other"; "In order to unfold their being existentially, colors require extension"; and "Every value demands an adequate response on the part of the person to whom it is revealed." Examples of the mere observations are: "Here stands a tree" or "Today the sun is shining." When we deal with mere facts

THE OBJECT OF PHILOSOPHICAL KNOWLEDGE 139

we bump something head on, as it were. Our mind falls bluntly on something external over which it cannot go. On the other hand, when we deal with necessary unities which cannot be deduced from anything else, we deeply penetrate the object with our mind. The unity discloses itself in a luminous manner. It becomes evident. We intuit it. This is the pole diametrically opposite to the mere observation of an actual fact. It is the insight that something is necessarily grounded in an intuitively graspable essence. The two really opposite poles of all our knowledge lie in mere observation and in the direct grasping of an ultimate, necessary unity. The latter is much closer to the source of all *ratio* than is any deduction. Indeed, we can directly understand the intelligibility of the springs that feed all deductive reasoning, for they are the nondeducible essential principles of logic. The real strictness of a deduction depends, moreover, on the essential necessity of the premises and, therefore, on the element which is given in the highest potency in the case of the essential facts which cannot be deduced from anything else. Intelligibility and rationality *par excellence* are to be found not only in the direct knowledge of a necessary state of facts, but also in the wedding of our mind with the object. This takes place in the intuitive "having" of the necessary essence, whether it happens in the very beginning of the essence-analysis or comes only after we have known all the essential truths grounded in the essence. For this "having" is not a dark and hidden affair. It is, rather, the most enlightened intellectual penetration into the heart of the object. When the analysis begins, it is present in its budding state and, when it ends, in its full unfolding.

It is well here to pause and realize a supremely important fruit of our analysis of apriori knowledge. In pointing to the fact of apriori knowledge and in proving that man has a capacity to attain absolutely certain insights into essentially necessary and highly intelligible states of facts, we have dealt the death-blow to all shapes and kinds of subjective idealism. For in each of our apriori insights we definitely and undoubtedly transcend the frame of any "relation" to our own mind. In this kind of knowledge we touch a fully autonomous being. We are admitted to the world of full objectivity and objective validity. The absolutely certain insights into necessary essences which are bathed in a luminous intelligibility are the blows that topple all relativistic theories of knowledge. They once and for all refute the thesis which would imprison our knowledge in the realm of our own mind, which claims that we can never transcend its relativity, and that we are forever cut off from a knowledge of something fully objective and completely independent of our mind. Our knowledge of apriori truths is the real Archimedean point for the evaluation of our knowledge as a whole. Apriori knowledge is the basis which no methodic doubt can shake. It is a serene, eternal gate which bars for all time every form of skepticism, subjectivism, relativism and subjective idealism. The force of apriori knowledge even precedes the *si fallor, sum* and its heavy armor. Thus, idealism is first refuted by the fact of apriori knowledge. The second blow is struck by the arguments of St. Augustine and Descartes: even the fact of my erring in all things is certain proof that I exist. This refutes idealism insofar as it tries to bar us from knowledge of *real* concrete existents.

5. *The object of philosophy*

Returning to our starting point, we can now determine the object of philosophy.

1. Philosophy deals almost exclusively with apriori knowledge. It aims at a knowledge taken in the sense of the enlightened penetration of the object from within, which is possible only in the case of contents whose luminously intelligible essences can be seen intuitively. The proper domain of philosophy is,

therefore, that of penetration into necessary essences and the knowledge of essentially necessary and absolutely certain states of facts.

2. The realm of philosophy, nevertheless, is not coextensive with the realm of the apriori in general. For there are apriori states of facts which lie outside of the object-domain of philosophy. Conversely, there are objects of philosophy which lie outside the territory of the apriori.

An example of the first case is given by mathematics. Such apriori truths as "Two times two equals four," and the Pythagorean theorem are not objects of philosophy. Examples for the second case are found in questions inquiring about the real existence of the outer world, the teleological order in the outer world, or, most important of all, the existence of God.

The realm of the apriori is not coextensive with that of philosophy, because there are still constitutive characteristics that determine whether or not something belongs to the object-territory of philosophy. One of these characteristics hinges on the specific type of intelligibility which an essence possesses.

Our concern up to now has been with the type of essence demanded by apriori knowledge. We had asked ourselves what kind of being possessed a such-being which could be the object of apriori knowledge. We therefore enumerated various examples which fully met the requirements of apriori objects since they all possessed a necessary, highly intelligible, such-being unity. Moral values, truth, knowledge, willing, a triangle, the number two, color in general, the color red: all of these were seen to be possible objects of apriori knowledge. When we listed these essences, we meant to point to a difference among all the such-beings given in experience and to show that some of them, namely, the necessary unities, afforded us the opportunity for an absolutely certain grasp of states of facts rooted in them, whereas others, the morphic unities for example, like gold, diamond, water, and so forth, afforded us no such opportunity.

With these morphic unities we have to be content with only highly probable "laws" of nature.

We now want to sift the realm of apriori objects and to point to outstanding differences *within* this realm. One such difference concerns the intelligibility of objects. The intelligibility which a number possesses, for example, differs from that of a color. Numbers are much "thinner" in their essence. They have a kind of linear essence. They are much more abstract, and their intelligibility is also affected by this character, for it has a specifically transparent nature. The way in which facts such as two and two equal four are rooted in the nature of two and four is a specifically formal one. To see it requires no delving into the nature of the numbers in question. In truth, these essences are too thin to allow us the opportunity of delving into them. When we consider numbers added to numbers, or numbers otherwise related to other numbers, we are always confronted with this inevitable thinness which numbers possess as essences. When, however, the question shifts from the mere immanent relations among numbers themselves to the inquiry into the nature of numbers as such, a new depth is possible. Thus, the philosophical question: "*What* is a number?" offers a real opportunity for delving into a quite mysterious essence. This philosophical question is completely different from the mathematical question which asks, "What is the sum of two and five?" or "Is it possible to find the exact square root of the number three?"

Numbers, as employed by mathematicians, have a specific rational intelligibility, a transparence which leaves no room for mystery. Furthermore, their abstract character excludes any kind of knowledge other than an apriori one. Hence, arithmetic has no empirical characteristics.

Totally different from numbers are the essences of color in general and the color red. Red has neither the abstract, formal character of numbers nor the thinness of essence. It has a *qualitative* plenitude. It is, therefore, not simply linear like numbers. Still, it is limited, as it were, to but two dimensions. It has not the transparent intelligibility of numbers and lends itself to very few apriori insights. It leaves room, moreover, for many empirical statements about its nature. Thus colors are objects both for science with its empirical observations and for philosophy with its apriori insights.

When we turn from numbers and colors to entities such as person, love, will, justice, efficient causality, final causality, promising, and so on, we clearly see that these entities are completely different from colors and numbers by reason of their three-dimensional fullness and their depth. Many differences are to be found among these entities themselves. Still, all of them have in common a depth and plenitude which clearly distinguishes them from the type of unity to be found in colors and numbers.

Apart from both their ontological superiority and their superiority in value, these necessary unities possess still another advantage, this time from the epistemological point of view. Their intelligibility is neither thin and transparent, such as we find in numbers, nor two-dimensional like that of colors. Rather, it combines a mysterious depth with an incomparably richer and more meaningful intelligibility. Here the depth of the object offers us the possibility of delving into it, of drawing from it necessary and essential states of facts, of tapping its plenitude again and again and always being rewarded with new and richer insights. And as far as the knowing subject is concerned, something completely new in the way of understanding and penetration is reached thanks to our concerting with these incomparably more meaningful objects, that embody in a matchless way the luminous rationality of the *logos* in question.

Let us summarize our results. States of facts which are grasped as rooted in the essence of a number or a color are similar to states of facts rooted in necessary unities, such as love or person, insofar as both are intrinsically necessary and can be grasped with absolute certainty. In their intelligibility, however, they differ. Though they all possess an intelligibility, absent in the morphic unities like gold, water, and carbon which is the presupposition for a "grasping from within," and therefore the presupposition for apriori knowledge, nevertheless the intelligibility of the fact, "Moral values presuppose a person," differs from that of the fact, "Two added to two is four," in respect to depth, plenitude, and type of rational lucidity. Again, the former fact about moral values is easily seen to differ from a state of facts such as: "In the order of similarity orange lies between red and yellow." There is a difference here of depth and rational lucidity.

As soon as we mention the differences to be found among apriori objects with respect to their kind of intelligibility, we realize a sobering fact. There is a vast field here which remains to be explored philosophically. There are countless problems which have not yet received any attention, much less the minute analysis they deserve. Once the frontiers of intelligibility have been marked off by the all-important and clear-cut distinction between the morphic unities and the necessary essences, once we have achieved the separation of empirical from apriori knowledge, then we are ready to advance into this new field and to make the decisive and important distinctions within the framework of the necessary essences themselves. To think of the magnitude of this projected task is to realize how much philosophy (I mean, true and adequate philosophy) is still only at the threshold of many fields of exploration.

Another characteristic that determines whether or not something belongs to the province of philosophy revolves around a certain essential significance and central importance to be found in the contents of some objects. Philosophy is interested only in those objects which in their essence stand somehow in a

THE OBJECT OF PHILOSOPHICAL KNOWLEDGE 145

very deep relation to the focus of reality. This relation can be manifold.

It can originate in the stage of generality of the object in question, or in the essential importance which is structurally grounded in the object and which links it to the focal point of reality. For example, the essence of number in general and the states of facts necessarily grounded in this general essence pertain to philosophy. The essence, however, of the number four or twelve, as well as the facts necessarily grounded in their specific essence, do not pertain to philosophy. Again, the essence of space, together with the facts necessarily grounded in space as such, is indeed an object for philosophy although the essence of single spatial entities, e.g., triangle, is not. Thus, ontology embraces all spheres of being in which a necessary unity is to be found, but only on a high level of generality.

The relation to the central point of reality can also be given by reason of the depth of content and qualitative meaningfulness of the object under consideration. This happens in the fields of ethics and aesthetics and in the philosophy of the person, among others. To the territory of philosophy belong also the most concrete essences that may be found in these fields, as well as the essential facts necessarily grounded in them. Hence to philosophy belong the essences of faithfulness, joy, the tragic, and so on. For in these fields the theme is qualitatively so important that a relation to the central focus of reality is possessed not only by the high stage of generality and its structural import, but also by every intuitively graspable and necessary essence.

With respect to these two kinds of objects which, for very different reasons, are related to the focus of reality, philosophy is interested only in what is essentially rooted in necessary, essential unities and thus makes apriori knowledge possible. For only these elements in the object possess essential import and are intrinsically united with the focus of the cosmos. There are, to be sure, empirical questions which we may ask about objects of apriori knowledge. For example, the nature of lying is certainly an object of apriori knowledge. But the influence of lying on the body, which is disclosed by the lie detector, is patently of an empirical nature. These empirical questions and the facts that answer them lack the prerequisites mentioned above to become objects for philosophy.

3. Philosophy, however, intends not only to know centrally important objects, but also to know them in a centrally significant manner. But only apriori knowledge can grant this kind of knowledge-contact toward which, as we have already seen, philosophical knowledge tends.

It would be of no avail to philosophy if the knowledge which it intends should proceed from without, detouring around centrally important objects, as the empirical sciences are forced to do in their observation and induction. Philosophy intends to know the essences of its objects. It means to penetrate these essences from within. For this reason also, with respect to these objects, philosophy is limited solely to those things which can be known in an apriori manner.

But because philosophy is so concerned with apriori knowledge of necessary and intelligible essences, we are not allowed to claim that it has no interest in real, concrete existence. On the contrary, several key questions about real existence are eminently philosophical topics. First, philosophy analyzes the knowledge that man has of really existing things and inquires about the degree of certitude which this knowledge can attain. The *si fallor, sum* of St. Augustine, as well as the *cogito, ergo sum* of Descartes, are both eminently philosophical truths, or rather, both are expressions of one completely philosophical truth: the concrete fact, known with absolute certainty, of the thinker's real existence. Because this truth concerns real existence, there is no reason to claim it is an "empirical" statement.

No, it is at once highly philosophical and still concerned with real, concrete existence. Again, the question, "Can we doubt the real existence of the exterior world?" is a philosophical question. So too is the question which asks whether we can reach an adequate knowledge of the world. It is, therefore, a philosophical question to inquire whether Kant is right when he claims that we cannot know "things-as-they-really-are-in-themselves."

Though all these questions concern existence, which cannot itself be known apriori, philosophy nonetheless proceeds to answer them by means of apriori facts, and not by any empirical or inductive method. It does not use experiments or induction in trying to answer the question of the real existence of the exterior world. Indeed, what possible experiment, what possible "scientific" apparatus, what possible series of observations and inductions could throw any light on this question?[12] In all such questions about real existence, philosophy proceeds as in the case of the *si fallor, sum*. Philosophy shows by means of an apriori insight that the fact of our own existence can never be dragged down into the whirl of dethronement which threatens the content of all our other knowledge of real existence. Whatever may be the chance or error or deception, I am still absolutely certain of my own real existence — my fully real existence. I am absolutely certain that the same "thing" which may possibly doubt the existence of all other beings apparently present to consciousness is a *person* who knows that his own existence as a full fact is not a whit shaken by the possibility of error and deception. My confidence is based on the truth that the real metaphysical existence of a personal being is always presupposed and always affirmed anew, even when this being worries about the possibility of error or deception.

This is without doubt an insight into a necessary and highly intelligible, as well as absolutely certain, fact. Once we delve

---

[12] Realizing that no scientific experiment can solve such questions, logical positivism dismisses them as "meaningless" — a rather convenient way to dispose of many serious problems not susceptible to empirical analysis.

into this fact, we grasp it as self-evident. We do not proceed by observation and induction in order to discover its truth. Nor do we need any confirmation and verification through new experiences to establish its truth. It would be shamefully ridiculous to assert: "In all cases so far examined, it has been observed that doubt and worry about deception have always existed in the consciousness of an existing personal being; it is therefore so far verified, and consequently highly probable from a scientific standpoint, that whenever doubt exists, a really existing and conscious person is also to be found." This is the mock "scientific" language of the pseudo philosophers, the men whom we mentioned in our introduction, the men who are so enamored of the method of science that they declare as meaningless anything not susceptible to empirical experiment and blunt observation.

Hence, philosophical insight, not blunt observation, brings to light the essential and intelligible relation between the possibility of deception and the certainty of a person's existence, that is, the relation which allows me to draw a necessary implication from the possibility of deception. Also philosophical is the full and intuitive grasp of the reality of the ego — as self-conscious *subject* of doubts, desires, will-acts, loves, sorrows, joys, and memories. The question of the real existence of the exterior world is also answered by philosophical knowledge and never by any blunt induction or observation. And above all, the supreme question of all real existence, the question as to whether or not an infinite Person exists who is the ground and source of all existence and all essence, the question of God's existence, which is the very climax of all philosophical inquiry, is answered by philosophical knowledge and not by empirical or inductive knowledge.

In all such cases we always aim at insight into essential facts. Even when, in a special case, we are forced to admit that no absolute certainty but only a high probability can be found,

THE OBJECT OF PHILOSOPHICAL KNOWLEDGE   149

this admission is the result of an insight into the epistemological character of the object.

The knowledge of real existence, as discussed above, even though it is not apriori, is likewise not empirical in the ordinary sense.[13] The method of the traditional and classical proofs for God's existence, especially the cosmological proof, is not empirical in the sense of induction. To be sure, we require as our starting point the observation of an actually existing being. Some finite being must be observed as existing. But the inference to God's existence, in the cosmological proof, is based on the essential relation which every finite being has to the ground and reason for its existence. Since the stating of any finite reason only postpones the problem, the positing of an infinite, extramundane being is strictly necessary. The conclusion from the existence of a finite being to the existence of an infinite being is, therefore, not of an inductive nature. It does not proceed from many observations. Nor is it marked by the essential gap which, as we saw before, every inductive conclusion possesses. It is a strict conclusion, without a gap. The argument rises to its conclusion because of an apriori and essential relation. It proceeds from the general essence of a being that has been observed to be an existing being. It proceeds from the *essence* and is, therefore, a knowledge "from within" and not, as in the case of a real induction, a knowledge "from without," based on the empirical characteristics of many cases. Only the first premise, the actual existence of a finite being, is empirical in the sense of being something observed. It is not, however, simply one common or ordinary observation among others. Rather, it is concerned with the prime question of the actual existence of something in general. If for this first premise we make use of

---
[13] In the case of our knowledge of God, we are concerned with something that cannot be known apriori only with respect to us. In itself the existence of God is not contingent, but, on the contrary, is essentially necessary. To use the classical terminology, *quoad nos,* the existence of God is contingent in the sense that it has to be reached through the knowledge of an existing finite being; *quoad se,* it is absolutely necessary.

the actual existence of our own selves, as given in the *cogito*, then even our first premise is an absolutely certain observation, and our knowledge of the Absolute Being reaches the same knowledge dignity as do apriori states of facts, at least with respect to the degree of certainty.

There is yet one more point to consider about the object of philosophy. Philosophy may make use of scientific, empirical results for the analysis of certain problems, such as the relation between soul and body, between the brain and the mind, and even indirectly for the problem of the immortality of the soul. Bergson's extraordinary analysis of memory was based on a series of thorough and minute empirical observations and resulted in many important distinctions concerning the general topic of memory. But even here it is not simply an empirical knowledge in the ordinary sense. The empirical observations here are not a starting point for inductions. Rather, a specifically philosophical knowledge begins with the interpretation of these empirical observations, an interpretation which again makes use of apriori insights and proceeds by way of a distinctly philosophical speculation.

Philosophy is also forced to make use of hypotheses from time to time. None of these hypotheses has the character of apriori knowledge. Yet they are certainly not empirical either, although they may be based on empirical statements. The real reason why these hypotheses are nonempirical, however, is that they are speculations — instead of being intuitive insights into necessary and intelligible states of facts. Not every philosophical problem can be answered by an apriori insight. Sometimes the fact which philosophy searches for is not accessible to an intuitive delving into the essence of the things in question. Even if the fact as such is necessarily rooted in the essence, it may be that the essence is not accessible to our mind. In all such cases, philosophy will not be able to reach an absolutely certain answer

THE OBJECT OF PHILOSOPHICAL KNOWLEDGE 151

but must content itself with highly plausible and adequate hypotheses.

Let us not be deceived about these problems which refuse to yield absolutely certain insights to answer our philosophical inquiries. The fact that no apriori insight is granted to us concerning these problems, some of them very fundamental and vital, does not eliminate them from the realm of philosophy. Still less does it transfer them to science's domain. Let us take, for example, the classical problem, so thoroughly discussed in the seventeenth century, about the relation between soul and body. How does extended matter act on the soul, which has no extension? How explain the fact that a spiritual, nonextended reality, such as my willing to raise my arm, can influence the world of extended things and actually cause my arm to be raised? Apriori knowledge is impossible here. We are granted no intuitive insight into the relation between soul and body. But the problem remains in philosophy. This problem and all similar ones are eminently philosophical because of their content. Although they are not open to apriori solutions, still less are they fit objects for scientific research. In short, their non-apriori nature does not make them empirical. We cannot attain to apriori answers because these questions concern things of which we do not even have a such-being experience. They are beyond experience and bear the character of opaque mysteries.

So we see how, without prejudice to their distinction, apriori knowledge and philosophical knowledge are deeply connected with each other. We see that a knowledge of the nature of philosophy, its object, its kind of knowledge and type of inquiring, is impossible without a thorough clarification of the essence of apriori knowledge, which we have sketched here in its broad outlines.

CHAPTER V

OBJECTIVITY AND INDEPENDENCE

We have seen that man is capable of an objectively valid knowledge, that he can grasp with an absolute certainty a truth which is in no way relative to his mind. We saw that the highly intelligible and absolutely necessary unities, the genuine essences, are objective in the fullest sense. Their objectivity implies an absolute independence from our mind, not only from my individual mind, but also from man's mind in general. We saw that these essences are in no way relative to man's mind.

The question however arises: Does validity in all cases require the same independence from the subject? If a proposition requires a full independence from man's mind in order to be objectively true, we may ask ourselves if this is also required for every aspect.

When we say that a world of real beings objectively exists, that it includes houses, the soil, animals, other persons, we of course imply independence from man's mind. When we claim the objective existence of an animal or another person, we mean that these things exist autonomously, whether we know of them or not. In these cases, objectivity necessarily implies full independence from our mind. If a tree or dog should exist only for an individual consciousness, in a dream or an illusion, we would deny it any objectivity and consider it as completely "subjective" — which in this case means "without foundation in objective reality." Again, on the supposition that all objects are "phenomena" in Kant's sense, that is,

OBJECTIVITY AND INDEPENDENCE 153

they are "appearances" relative, not to this or that individual mind, but to the mind of man in general, even on this supposition, we should deny a full objectivity to such a world of objects.

Granted, therefore, that in all the cases discussed above objectivity means a full independence from man's mind, the question remains: Is this independence required for the objectivity of all data? Would a thing become nonobjective for the reason that it in some way depends on the mind of man? If a certain aspect of a real thing presupposes a human mind, must we say that this aspect is "subjective" in the sense that it has no validity and no foundation in reality?

Let us take a concrete case. We often speak of things as being above or below other things. Science tells us that if we prescind from a human mind there really is no such reality as "above" or "below." Hence we ask: If we grant that the notions of above and below presuppose a human mind in order to have meaning, must we claim that these notions are merely subjective? Are they semblances which pretend to be valid, like dreams, but are not? Or again, assume that colors constitute themselves only for a human mind and that independently of a human mind and without the co-operation of human senses only vibrations would exist, must we say that colors are no longer objective and valid and must we relegate all the colors to the level of a mere semblance?

Before we begin to analyze this problem we must, however, clarify the term "subjective" and unearth several equivocations buried in it. Several meanings of the term "subjective" and its correlative "objective" exist, and these are often indiscriminately used, to the prejudice of clarity and truth.

To be subjective may mean, first of all, to pertain to the personal world, as opposed to the impersonal world; it would mean something belonging to the personal *subject* of knowing, willing, loving, and so forth. In this sense everything which is a real "part" of a person may be called "subjective." An act of knowledge, an act of will, an act of love or joy are all subjective in this sense; a rock or a tree would not be subjective in the same sense. But let it be clearly marked and known: the acts of knowing, love, and so forth are fully objective *realities*. They are at least as "real" as a stone or a tree. Thus the term "subjective" refers to the ontological feature of being a "subject," a person, and not to the epistemological feature of being an appearance for a subject.[1]

That a being is subjective in this first sense evidently implies nothing pejorative or restrictive, no lesser degree of validity, no inferiority to the contrasted nonpersonal beings which in this context are called "objective." We may go still further and say that these subjective beings, these personal entities, are superior in being to the objective, nonpersonal beings. They possess a higher being and are even more "real." When subjective is used in this ontological sense of personal, it clearly escapes all the suspicions attaching to the epistemological use of the term. Unfortunately, this has not always been clearly understood. For many people, even for certain philosophers, the term "subjective," even when it refers to such objective realities as acts of will and joy or the person himself, connotes something less real, something more suspicious, something which exists only in the "mind" of a person — a mere reality *in mente*.

That the term "subjective" should have this unfortunate connotation rests at bottom on the confusion between the ontological and the epistemological sense of the term. We may say that the house I dreamed about existed only in the mind, that it is a reality *in mente*; this means that a real house does not exist but only pretended to exist in the dream. We may also say that my joy or sorrow or love is a reality *in mente*. But by this we by no means intend to say that the joy only pretends

---
[1] The very term "subjective" is unfortunate because of its inevitable epistemological flavor; on the other hand, the term "subjectivity" is much clearer and unambiguous and is easily understood as referring to the person as subject.

to exist, that it is a fiction, like the house I dreamed about. Ontologically speaking, houses are destined to be "extramental" realities — to exist independent of my mind. When an allegedly existing house has no objective existence in this sense, we rightly say its presence is "subjective" — that is, due to the activity of the subject. Here subjective refers to the suspicious epistemological dignity of something not truly real. The case is quite different with joy, willing, knowing, and all acts and parts of the person. These realities, when they are accomplished, are real "parts" of the ontological reality, the person. They are destined to be *conscious beings* whenever they exist. To call them subjective in the pejorative epistemological sense, to cast suspicion on them as if they were not fully "real," as if they were like the house we dreamed about, is clearly to confuse their ontological status as real parts of a subject with the above-mentioned epistemological deception.

There is a slogan as well known as it is unfortunate, which abruptly dismisses all personal data like joy, conviction, love, and so forth. This slogan runs: "These things are merely psychological and no longer metaphysical." Away then with love and conviction and other such suspicious realities! Let us stick to the more "real," more "metaphysical" realities like the motion of a stone, the matter of a pear, the potential being of an oak tree in an acorn. This sad misunderstanding of personal realities is based on the pejorative meaning of the term "subjective," which leads one to look upon personal acts as embodying lower degrees of being than a movement in the cosmos. Let us once and for all state here and clearly grasp that if the term "objective" indicates the dignity and rank of reality, then such "subjective" realities as personal acts, joy, love, conviction, faith, and knowledge are fully objective realities, and are more "metaphysical" than stones and events in the material cosmos.

There is a second meaning of subjective to which we must now attend. It too concerns human acts, but in a completely different way. Suppose a man judges a poem and finds fault with it exclusively because the poet is his rival. We should call this judgment "subjective," meaning that it is determined by the personal prejudice of the judge, not by the objective theme, by the objective reality. The judge has allowed something alien to the object to interfere with his judgment of it. All prejudices are subjective in this sense. Again, if a man fails to promote a very gifted employee because of a personal grudge, we say that his attitude is typically unobjective: it is not based on objective grounds, namely, the merits and qualification of the employee. Here the term "subjective" implies something blameworthy. It is therefore synonymous with such pejorative terms as non-objective, inadequate, prejudiced, nonvalid.

There is yet a third meaning of subjective which, like the second, is a pejorative one. It refers to a kind of egocentric self-reflection. An introvert, a person who is always centered around himself, who lacks any real interest for anything on the object side, whether it be persons, nature, art, or science, may be termed "subjective" in this third sense. The term refers to a certain perversion or unhealthy distortion in a person's life.[2]

So far we have discussed three meanings of the term "subjective." Each was concerned with acts or attitudes of the person. There are three additional meanings which concern, not the acts of the person, but rather the content of a person's knowledge, the existence of an object of our knowledge, or the validity of our knowledge. Let us examine these three new meanings one at a time.

The house that we grasp in an hallucination or a dream is subjective in this new, fourth sense. For instead of existing in reality, it is an illusion that exists only in the mind of the

---

[2] We prescind here from the perversion of human acts and attitudes which is meant when we refer to a sham joy, a sham enthusiasm, a love that rings false, etc. These are the perversions typical of hysterical people. The invalidity and sham reality of these acts is adequately indicated by the term "ungenuine" or "intrinsically false." To call such perversions "subjective" is therefore an unwarranted extension of the latter term.

subject, the knower. Whereas it pretends to exist as a real object in the real world, its entire reality is simply to be the object of a grasping. It is a mere semblance, a "subjective" thing, therefore, because it does not stand in the world of real objects. Here "subjective" points to the nonreality of the object, to the contradiction between what it claims to be and what it really is, and to the invalidity of the knowledge or other act whose object it is. Here too "subjective" means that the object is relative to my individual mind at a given moment.

When "subjective" is used to refer to the relativity of an object to the mind of man in general and at all times, as distinct from relativity to an individual mind at a given moment, we have a still new sense, the fifth, for the term. It is in this sense that knowledge is subjective for Kant. The full objective reality, the so-called "noumenon," the object as it really exists in itself, is inaccessible to us, according to Kant. All our knowledge is limited to phenomena, to things insofar as they appear to the mind of men. For Kant the world which experience offers is, in all its articulation and form, a product of man's mind. Hence, it follows that the validity of all the "truth" we can attain is relative to that mind, not to the mind of this or that individual at a given time, but to the mind of man as such — to all men at all time. This is idealistic subjectivity and is the fifth meaning for the term "subjective." It clearly differs from the fourth meaning which refers to things that are mere semblances. Within the framework of this idealistic subjectivism, the difference between a mere hallucination and a genuine perception keeps its full place. So too the difference between a merely "subjective" view of an individual and a generally valid truth. The difference between a true and a false statement also retains its full meaning in this idealistic scheme, although all true statements are true only *for* man's mind.

But what has no place in the idealistic scheme is the absolute truth, a proposition which would be true, equally true, and true in the same sense, whether or not the human mind exists. For idealism, the proposition refers to objects which would be different as soon as we prescind from man's mind; moreover, in its very validity the proposition is relative to a human mind — to the way *men* are constructed as opposed to other beings who might be knowers. From this it follows that all metaphysical facts are inaccessible to our mind. Man cannot attain eternal verities in the Augustinian sense. Idealism of this kind has, therefore, by reason of its doctrine of "subjective" validity, a restrictive and negative character. Even so, its meaning for "subjective" is not at all the same as the fourth meaning — that of a mere semblance.

The sixth and final meaning of "subjective" refers to what is the topic of this chapter, the fact, namely, that the co-operation of a human mind is presupposed for certain data, such as the notions of "above" and "below." This co-operation refers only to an aspect or appearance of certain objects in the exterior, extended world. These aspects constitute themselves only for a human mind and are, therefore, in some sense subjective; for they cannot be regarded as properties of beings independent of the human mind. Because this meaning of the term "subjective" involves the question of how the aspects "actually are," it rightly includes an epistemological feature.[3]

In this chapter we simply want to ask: Is this type of dependence upon man's mind incompatible with objective validity?

---

[3] We prescind here from the extremely important meaning of "subjective" as referring to all the realities which are constituted for an individual person. The value which an object has for us because we received it from a beloved one is, on the one hand, completely valid, but, on the other hand, this value exists only for me, and not as such, independently of the fact that it was a manifestation of love of a certain person, whom we love. This meaning of "subjective" is, as we can easily see, in no way opposed to validity, and has no pejorative connotation whatever. Our appreciation of this gift is most objective, i.e., it is the objectively right attitude toward it. Being a manifestation of the love of a beloved person, the object really assumes a great preciousness. It is true that this preciousness exists only for me, but this does not efface its full validity because objectively it *should* be precious to me. This meaning of subjective and subjectivity is extremely important and plays a great role in Kierkegaard and existential philosophy.

OBJECTIVITY AND INDEPENDENCE

Must we say that colors, that notions like *above* and *below*, are "subjective" in the sense of "nonobjective" semblances, or in the sense of "relative to man's mind"? Shall we say that the blue color of the sky is only a mere semblance, a kind of optical deception? Shall we thereby deny it any objectivity and validity? Human experience offers us as aspects of the exterior world a universe of colorful, sounding, odorous things. Is this world less objective than the one offered by physics and chemistry? In the words of Gustav Fechner: "Is the *Nachtansicht* (night view) more objective and more real than the *Tagansicht* (day view)?"

The question of objective validity of aspects depends, of course, upon the aspects themselves and varies with their specific nature. For the moment, however, we limit ourselves to this general question: Is it true that the objective validity and reality of an aspect is the same as its independence from man's mind? It will become clear that this is not true if we start with something that is indeed merely a subjective semblance and contrast it with the aspects that are our topic here.

The most radical case of a merely subjective semblance is an object of a dream. True, if in a dream we grasp the fact, both necessary and highly intelligible, that "Moral values presuppose a person as bearer," the truth and validity of this fact are in no way prejudiced by our having grasped it in a dream instead of in the waking state. When, however, not a necessary and essential fact, but rather an event, a deed, or a person is given in a dream, then these things are stripped and deprived of all objective validity and are rightly regarded as mere semblances.

If a person we know suddenly looks different in a dream, has blond hair instead of black, is tall instead of small, this aspect is definitely a pure semblance.[4] The same applies analogously to an hallucination.

---

[4] The psychological, symptomatic meaning of dreams obviously goes in a completely different direction.

Something different, though equally invalid, is at stake when we turn to mere semblances due to an optical or acoustical deception. Suppose we look at an oar in the water: it seems broken. Here we are not completely cut off from reality as in the case of dreaming or hallucination. The oar is an object which belongs to authentic reality. But it offers an aspect, in this case the rupture, which does not correspond to reality. We need only remove it from the water in order to see that this aspect was deceptive.

In this case, as in the forementioned ones, it is the dependence upon our mind that makes these appearances merely invalid semblances. The difference between this optical deception and the dream or hallucination consists in the fact that this semblance is determined by the structure of man's sight and by certain elements on the side of the object and is not a mere semblance restricted to an individual person. Every man sees the oar as broken, whereas the semblances in a dream or hallucination vary according to the individual person.

Although this deception is general and rooted in man's sense-structure, what it presents to us is clearly an invalid semblance with no claim to reality, a fact which is plainly manifested by the term *deception*.

Let us now compare the blue color of mountains seen from afar with this optical deception. The blue color is also a mere semblance, insofar as the mountains, on drawing near to them, are green. One perception of the mountains contradicts the other, and we do not hesitate to consider the nearer sight to be more authentic and to assume that green is their real color. But is the blue color a mere deception? Is this semblance on the same level as the one of the rupture of the oar? Certainly not.

First, the semblance of an oar in the water contradicts reality quite different than does the blue color of the mountain. That an object changes color in a different light is normal. By its very

OBJECTIVITY AND INDEPENDENCE

nature color refers to the way a thing looks, and the fact that one and the same thing appears differently colored does not imply a contradiction like that between a broken and an unbroken oar. But there is a still more important difference. The semblance of the broken oar includes no contribution to reality. It does not enrich the world, nor does it form a member in the chain of elements which build up a meaningful aspect of the exterior world and are bearers of its beauty. But this all applies to the blue color of the mountains.

The blue color of mountains seen from afar is a great enrichment of the world. It definitely has an important function in the beauty of nature; it contains a "word" full of significance, a message frequently the theme of poets. It fits meaningfully and organically into the general aspect of nature and especially of the landscape. It includes a specific meaningful message, whereas the appearance of the broken oar is a mere deception.

The blue color of mountains seen from afar definitely cannot be placed on the level with the appearance of the broken oar. It would be impossible to consider the former a mere deception.

The question now arises: What place has this blue color in reality? It certainly presupposes a human spectator, and does this fact deprive it of all objectivity and validity, and exile it from reality?

Are we not here confronted with a case in which the dependence of something upon man's mind does *not* deprive it of its objective validity and its place in reality?

It seems that we must distinguish between two radically different types of dependence upon man's mind or two different types of subjectivity: the first is due to a limitation of man's mind and consists in a deformation of reality or in semblances which are completely cut off from reality.

The second is an appearance of reality which implies a meaningful message directed to man. We could say of the second type that the object *should* have this appearance; it belongs to its very meaning. It is meant to look so, to present itself to man in this way. And by that it acquires a full validity and is withdrawn from merely negative subjectivity.

We already saw in Chapter IV that color, because of its intelligible and necessary essence and its "ideal existence," retains its character of objective reality as an aspect of the exterior world, and that even when it is given in an hallucination it does not sink to the level of a mere "object of our mind." Afortiori, color possesses a full validity when it is found, not in an hallucination, but as an element of the real appearance of the exterior world. Not all aspects, of course, need possess a necessary, intelligible essence as color does. Certain aspects may present only a meaningful but nonnecessary such-being.

Our point is that the existential role in the human universe of all meaningful aspects, whether necessary essences or not, prevents us from looking upon them as a kind of deception. Their value and the meaningful message they contain are obviously opposed to deception or something which results from a limitation of man's mind. Furthermore, as we shall see later on, these aspects clearly differ from all meaningful and value-endowed fictions and products of human imagination and phantasy.

The objective validity of these appearances is thrown into relief in a specific way if we look upon the world as a creation of God and if we understand the role of man as Lord of creation.[5] Against the background of these two fundamental

---

[5] If we introduce a reference to God as Creator of the world, we do not for that reason leave the strictly philosophical or phenomenological realm. For the existence of God is a topic of philosophical exploration and there are, as we mentioned above, philosophical proofs of God's existence. Thus, in any case, a reference to God's existence would never imply an abandonment of the level of rational knowledge and a leap to religion. Furthermore, the "message-character" of certain appearances in the world exists and can be grasped even if we prescind from God's existence and from the world as His creation. Our reference to God

facts, the different objects of this world imply a message from God to man, and the decisive question which divides reality from error, which divides deception or mere subjective semblances from an objective, valid appearance, is whether or not such a valid message is at stake.

Here the fact that something looks so for man does not imply that the way it is, if we prescind from man's mind, is the more authentic and more real, the more objectively valid. No, the appearance it offers to man belongs to its objective meaning, because God has created "this" world for man.

Wave vibrations are not more real or valid than colors, but one of the reasons for their existence is to afford a basis for the appearance of colors. We will understand better the nature of this "message objectivity," if we think of a work of art. The artist uses many means in order to bring certain effects into existence. These effects, the real artistic content, are the *raison d'être* for all the means used to achieve them. If someone does not grasp the artistic content, he has missed the point; that is, he has not grasped the real meaning and theme of the work of art. If someone hears a symphony and pretends that only the musicians and their instruments and the movements which they make are real, and that the music is merely a subjective offshoot, he obviously reverses the entire objective meaning of the symphony. The movements of the musicians are senseless and ridiculous if one prescinds from the music which they are destined to produce. Their *raison d'être* is the music. Analogously, the aspect of nature which is a meaningful bearer of values and which implies a specific message to man's mind

---

as Creator has a twofold function here. First, it should throw into relief what is already given to us, namely, the message-character of the aspects. We do not deduce this character from the fact of creation; rather, we grasp it directly. Yet it shines forth in a specific clarity when looked at in the light of Creation. To see the world as God's creation makes more visible the validity of certain aspects which are given to us as such. Second, our reference to God contributes a new argument for this validity to all those who, on the ground of the philosophical proofs for God's existence, look upon the world as God's creation.

is fully valid and belongs to reality, although it presupposes man's mind in order to be grasped or even to be constituted.

We have to stress that all this applies to an appearance or aspect of the real world. This dependence on man's mind or this form of subjectivity in no way refers to a kind of world in our imagination which could be opposed to the real world existing independently of us. Someone might argue: "God can also convey a meaningful message to us through a dream or any content which we have present in our imagination. Hence, the fact that a meaningful message is present in a phenomenon in no way grants to it a place in the real existing world. The real world which we aim to explore in natural science is one thing, and the subjective impressions are another world existing only in our mind. God can also use these impressions to convey a message to us but they do not for this reason assume the character of elements of the real exterior world surrounding us."

We say in answer that this is certainly true. But the contents in question are not a world apart from the real one; on the contrary, they are aspects of the real world surrounding us, pretending to belong to it, presenting themselves as the appearances of the real objects, their qualitative faces.

And it is in the frame of the appearances of the real world surrounding us, and existing independently of our mind, that we have to distinguish between merely subjective semblances, which are nothing but deceptions, and the valid appearances which belong to the real objects even though they include a reference to man's mind.

Here the fact that an appearance is meaningful, that it includes a significant contribution to the cosmos, and has a definite value — this fact permits us to consider it as a message of God, not in the sense of a direct word, but as the valid and authentic aspect of a real object. This message is not an inspiration, or a presentment; it is not some direct action of

God in our soul. It is not a message such as the warning to Joseph, in a dream, to go into Egypt. Message means here the God-given or God-willed aspect of an object of nature. In the comparison with the effect of a work of art, given above, the nature of this message discloses itself. The mountains *should* look blue from a distance, even as the perspective in a painting *should* give the impression of space, or as the contrast in a painting *should* throw certain colors more into relief. If the natural scientist tells us that the sky in reality is not blue, but black, it would be wrong to consider the black color as more authentic and the blue sky as a mere subjective semblance, a result of subjective limitations. The blue color of the sky has a fully objective character. It *should* look so; it is a deep, meaningful element in a world view which is classically human, but precisely for that reason more valid; only here does the specific message of God to man realize itself. The same applies to the form of the sky as firmament, as a vault, with the two dimensions of vertical and horizontal. The natural scientist may look at this as a mere subjective semblance. But the philosopher should not believe that this "subjectivity" deprives these elements of their full place in reality and their objective validity.

Again, it would be completely wrong to assert that the dimensions of "above" and "below" are merely subjective semblances having no place in reality. These two dimensions contain a message of specific depth and importance; they are analogies of two fundamental metaphysical categories. There is a deep meaning in the fact that the exterior world presents itself to man as containing these two dimensions. To look at them as mere deceptions, like the broken oar in the water, or as consequences of our merely subjective limitations, such as our inability to grasp a thing simultaneously on all its sides, betrays an absolute lack of philosophical understanding. If the scientist is right in stating that the categories "above" and "below" lose their meaning in the exterior world when once we prescind from a human mind, still this fact in no way prevents these categories from being valid and objective elements of reality. The exterior world *should* present itself in this way to man; it is meant to look so, it corresponds to the aspect of the Creator's intention; it is the valid aspect of the world. The aspect which is the object of science, far from being more objective, is only a section of reality.

Sometimes we even encounter the opinion that the microscope shows us how a hand is in reality; the way a hand looks to our naked eye is only a subjective impression, a kind of illusion. Here it is especially easy to see that there is no reason whatever to consider that the aspect offered by the microscope is more authentic or valid. Why should the aspect of the details be more authentic than the one which we grasp with our eyes? But the aspect of a hand disclosed by the microscope is not closer to the being of the hand, is not more its property than the aspect given to the naked eye.

It is of the utmost importance to understand the radical difference between this kind of dependence upon man's mind and the one which in subjective idealism applies to all objects of knowledge. It is not enough to distinguish the subjectivity of a valid aspect from a mere semblance, such as the object of an illusion or an hallucination; it is also necessary to distinguish it from the subjectivity of idealism as well. We must see why, in the case of these aspects, dependence upon our mind does not invalidate the object and deprive it of a full place in reality, although dependence on man's mind is precisely the reason why we declare the objects of subjective idealism to be invalid.

Let us note, first of all, that the subjectivity which is our topic here concerns only corporeal bodies or at most the whole spatial exterior world, whereas the subjectivity of Kant's idealism extends to all objects of experience, whether corporeal or spiritual, and likewise to the entire sphere of metaphysical facts and truths.

Second, the subjectivity in which we are interested implies no contradiction to full validity; it refers only to *aspects* of corporeal beings (in the largest sense of the word) and does not extend to their entire such-being as does the subjectivity of idealism. When we say that the aspect of a hand offered to the naked eye is the valid aspect in comparison with the aspect disclosed under a microscope, we in no way deny the reality of what we see under the microscope. The physiological features of our hand, the pores, tissues, nerve endings, and so forth, are strictly objective things in our scheme and in no sense depend upon the mind. Hence the subjectivity of the valid aspect neither denies the possibility of a knowledge of features of the exterior world which are independent of our mind, nor does it imply that the superiority, so far as validity goes, of the subjective aspect excludes the reality of those aspects which a scientific exploration discloses.

The subjectivity of idealism, on the contrary, declares every object, whether of experience or of scientific research, to be subjective. Everything which we can reach with our consciousness is to a great extent a product of our mind. We can never and in no way reach a reality which is completely independent of our mind; we cannot reach the object such as it is objectively.

Third, the subjectivity of an aspect in our context does not detach this aspect from the real object which is as such completely independent of our mind. It does not make of this aspect an accidental, or even a necessary, image which exists as a "second world" apart from the real one; but it considers the valid, subjective aspect to be in a deep meaningful relation to the object — to be, indeed, a valid aspect of the real object.

The difference between our position and that of the idealists is, therefore, fully clear. Lest, however, our thesis that certain subjective aspects are fully valid be construed as favoring the idealistic interpretation of knowledge, we shall now take pains to outline the sharp and profound difference between our stand and that of the idealists like Kant. What we shall now say is merely a new approach and a stronger restatement of what we have mentioned above.

For the idealist, our knowledge as such cannot reach farther than objects which are relative to man's mind. Every truth is valid merely for man. Absolute autonomy and objectivity and absolute validity find no place in idealistic subjectivity. On the contrary, we claim the possibility of an absolute knowledge, of absolutely certain insight into highly intelligible and necessary facts. Knowledge of this kind excludes any relativity whatsoever. This is the first point of our radical difference from idealism.

We claim, furthermore, the possibility of grasping with an absolute certainty the real existence of concrete individual beings; this subjective idealism denies. We claim, moreover, the possibility of a knowledge of the exterior world that does justice to its real such-being. At this point we pause, however, to distinguish different strata in the aspects offered by the corporeal world. We then claim that the aspect which is dependent upon man's mind, and which moreover presents itself to man in naïve experience, is the objectively more valid aspect — because it is the aspect which the objective being is destined and is meant to convey to us.

Thus, idealism means to restrict *all* our knowledge by claiming it has only relative, and not absolute, validity. Idealism sees all knowledge as dependent upon man's mind and, therefore, as relative to it. We, on the other hand, show that our knowledge of essences and of concrete individual beings is absolute. We then go further. We say that even in those cases where an aspect really does depend upon man's mind, we refuse to see in this dependence a reason or symptom of invalidity.

OBJECTIVITY AND INDEPENDENCE 169

Idealism claims that all objects depend on, and are relative to, our mind; whereas we concede this dependence and relativity only for the aspects of the corporeal world. Idealism impairs the validity of all objects because of their dependence on our mind; we extend validity even to the aspect which in a certain way depends on man's mind. Our position is just the opposite of idealism: in idealism every content of our knowledge is reduced to a subjectivity which is in marked contrast to objectivity. In our scheme, even certain contents which depend upon our mind, and are in this sense subjective, share in the objective validity.

It is clearly impossible, therefore, to gain support for subjective idealism by applying our arguments for the objective validity of the human aspects of the exterior world.[6]

Let us consider a further argument. When we grant objective validity to certain aspects of the exterior world, we see that the very possibility of this validity depends upon the aspect's being framed against the background of an objective reality which is in its existence completely independent of our mind and which can be known by us. Our view does not point to any grand discrepancy between "things-as-they-really-are" and "things-as-they-appear-to-man" in any and all possible experiences. This is the axis of Kant's idealism, but it has nothing to do with our view on the validity of certain subjective aspects. The discrepancy we notice is a limited and local one: between the aspect which corporeal beings afford us in a naïve experience and the one afforded in a scientific experience. Naïve

---

[6] The contrast of our position with the idealistic one discloses itself drastically when once we realize how impossible it would be on idealistic principles to interpret the aspects of corporeal phenomena as valid messages from God. If idealism were true, the merely subjective categories and the entire aspect of experience which they afford us could never be considered as valid messages from God. Even more, subjectivistic idealism bars the possibility of our knowing God's existence since it denies the possibility of our knowing something transcendent. In such a scheme, therefore, there is no possible ground to state that certain things dependent upon man's mind are nonetheless valid because they are messages of God.

experience shows us a red rose, an orange marigold. Scientific experience seems to suggest that underlying both these colors is a pattern of vibrations. Differences in the wave lengths of these vibrations seem to account for the differences in the color perceived in the naïve experience.

We have compared this duality of aspects with that of the artistic content. Just as the painter or composer uses several means to build up a certain aspect, and just as the *raison d'être* of all the means is precisely this intended aspect, so too in nature, the reality with which science deals, the vibrations in this case, is a means whose true *raison d'être* is to offer an intended aspect to us in a naïve experience. Hence the end product, the aspect offered in naïve experience, is the more valid one since it is the "effect" intended and meant by the Creator. It conveys an important and meaningful message to man and is superior in meaning and value to the underlying reality which is its bearer. But it clearly belongs to the nature of this aspect that the reality underlying it is independent of our mind.

The idealist's world cannot in the same way be compared to a work of art. What sense would there be to the argument that God constructs man's mind in such a way that all truth, meaning, and values exist only as products of man's mind and that man is absolutely cut off from any being that exists independently of his mind? To assert this is really to deny the character of a meaningful valid message from God.

We have repeatedly said that the inner meaningfulness and value of an aspect is an argument for its validity and reality. Perhaps someone might object: "Imaginations and fictions can also be meaningful and beautiful without thereby gaining any reality." This is certainly true. The mere fact that something is endowed with meaningfulness and is beautiful does not insert it into reality. But it is easy to see that a fiction or mere object of our imagination differs completely from an *aspect of reality*. We are not forced to abandon our argument that meaningful aspects are valid. For this argument does not imply that anything meaningful is a valid reality. No, it is limited to meaningful aspects of the real world.

In the way in which they are consciously accomplished, fictions and imaginations differ from any aspect which imposes itself upon us. Fictions present themselves to us as products of our imagination; they are experienced as belonging to a world of phantasy, which is clearly distinguished from the real world in which we live. Whether this imaginary content is beautiful or not, whether or not it has any value, does not alter the fact that the bearer of these values, in contrast to the values themselves, is definitely not real and not existent.

If it should happen that a certain man understands fictions, not in their true nature as being imaginary things, but in a superstitious way; if he should believe that witches, nymphs, and centaurs really exist, they nevertheless are still separated by a world from the aspects of the exterior world which concern us here.

These fictions are in obvious contrast to the classical aspect of nature; they bear the seal of the mythical, of the extraordinary, of a foreign body. They are often deprived of any value, and they always lack the character of deep, meaningful analogies and classical categories of reality. Neither can they be considered as specific messages from God, nor are they in any way the aspects of real things in nature.

CHAPTER VI

THE TWO BASIC THEMES OF KNOWLEDGE

Before we elaborate upon the difference between philosophical and scientific knowledge, we must first analyze two different themes of knowledge in general, namely, the notional and the contemplative. We mentioned these two themes at the end of Chapter II, in which we dealt with the difference between taking cognizance of something and knowing. They disclose themselves when we concentrate on perception and take notice of the two basically different advantages afforded by perception.

By *perception* we mean every form of taking cognizance of something wherein the object is self-present and discloses itself intuitively to our mind. We thus include in our notion of perception more than mere sense perception. In our sense of perception, when we hear the *Fourth Symphony* of Beethoven we perceive not only the tones but also the melody, harmonies, the entire structure of the symphony; above all, we perceive its beauty. All these contents are given in self-presence and disclose themselves to our mind while we hear the symphony. Perception in this precise sense of the term is characterized by the following three features:

First, the object of which I take cognizance is self-present and given as such, as itself. It is not reached indirectly by any means of induction or deduction, but it stands, as it were, in person before my mind. I am in direct, immediate contact with the very object itself.

Second, the object discloses itself to my mind in its existence and such-being. It speaks to me; it informs me about itself. A unique contact with the object is established. The perceived object fecundates my mind; it bestows a "knowing" on my mind.

Third, the object is intuitively given, that is, it unfolds its such-being before my mind. We shall understand more clearly the nature of these three marks of perception when we compare perception with other forms of "consciousness of" something.

We have already mentioned that the self-present givenness of the object distinguishes perception from any kind of inferring. In the perception of a fire, the fire is itself given to me as really present. When I see smoke and infer that there must be a fire somewhere, only the smoke is given in its self-presence. The fire, on the contrary, is not given in this way.

Again, when I learn something through another person, the object learned is even still less given as self-present. If someone tells me that there is a fire around the corner, I perceive the man who tells me about the fire. I hear his words. I understand their meaning. But the fact that there is a fire is not given in its self-presence.

Again, if I represent the face of a friend in imagination and actualize my knowledge of it, this face is not self-present. It is only represented. By means of the prefix "re," our language expresses the difference between this mere presence to our mind and the real self-presence of an object. I have the clear consciousness that the object I represent is not itself really standing in front of me.

When we thus contrast perception with other forms of taking cognizance, such as inferring and learning, or with mere representation, which is a specific type of actualizing our "having knowledge of something,"[1] we mean to clarify the nature of the first mark of perception, namely, the self-present givenness of the object.

The second mark of perception, which we can call the fecundating contact between the object and my mind, is thrown into relief especially by comparing perception with representation. An object given in representation does not bestow a new "knowing" on my mind. The object does not disclose itself. The contact between the object and the human mind is not such that the object speaks to me and fecundates my mind. I do not learn anything new, but I merely actualize in a specifically intuitive manner my knowledge of the object.

So far the fecundating contact with the object is a mark which seems to distinguish all forms of taking cognizance from all forms of actualizing a "knowing" of an object. Thus, in inferring we learn something new. We take cognizance of a state of facts and thereby allow the object to fecundate our mind. Something analogous applies to the case in which we learn something through another person. Nevertheless, we must see that the fecundating contact in perception differs from that in all other forms of taking cognizance of something because it is an immediate contact, because the object itself speaks to us and discloses itself to our mind without any intermediate element. This immediacy gives to the fecundating contact a unique character. Because the object or state of facts itself speaks to our mind and engenders a knowing of it in our intellect, the fecundation proper to perception has an incomparable plenitude and intimacy. Thus, the second characteristic of perception, fecundating contact, though found in an analogous sense in all forms of taking cognizance, is a distinguishing mark of perception by reason of its immediacy.

The third mark of perception, its intuitive character, is thrown into relief most drastically when we compare perception with

---
[1] Cf. Chap. II.

the act of meaning. In every declarative sentence that we utter we are directed toward a state of facts. We refer to it in a very precise way. Through the concepts of the subject and predicate, moreover, we refer to certain objects. But the objects are not given to us. We only direct ourselves in a very precise way to the objects. We do not perceive them; we *mean* them.

We mentioned in Chapter I the difference between taking cognizance and affirming or judging in the strict sense. We stressed that in taking cognizance the object is in some way given to us, though not always in self-presence, whereas in the act of affirmation, the state of facts which we affirm is in no way given. We pose it, as it were. We affirm it through the proposition. Affirmation implies the act of meaning whereby we indicate through words the different members of the state of facts.

We are now concerned with this act of meaning insofar as it exemplifies the absence of all intuition. In giving a lecture we refer meaningfully to a certain object with every word uttered in the continuous flow of speech. Though we refer to it in a very precise and highly rational way, the object is not thereby unfolded in its such-being. It is reached through the medium of a concept and circumscribed by it in a most precise way. If we contrast the situation present in meaning to that present in a representation of the object, we clearly grasp the nature of an intuitive givenness. In thinking of a friend we may try to represent his face. We do this in order to reach an intuitive contact with him and gain thereby a greater intimacy, a closer contact with his personality than in the mere "meaning" him when we refer to him in our thought. Compared with the mere meaning, the representation has an intuitive character, though the meaning has its own advantage in being more specific and precise.

The intuitive character of perception is evidently incomparably more perfect than that pertaining to representation. Yet the contrast between representation and meaning serves to clarify the nature of this third perfection of perception, its intuitive character. We point to the intuitive character of perception when we state that representation and imagination share this intuitive character with it, though in a less perfect way, whereas the contact with an object in "meaning" it is radically nonintuitive. Yet not only in meaning, but also in inferring, is the intuitive character absent. The object whose knowledge is reached by inference is not thereby disclosed to my mind in an intuitive manner. Compare the knowledge of the fire which I see with the one which I possess because I hear the sirens of the fire engines. Only in the former case does the object, the real fire, disclose its such-being to my mind.

After this brief look at the nature of perception, we can now proceed to the topic of this chapter, the two basic themes of knowledge. To do this we must distinguish two perfections of perception. The first consists in the fact that perception is the most original and perfect way of taking cognizance of reality. The existence of something is disclosed to my mind in the most direct way when I perceive it. The self-present givenness of the object informs me in the most immediate way about its existence and such-being.[2] In this respect perception has a privileged position among all forms of taking cognizance of something.[3]

This perfection of perception refers to the appropriation by the mind of an object. It also applies to the "knowing" which perception engenders in our mind. It refers to the notional theme which, as we saw, dominates taking cognizance as well as knowing.

But perception has still another, a second, basic perfection.

---

[2] This does not mean, of course, that the very first perception of an object suffices to inform me about its entire such-being. In many cases, as we saw before, a complicated research alone can inform me about a certain such-being. Yet in this process of research, in experiments, for instance, perception will always have a privileged position.

[3] We shall see later on that with respect to certain objects, intellectual intuition is the most privileged form of taking cognizance of their such-being.

THE TWO BASIC THEMES OF KNOWLEDGE

It is as such the most intimate contact with the object. Even if I know an object through and through, so that its perception could add nothing to my knowledge, nonetheless, to grasp it in its self-presence, to touch it with my mind, and to "have" it thereby in an incomparable way, implies an intimacy of contact which is a perfection of its own. Knowledge as such is a unique form of spiritual union with the object. But our point in this chapter is to show that this union implies two different dimensions. The first one goes in the direction of the most perfect knowing. The second in the direction of the intimate real contact of *having* the object in a most immediate and full possession, of touching it with our mind, of confronting the object "face to face."

The first dimension of union displays itself in our appropriation of the object. This comes to pass in taking cognizance of something and subsists in our knowing, whether the knowing be superactual or actual. This first perfection of perception consists in its being a privileged source of taking cognizance and of acquiring knowing thereby. This perfection refers to what we have called the "notional theme" of perception.

The second dimension of union displays a new perfection of perception. Even if taking cognizance of something is fully accomplished, and perfect knowing is attained, the continued perception of the object results in a special, intimate, and immediate union with the real object, in contrast to the merely superactual knowing, which can subsist even when the object is no longer self-present to the mind.

Knowing, even the most perfect, could never substitute for the dimension of contact and union with the object that perception affords, the "dwelling-in" the object that is thus made possible.

In this "dwelling-in," we are no longer concerned with the question, "How is it?" or with the answer, "It is so," but exclusively with union with the object, with the union, face to face, which perception affords, above and beyond its capacity to bestow on us a knowing of the object.

This perfection of perception fulfills another theme, the contemplative theme, a spiritual "wedding" with the object.

In short, there are two basic kinds of spiritual contact with an object. The first is climaxed in the knowledge of the object and the other in the spiritual wedding with the self-present object. There are, consequently, two fundamental directions of knowledge in the broadest sense, two kinds of spiritual possession of being toward which our mind tends. Perception is the basis for both. For a "knowing-possession," it is the starting point. For a wedding with the object, it is the fulfillment.

Perception, therefore, entails two completely different perfections. It displays two advantages. The first is the ability to engender a knowledge in the person about the perceived object, and thereby to produce an entirely unique form of spiritual possession of the object: "knowing." Second, in the perception itself, once the unfolding of the object is accomplished, there is an intimate living contact with the real object, a fully static possession which cannot be replaced by any other relation to the object.

Despite the great difference between the notional and the contemplative themes, they are intimately linked. "Knowing" plays an important role for the contemplative "having" of the object. The more perfect our knowledge of a being and the more we know it, the more intimate will be the spiritual wedding with the self-present object in perception. For instance, when we hear a symphony, the union with the self-present object, though it cannot be replaced by the most perfect knowing, will evidently be much more perfect the better we know the symphony. Thus, for a face-to-face contemplative contact to be ideal, it is necessary to have reached already a perfect knowledge of the object. To put it differently, we can

THE TWO BASIC THEMES OF KNOWLEDGE

say that a perfect contemplative wedding demands a perfect and prior notional contact.

This contemplative "dwelling-in" the object, this most immediate and full possession, has a static character, as does knowing in contrast to taking cognizance of something. Nevertheless, it differs radically from the static knowing which we distinguished in Chapter II from taking cognizance of something. In truth, contemplative wedding differs both from taking cognizance of something and from knowing because it is no longer dominated by the notional theme which pervades both of them.

There are three things in question here: contemplative having, static knowing, and dynamic taking cognizance of something. Contemplative having agrees with knowing in that both have a static character, and with taking cognizance of something in that both are actual and fully conscious. But it radically differs from both static knowing and taking cognizance by reason of its theme. Whereas static knowing and taking cognizance are dominated by the notional theme, the contemplative having is dominated by the theme of a spiritual wedding with the object.

We must now, however, emphasize that the role of contemplation in our cognitive contact with being is restricted to certain beings.

When we wish to become acquainted with some practical thing, such as a machine, in order to use it purposefully, we are interested only in knowing about it, not in a spiritual wedding with it which only a perceptive intuition can give us. When we say this, we mean something different from saying that our pragmatic interest in the object limits our knowledge of it. The point at issue here is that, in our learning how to use the machine, we rightly see as important only the notional contact which leads to knowing, and not the contact that is given in full contemplative "having." When, on the other hand, we behold a work of art, the cognitive contact desired with the object is not given merely in "knowing" it, but instead in the full "having of" it in its self-presence. For only this cognitive contact, presupposed for the enjoyment of any work of art, admits of a wedding *in and through knowledge* with the object as it unfolds itself to us. All learning-to-know in cases like these has only the meaning of making possible the full having of the object, and the consequent enjoyment[4] of the same object. Not all beings which can be an object of our knowledge can become the object of contemplative having. The contemplative theme can refer to persons, even those known only through history, or to all objects endowed with qualitative values, such as a great work of art, a beautiful country, a lovely flower. It can also refer to many of those things which, because of their central importance, are objects of philosophy. Needless to say, the role of the contemplative theme reaches its climax in the religious sphere.

Taking cognizance of something and knowing bear a closer relation to being convinced and to affirming than does contemplative having, because the notional theme is found in conviction and affirmation although, it is true, in a totally different way. Conviction and eventually affirmation organically follow taking cognizance and knowing; they do not require a contemplative having of the object. What is given in contemplative having lies beyond what is at stake in conviction and affirmation. The interest of the notional theme in the "how-is-it" is the basis for the spontaneous "so-it-is" of conviction and affirmation — which are the "answers" we ourselves give. In contemplative having, on the other hand, the theme of "how-is-it" is very much subdued. The "so-it-is" no longer has the character of an answer to the question, "How is the thing?"

The contemplative theme, which is not, as such, concerned

---

[4] The Augustinian *frui* as opposed to *uti*.

THE TWO BASIC THEMES OF KNOWLEDGE 181

with affirmation and conviction, exhibits a new kind of relation to the object; it looks to the unfolding of the value of the object, beginning with the initial stage wherein the value radiates from the object and enters my consciousness, passing through the stage wherein I am touched or affected by the value, and ending with affective responses. The climax of this theme is, therefore, the Augustinian *frui* — the enjoyment of an unfolded value.

It will be recalled that we drew attention to perception in order to elaborate the nature of the contemplative theme in knowledge. The perfection of self-present givenness in perception helped us to throw this theme into relief. Yet it would be wrong to restrict contemplation to perception. The same theme can manifest itself in many cognitive acts, although it finds only a relative fulfillment in them. We have already mentioned the desire to establish a more intimate contact with a beloved person by representing his or her face, way of speaking, mannerisms. Such a desire is evidently not dominated by the notional theme. For we are not aiming at an enlargement of our knowledge of the beloved person, nor could a mere representation ever contribute anything to such an enlargement. This desire is exclusively directed to increasing and deepening our contact with the beloved person in the direction of the contemplative theme. Certainly representation is a very poor fulfillment of the contemplative theme when contrasted with perception of the beloved person, dwelling in his real presence, and seeing him face to face.

Between mere representation and seeing face to face, however, there are many stages of fulfillment of the contemplative theme.

The authentic recall of some past situation with the beloved person, going back with our mind to former experiences, offers us a much more intimate cognitive union with the beloved than does mere representation. The same applies in the case of a beautiful landscape or a beloved country. When we try to represent the landscape, we aim at a contemplative possession, a contact which only perception grants us in a perfect way. Now, if we recall our former days of dwelling in this country and seeing this landscape, if we "go back" to the original perceptions of this landscape, a higher degree of contemplative having is afforded.

A still higher degree of contemplative having may be reached when we immerse ourselves with all our mind in the personality of a beloved person or in the atmosphere of a beloved country. Certainly, the success of this immersion in establishing an intimate contact with the object does not depend exclusively on us. There is an element of gift in this contact. To immerse oneself with one's whole mind in the personality of a beloved person, or the atmosphere of a beloved country, may or may not be successful. If successful, it is a deeper fulfillment of the contemplative theme than mere representation.

It is especially in religious life that the contemplative theme of knowledge plays a great role and that we may clearly grasp the difference between this theme and the notional theme. Thus, if a theologian studies the passion of Christ in order to learn something about it, the notional theme dominates his mind. If, on the contrary, he meditates on the passion of Christ in mental prayer and, still more, if the passion of Christ is the object of his contemplation in the religious sense of the term, then the contemplative theme is exclusively at stake. The longing to see Christ face to face, the great desire of the Christian which he hopes will be fulfilled in eternity, manifests itself in religious meditation and contemplation.

To be sure, in one respect the Beatific Vision is also the fulfillment of the notional theme. When St. Augustine exclaims: "That I may know Thee, that I may know myself," he expresses the desire for a knowledge of God, the fulfillment of the notional theme. But when the same St. Augustine says:

"There we shall see, and we shall love," or when St. Thomas in his hymn *Adoro Te* says:

> Jesu quem velatum nunc aspicio;
> Oro fiat illum quod tam sitio
> Ut te revelata cernens facie
> Visu sim beatus tuae gloriae,

each refers to the fulfillment of the contemplative theme, to the wedding union afforded in the Vision.

We must, however, stress that a fulfillment of the contemplative theme with respect to certain objects can be reached without recourse to a perception in the strict sense. Insofar as necessary and highly intelligible essences are in question, intellectual intuition grants us an intimate union analogous to that granted by perception. This is so because essences enjoy a kind of self-presence analogous to the givenness of a concrete individual being. The contemplative having of an intelligible essence, the nature of justice or love, for example, displays itself in an intellectual intuition.

As we saw before, these highly intelligible necessary essences enable us to grasp intuitively the necessary states of facts rooted in them. Intellectual intuition is the way in which we analyze objects with these necessary essences. Although at least one perception of these objects is presupposed if we are to become acquainted with them, still, when we begin a philosophical analysis, we need not witness a real act of justice, or a real forgiving, we need not "perceive" these actual things in order to establish an immediate intuitive contact with the essence of justice or forgiveness. We may start with an example offered by history, or even by a novel. The essences of justice and forgiveness may be intuitively given to our mind even in a kind of self-presence although the bearers of these essences are not at the moment perceived. In short, to represent an act of justice is not to perceive it. Nevertheless, this merely represented act of justice, weak as it is, suffices to enable me to have an intuitive contact with the self-present necessary essence of justice.

Intellectual intuition into essences can inform us about their nature in a most direct and immediate way. What matters here in our context, however, is that the intellectual intuition is not only the source of fulfilling the notional theme regarding justice, not only the way for us to appropriate the nature of this essence to our mind, not only that which allows us to accomplish insights into necessary states of facts; it also allows us to fulfill the contemplative theme with respect to the essence. For intellectual intuition can grant us a union with the essence in question, a wedding contact, face to face. Such a wedding contact with respect to persons and all other concrete individual things is possible only in a perception. But with essences it is possible through an intellectual intuition. This intuition can grant us a contemplative having of the essences and a fulfillment, therefore, of the contemplative theme. This requires, of course, that we be not absorbed in the knowing process, that we be not preoccupied, so to speak, with the notional theme — as we are indeed preoccupied when we undertake a philosophical analysis. Only after we known an essence deeply, only after we have profoundly penetrated the nature of an essence and in a way "exhausted" the notional theme, only then can the contemplative theme rise to its full prominence — when we intend to immerse ourselves in the essence, to repose in its vision.

CHAPTER VII

DISTINGUISHING MARK OF PHILOSOPHICAL KNOWLEDGE AND INQUIRY

When we discussed the object of philosophy, we were already deeply immersed in the singular way in which philosophy directs its glance and poses questions. Now we shall take up more fully the nature of philosophic inquiry.

1. The dominant themes of philosophic inquiry

First of all, philosophy is interested only in certain centrally significant objects and is almost exclusively directed to knowledge of apriori states of facts. Another characteristic of philosophy is that it is dominated not only by the theme of knowledge but also by that of the object. We have seen the difference between knowledge-thematicity and object-thematicity earlier in this work. We saw that there are cases of naïve taking cognizance of something when there is an explicit thematicity of the object but none of knowledge. There are also cases, however, in which the knowledge-thematicity, as in most sciences, by far exceeds that of the object-thematicity. There is, of course, no instance in which there is purely interest in knowledge and none in the object, for knowledge is essentially related to objects and can never be completely independent of them without losing all content and seriousness. But it can happen that, in certain instances, the theme of knowledge has more importance than that of the object. This is the case in the basic attitude characteristic of the sciences.

Someone might object that the pragmatic character of certain sciences, of a great part of physics for example, contradicts our statement that in science the object-thematicity is less than the knowledge-thematicity, for to be pragmatic means to be concerned with the object much more than with knowledge.

This objection, however, is based on a misunderstanding of the nature of pragmatic interest. Suppose I am interested in elevating an enormous weight of several hundred tons and I desire to exert only a small force to accomplish this. I immerse myself in the study of hydraulics and I devise a lift that operates on the familiar principle of hydraulics known to every automobile mechanic who has ever used a hydraulic jack. Is my interest in the laws of hydraulics pragmatic? Indeed it is. Is it therefore highly concerned with the object? Am I really interested in the mysterious fact that liquids may be only slightly compressed, that pressures on a small area can affect the entire volume of liquids, and so forth? Does the *object* itself draw me to itself and invite me to delve into its depth? No. Although a pragmatic approach in science means that the theme of knowledge is not very prominent, this does not therefore guarantee a full object-thematicity. The truth is that in such a case of pragmatic interest, the object is looked upon simply as a *means* to something else. Hence we are not preoccupied with it as such: its nature, meaning, and value. Rather, our interest is fixed on something else, the end for which the object in question is a means. Thus, the entire question of hydraulic systems does not interest me in its own right. I study hydraulics simply to accomplish something else which does interest me, namely, the elevating of the enormous weight.

It is true that the pragmatic approach, by putting little value on knowledge as such stands in sharp contrast to a real knowledge-thematicity. But this does not mean that the pragmatic approach is closer to object-thematicity. It is, rather, antithetical to it, only it goes in a direction different from that of an approach chiefly dominated by the theme of knowledge. Any possible object-thematicity is undermined in the pragmatic approach by the fact that the object assumes the character of a mere means. The pragmatic theme is always interested in *achievement*. It is concerned with bringing into existence something not-yet-real by means of our intelligent activity. How then can the object be thematic when it interests us only because of the end we hope to realize by using it? The end, rather, is thematic, and not the means.

We are faced now with three different themes that may determine the relation we have toward an object in knowledge. The first holds the object in high prominence, because of its value and meaning. The second gives the palm to knowledge as such and extends a secondary nod to the object. The third looks at the object only because it desires something else which can be attained with the aid of the object. The difference between this third, pragmatic theme, and the first, the object-theme, is much more radical than the difference between the first and the second themes. For the first two may fully coexist, and they do fully coexist in genuine philosophical knowledge. But the third theme is by its nature hostile to the first. The pragmatic approach inevitably corrodes object-thematicity. It may, however, coexist with knowledge-thematicity, especially as a motive for undertaking research. What plainly divides the first from the third theme is that object-thematicity implies the presence to a certain extent of the aforementioned contemplative theme, whereas the pragmatic approach excludes this theme from the start.

In science, the desire for knowledge is one jump ahead of any interest in the object as such. The thoroughness and the systematic and critical character of knowledge about the object stands more in the foreground than does the object itself. History and philology, for example, attest to the fact that moments which are of relatively slight importance are investigated with the same seriousness, and treated as of the same weight, as objects having much more important contents.

With respect to philosophical inquiry and knowledge, however, there is a highpoint of both object-thematicity and knowledge-thematicity. Yet, despite the high stress on knowledge in philosophy, greatly exceeding that in the other sciences, for philosophy the object is one jump ahead in thematicity.

The centrally important objects, which alone are the concern of philosophy, stand with their ontological weight totally before the spiritual eye of the philosophical searcher and knower. They always mean more to him than mere objects of knowledge. Hence, the unique reverence that is found in philosophical inquiry and also the solemn character of philosophical knowledge. Philosophy is essentially not so "neutral" as are the other sciences with respect to their own proper objects.

A further characteristic of the philosophical attitude stems from this fact. Whereas the notional theme predominates in all other scientific knowledge; in the case of philosophy the contemplative theme plays a decisive role. Philosophical inquiring yearns not only for a conscious, explicit, and profound knowledge of the object, but also for something beyond this — a contemplative possessing of the object, a spiritual wedding with it. Naturally this is very much graduated, either up or down, according to the height of meaning of the knowledge-object. The higher the form of God's image in a being, the greater is the role played by this contemplative theme. Philosophical longing, or eros, aims not only at the spiritual possession of the world of ethical values, for example, which possession is fulfilled in a clear and deep knowledge about the essential states of facts of this world, in a profound and thorough knowledge of ethical values, but also at the spiritual wedding of the mind with this world, which is brought about in the vision of the world of ethical values. The direction of this *eros* depends on the fact that philosophy grasps every object in its relation to the focus of reality, that philosophy sees in each object its function of reflecting God in some way. The cognitive glances of philosophy do not look at reality simply in its breadth. They do not travel over the world of being step by step until the entire dimension of breadth is covered. Rather, philosophy looks at every knowledge-object from the point of view of its depth. It follows the path which, in the case of every object-territory, leads to the absolute, to the original ground and source of all being. This attitude is already displayed in the questions about essences which philosophy asks. What is space, what is time, in their essence? What is the essence of faithfulness? of purity? of beauty? of the person? This is how it inquires. And in the *wonder* which is constitutive of its attitude, the wonder about being, there is always present a thoughtful consideration of the object *sub specie aeternitatis*, that is to say, in relation to the trace of God that is found in the specific content of this or that object.

Indeed, in the case of other types of scientific research also, something analogous to this can be found, but it lies completely beyond the respective science and its formal object. The physicist also can immerse himself contemplatively in the mysterious world of force. The historian can rest in the world, present now to his mind, of an epoch of culture, or in the special character of a great personality. But these contacts with knowledge-objects go beyond the respective attitudes proper to the sciences in question. They are extrascientific, in the sense that they properly come under either philosophy or a lived contact with being. So far as philosophy itself goes, however, its longing for a contemplative knowing-wedding with the object belongs to its most basic and ultimate attitude. This longing penetrates its entire knowledge process, and it is this which gives to philosophy its characteristic solemnity.

The contact with truth which philosophy desires is, therefore, of a nature different from that of the other sciences. The philosophical seeker intends ultimately to rest in a contemplative vision of truth. Philosophical knowledge is, therefore, the most extreme antithesis to every kind of knowledge which, as it were, "abandons" the object after having reached a knowledge of it. It distinguishes itself from the kind of knowledge-attitude for which knowledge is a sort of conquest of being with the result that one gains a superior position to the object by having known it or "seen through it." Of course, every other serious science likewise disowns this disrespectful knowledge-attitude, which from the start prohibits any real penetration into the essence of the object and which advertises its boast of "seeing through" the object only because it suffers from an illusion. But the philosophical attitude is the most extreme antithesis to it. Philosophy does not pretend to assume a position superior to the being it intends to know. Rather, it considers this being as a "partner" in which it wants to participate. It seeks to know the object, not in order to abandon it triumphantly when conquered, but to be able to be devoted to it more deeply and authentically. For this reason, a truth that is already known never becomes old or outdated for philosophy — not even in the sense in which something true becomes obsolete for the other genuine sciences. Philosophy is not content with the contact with the object that is given in the mere knowing of it, but it seeks also a wedding with the object that is given in the contemplative having of it. Hence, in the most ideal knowledge-penetration of an object, the object never ceases to possess a real interest to the knower.

Thus philosophical knowledge is marked by a threefold thematicity in its ordination to the world of centrally important objects. Philosophy embodies, first, the highest and purest knowledge-thematicity, in the sense of the "notional" theme; second, the full object-thematicity; and, third, the thematicity of a wedding with the object in contemplation.

2. The depth dimension and depragmatization of the philosophical knowledge of essences

Philosophical inquiry wants to push forward into an essentially deeper layer of the object than is sought after by the other sciences. If we supposed that all questions and problems of the other sciences were resolved, still nothing would be asked or answered with respect to the depth-dimension in which philosophy is interested.

This difference in depth is determined by the difference in approach between philosophy and the other sciences. But it is also determined by the difference in their respective objects.

We have already seen that the nature of the *object* in each case determines the difference between apriori and empirical knowledge. Apriori knowledge is possible only with objects having a necessary, highly intelligible essence. We have also seen, moreover, that even with respect to an object possessing a necessary and intelligible essence, not every fact which we may wish to know is accessible to apriori insight. Joy is a good example of this. It possesses a necessary and intelligible essence. We can, consequently, grasp with absolute certainty several truths rooted in the essence of joy. We can understand that it is an intentional experience, which presupposes a knowledge of the object as well as of the importance of the object, and, likewise, that the object of joy may be a value, an objective good for the person, or it may be something only subjectively satisfying. Other facts about joy, however, are not accessible to apriori knowledge, for example, the influence of joy on the health and the body of a person.

Again, the object, "man," has a necessary and intelligible

essence and is thus an eminent object of apriori knowledge. At the same time, however, many facts about man are in no way rooted in his intelligible essence as a person. Hence, they cannot be grasped in an insight. These facts require empirical observation and investigation. All the facts of man's physiological nature fall into this empirical and nonintelligible category, as well as all psychophysical and psychological facts.

It follows that apriori knowledge makes a twofold demand. The object it deals with must have a necessary and intelligible essence, and the facts it discovers must be essentially and intelligibly rooted in this essence. Empirical knowledge, on the other hand, claims as its object all those beings that have a morphic unity, and not only these, but also all those "opaque" facts which may belong to beings that have a necessary essence. To put this in another way, we may say that as far as states of facts are concerned, the object of an apriori knowledge is always different from the object of empirical knowledge. But as far as beings and real substances are concerned, one and the same being may present an intelligible essence and many intelligible states of facts rooted in the essence, and present likewise an opaque such-being which is not intelligible and which must be subjected to empirical study. It can happen, therefore, and it is indeed very often the case, that one and the same substance is investigated by both apriori and empirical methods. Thus, both rational and experimental psychology study man.

In a broad sense we may say that "man" is the object of both these studies and that, therefore, they have the "same" object. But, strictly speaking, this is false. The real and immediate object of apriori knowledge is always something different from the immediate object of empirical knowledge. The results of these two kinds of knowledge likewise differ. The eternal verities, the luminous insights afforded by apriori knowledge, can be reached only in this apriori way. They can never be the result of any empirical knowledge. Nor, on the other hand, can empirical truths ever be reached by apriori knowledge.

What obtains between the different objects of apriori and empirical knowledge obtains in an analogous way between the objects of philosophy and the sciences. In many cases what makes a scientific result different from a philosophical one is exactly equivalent to what makes an empirical object different from an apriori object. In many cases, but not always. As we saw previously, for a given being to be an object of philosophical analysis, it must have other features in addition to the prime one of possessing an intelligible and necessary essence. Not every apriori fact is a philosophical one. The fact that two and two equals four is certainly apriori. It is not philosophical, however, because it lacks the note of central importance which every object of philosophy must possess.

We have also seen that, although individual numbers and number combinations fall outside the scope of philosophy because they are not centrally important, the nature of number in general is a specifically philosophical topic. Now we must notice that the state of facts in question when philosophy inquires about the nature of number in general is completely different from the state of facts at stake when mathematics analyzes specific numbers and number combinations. The questions asked are different and the results obtained are different. Philosophy plainly wants to know something different from what mathematics can offer when philosophy asks, "What is number?" "What kind of entity is number?" "What is the relation of number to the real world?" "What is the difference between ontological unity and oneness in the numerical sense?" "What is the difference between number and the ontological 'accident' of quantity?"

Even here, therefore, it remains true that the immediate object of philosophy is always something different from that of the other sciences, no matter how closely related both objects are to the one being that is approached from the two different viewpoints. This difference in immediate object must be kept in mind. It will help us to see how the difference in depth between philosophy and the other sciences rests on the fact that philosophy is interested in beings having a necessary essence only insofar as intelligible and necessary facts are intelligibly and necessarily rooted in these beings and, moreover, only insofar as such facts are of a central importance and have a relation to the universe of being.

In philosophizing, the human mind awakes to a thoroughly new stage of awareness and is rooted in a "deactualized" standpoint, from which it looks out upon being. Compared to this, the other sciences move *among* beings and rub familiar shoulders, so to speak, with the beings investigated. Not so philosophy. The philosophical putting of a question confronts the objects with the light of the absolute, as it were, and, therefore, considers the being not only from the depragmatized and deactualized position but also from the point of view which depends on the main theme of the object and the objectterritory.

Most sciences observe their respective objects from a certain point of view, and it is not necessary that this point of view be dictated by the main theme of the object in question. Physics and chemistry consider different cross sections of the world of material being. Such cross sections imply no deformation of the object inasmuch as they are made with a *fundamentum in re*, and not arbitrarily. But they do imply a *limitation* of the object since they depend only on a segment of it. History likewise considers its object from a certain point of view, that of the factual order and interconnection of events. History does not inquire about the essence of heroes and saints but about the concrete factual appearances of such men, about their lives, works, deeds, and the like. Neither does it ask about the natural laws which lie at the root of the burial of Herculaneum and Pompeii. It asks only about the facts themselves and their historical importance. Characteristic of the philosophical attitude is that its point of view not only has a *fundamentum in re*, as is true of all other genuine intellectual disciplines, but also is oriented around the main theme of the object or object-territory. The factual themes around which our knowledge can be oriented do not simply stand with equal rights, one beside the other. On the contrary, they have an order of rank, a hierarchy, according to their relation to the real meaning-axis of the object. I can look, for example, upon a landscape from the aesthetic point of view, the economic, the geological, the zoological, the botanical, the historical, the strategical, and many others, but always from a special point of view. None of these points of view is arbitrary, to be sure. It is also true that there is a difference in the content of the object revealed under these viewpoints, a content which rests on the fact that some of these points of view are of purely knowledge-interest, whereas others have pragmatic interest. Prescinding from this difference, we still notice that the various themes of pure knowledge-interest do not stand on the same level. For the question which seeks the main and the subordinate points of view is given objectively, independent of our knowledge interests. Thus the strategical and economic viewpoints, inasmuch as they are pragmatic, are already much further removed from the fullness of the main theme. Of the two, the economic is indeed incomparably less impoverished, arbitrary, and external. For the need it serves is by far the more classical and it touches a point lying much closer to the meaning of the object than does the strategical.

Thus, the botanical point of view is more pertinent than the historical to the full main theme of a landscape. Again, if we think of a literary work of art, we can consider it aesthetically, historically, scientifically, or ethically. Here the main theme of the object unequivocally dictates that the aesthetic point of view is primary.

If an object is considered from only one point of view, there necessarily follows a limitation of the aspects given by the object. But this limitation will mean one thing when the viewpoint is centered around the main theme of the object, and something totally different when the viewpoint is oriented around a subordinate theme of the object. A strict one-sidedness is not implied by our considering an object from the viewpoint of its substantial and primary theme. Strictly speaking, of course, we can say that a new object comes into focus whenever we change our point of view. The historical consideration of a work of art looks upon the origin of the work, the influences which affected the artist, his subjective intentions, and so forth. The aesthetic consideration looks upon the work of art itself, its value, and the like. Although each of these different aspects of the object belongs to diverse areas of knowledge-interest, they all are linked in reality, and one aspect is the center and supporter for all the rest. The extraction in knowledge of an accidental feature of an object leads, to be sure, to a new object of knowledge in the strict sense, but it does not eliminate the central unity underlying all the objects of knowledge which can be based upon it. Consequently it remains true that the various possible viewpoints in knowledge can and must be measured by the relevant weight of the theme upon which the point of view is based. The philosophical viewpoint is distinguished by the fact that it not only follows the highest theme within the object and, therefore, asks only about centrally important things, but also inquires about the main theme of the object of knowledge in question. Thus, of all knowledges, philosophical is the least one-sided, least limited, and least pragmatic. It is the knowledge most purely and exclusively determined by the complete such-being of an object, for it is always directed toward that essence.

PHILOSOPHICAL KNOWLEDGE AND INQUIRY

The attitude of philosophical knowledge is not only completely free from any pragmatic concern, but also from every limitation and one-sidedness springing from a point of view oriented around a theme that is not central and principal to the object. This same characteristic of philosophical knowledge follows from its spiritual position with respect to its object. Philosophy occupies a position removed from actuality, whereas, in comparison, the sciences "move between" many actual, concrete beings. This position of philosophic knowledge does not imply, however, that such knowledge is removed from a lived contact with the object. It means, rather, a distance which enables us to approach the object in the way objectively determined by the main theme. It means, finally, that even in posing a question about the object, philosophy is completely concerned with its principal theme.

Philosophy implies a *wondering* about its object. In philosophy one "wakes up" in a special way. When a man embarks upon a philosophical analysis of the world, he begins to stare at the world in wonder, instead of taking it for granted. He emancipates himself, as it were, from the entanglements of the concrete situation and removes himself a certain distance from it. He no longer moves among things but places himself, as it were, at the axis of truth. Now his stand is freed from all preoccupations which do not originate from the objective meaning and essence of the being. His standpoint is free from the whirl of the actual. It is also unpragmatic. From this standpoint he looks at the being and takes it seriously for what it is and means in itself.

The philosophic stand is the very antithesis, however, of that "distance" from the object which results from our dwelling in abstract concepts instead of our delving into the reality in its full existential flavor. This "conceptual" attitude, although it can be found in many philosophers, is in itself contrary to the very meaning and genius of philosophy.

True and genuine philosophy, as we shall see later on, requires a continuous and most intimate contact with reality, with all beings that are accessible to philosophical analysis. We here merely notice that the "distance" from the object proper to philosophy is the very opposite of the blind haughtiness of certain philosophers who neglect all intimate contact with the objects in question, and who are content to go from concept to concept. This kind of distance, far from aiding philosophy by allowing it to see the object in an unpragmatic way, really serves to kill philosophy. For to remain within the sphere of already known and defined concepts means that we have severed the life-giving, life-sustaining, always fruitful link between our mind and the world of being, soaked in infinite and mysterious plenitude.

The philosophical stand, with its unpragmatic "objectivity," is also the very antithesis to that attitude whereby one looks at the object from without, in a "disinterested" or "neutral" manner, in the so-called "laboratory" spirit. This kind of neutral attitude, whereby one places the objects in question on a plate, as it were, and looks at them with the mere curiosity of knowing, is incompatible with the object-thematicity which, as we saw before, is proper to philosophy. Because in philosophy the knowledge-thematicity never surpasses the object-thematicity, it is impossible that philosophy could adopt this "neutrality" toward the object which we find in science.

The philosopher, thanks to his "distance" from the object and to his freedom from the whirl of actuality, is able to enjoy a deeper and more intimate contact with the object. As paradoxical as it may seem, distance in this sense is an aid to intimate contact. By placing himself at the axis of truth, by staring at the object in the light of truth, by his attitude of solemnity and reverent wondering, the philosopher frees himself from all obstacles that hinder his mind from "listening" to the voice of being and that prevent the object from disclosing itself in all its plenitude and mysterious depth. By reason of this freedom, this emerging from all interests not engendered by the object itself, the philosopher acquires a closeness or proximity to the object which surpasses the closeness that existed before the emerging from actuality took place. This new proximity and closeness gives, in a certain sense, to the object a unique "actuality" of its own. It hovers before us, as, analogously, the beloved stands in a unique light before the lover.

The universe is mysteriously deep and solemn. Deep also are the centrally important objects of philosophy. It is to the depth of these things that we awaken when we emerge from practical closeness to the object and from entanglement in accidental situations. We in no sense emerge to the neutral objectivity proper to the sciences. Adequate in the sciences, this neutrality is inadequate, we might say fatal, in philosophy. The depth-dimension of the objects of philosophy calls for a deep and reverent wondering and it discloses itself to this attitude and to this attitude alone.

Let us take another look at this philosophical distance from the object. We must consider and distinguish two ways in which an object may be "close" to us. In the first way, we are close to objects when we move among them, become entangled with them, when we approach them with a pragmatic interest. In the second way, we are close to certain objects because of an existential contact with them, because of a lived contact in the depths of our spiritual life. As we shall see, the distance in philosophy opposes the first kind of closeness but not the second.

The first kind of closeness exists with respect to all objects that have a practical function in our lives. The water we wash with, the towels we use to dry ourselves, the chair we sit on, the taxi we ride in, the pots we cook in, the glasses we drink from, and so on — these are close to us in the first sense. We approach all of them with a naïve pragmatic attitude. We take all of them for granted. They possess for us a familiarity which is not the result of a thorough thematic knowledge but of repeated use. We are too close to them, in the sense of their being too familiar to us, for us to pose questions concerning their nature, for us to be curious about them and, afortiori, to wonder about them. This attitude of being too familiar with certain things and taking them too much for granted is not restricted to practical things. The rhythmic changes of the moon in all its phases, the alternations of day and night, the rhythm of the seasons, the star-covered sky — all are also taken for granted in the ordinary course of life. Even life and death, two of the greatest mysteries in the universe, are accepted as routine events. We do not question the whence and the where of existence but take the whole of existence for granted: "It happens every day." We also turn this unquestioning familiarity upon certain persons who have a function in our lives, perhaps persons we meet in society, perhaps colleagues in our business or profession, perhaps the mailman, the milkman, the ticket seller at the railroad station, the policeman. We have not really awakened with respect to these things and persons. We have not yet gained that distance from the objects which all systematic knowledge requires, the scientific as well as the philosophical. This kind of closeness has the character of a *blind familiarity*.[1]

The second kind of closeness is completely different. This refers to deep existential contacts in our spiritual life, to the contact with being that is granted to us in all deep experiences, when something in nature or art discloses its beauty to us and moves us deeply, when we are profoundly touched by a great

---

[1] In a certain way children are exempt from this familiarity-blindness, no doubt partly because the things are *not* familiar enough to be taken for granted. This fact explains the astonishment and genuine delight that accompanies many of the perceptions of a child. Take him to the zoo and he stares with wonder and incredulity at the mysterious objects before him. The waves at the beach, the fact of rainfall, birth and death, all are eagerly and sincerely investigated. Although uncritical, the child's mind may nevertheless be called more "metaphysical" than the mind of an ordinary adult.

personality, by his charity or generosity, when we are impressed with the intellectual power and depth of insight in, say, a dialogue of Plato or the *Confessions* of St. Augustine, or when the personality of a beloved person reveals itself to us overwhelmingly, and our souls interpenetrate each other in a deep love.

In all cases like these, the object is grasped with an especial awakenedness. It is thrown into relief and in a certain way we emerge from the dull routine of the day, the ordinary course of life. We emerge from the pragmatic tension also, which impels us toward an end to be fulfilled. We break loose from the rhythm which pushes us from one occupation to another. Such emerging, it is true, does not imply any questioning on our part, any inquiry, as might be expected in a systematic kind of knowledge. There is here no full thematicity of knowledge. Our emerging from the deep sleep of ordinary routine is certainly different from our familiarity with things, but it differs in its own way from this blind familiarity and not by reason of its being systematic. Any systematic knowledge, and philosophy above all, is in direct antithesis to blind familiarity. But this emerging has not the same kind of antithesis. It is rather the awakenedness of immediate experience. It concerns the full thematicity of the object as such, inasmuch as the object discloses itself in an extraordinary way. This personal, lived, existential contact with the object is the precise opposite of the attitude of blind familiarity. There is a great scale of intimacy and closeness within the frame of this existential contact, but for our purposes here it is enough to stress the difference between this kind of "closeness" in general and the blind familiarity which we mentioned before.

In a previous chapter we hinted at the distinction in question here. There we distinguished the pragmatic approach to the object from the approach wherein the object becomes strongly thematic because of an intensely dramatic situation involving the object. Thus, when we see a man in danger of death, the value of human life flashes up with great impact. We grasp this object in a way radically different from any pragmatic approach. The being speaks to us in its full importance, in its existential garment. The situation in which this being is present to us is not dominated by the theme of knowledge, for the dramatic call to action stands in the foreground and overshadows all other considerations. Yet, this dramatic, practical theme of the situation does not frustrate or undermine our adequate perception and our deep understanding of the object as does the pragmatic approach.

The philosophical standpoint, from which we gaze at the universe in general and at specific objects, certainly differs from the closeness of the existential lived contact as well as from the closeness of blind familiarity. It differs because it has a high thematicity of knowledge, because it implies a "distance" from the object and a "deactualization." But whereas it forms an outspoken antithesis to the closeness of blind familiarity, it has many deep links to an existential lived contact. Although, as we saw when we showed that the philosophical stand places us at the axis of truth, philosophical "closeness" has roots different from the closeness of existential lived contact and is, therefore, only an analogous kind of closeness, nevertheless, philosophical closeness presupposes in many areas an existential lived contact.

In ethics, aesthetics, or philosophy of community, the success and even the possibility of a philosophical analysis depends upon a prephilosophical lived contact with the respective objects. Even though a man be eminently gifted in philosophy, even though he can offer brilliant and profound insights in such fields as epistemology, he may be a dismal failure in aesthetics or ethics if he lacks the necessary lived contact with the object. If the world of moral values has never disclosed itself in its majesty and depth to a man, what can this man possibly discover in ethics? How shall he be able to interpret the metaphysical call and challenge of moral values if he has never once had a deep moral experience? For ethics it is imperative that the philosopher's prephilosophical experience be profound enough to have brought him into contact with the existential reality of moral values. The greatest gift of intelligence cannot substitute for this lived contact.

Again, a philosopher's analysis of aesthetic problems would be of no interest, and would also most likely be absurd, if the beauty in nature and in art played no role in his life — if he had never had an authentic lived, existential contact with the world of beauty. No philosophical gifts of acuteness, intelligence, or sagacity could enable him to attain deep insights into the nature of beauty if the true and genuine beauty in nature and art had never touched his heart deeply. What he says would be as worthless as the remarks about color by a man who has been blind from birth.

Philosophy, therefore, in certain disciplines presupposes this existential lived contact with objects. Not only this, but in philosophical closeness we find several elements analogous to existential closeness. Both, for example, have the full thematicity of the object. Both have the intimacy of contact with its full qualitative flavor and its mystery. Again, both are opposed to blind familiarity. They differ, however, as we said before, by reason of the different root of closeness in each case, and also by reason of the knowledge-thematicity which is full in philosophical contact and nonexistent in the naïve, existential one. They differ also in that the closeness of the existential contact may surpass by far the closeness of any philosophical penetration.

We see, therefore, that philosophic "distance" from the objects of which it seeks knowledge forms the perfect antithesis to all "familiarity" with the object, in the sense of taking certain aspects for granted, to all mere intellectual "toying" with the object, to that closeness whereby we can no longer see the object in its totality. In no way does it imply an escape from the object, a distancing in which the living contact with the object, together with its atmosphere and self-revealing essence, is broken off so that the object becomes a merely neutral, peculiar phenomenon. This, in effect, would mean the ravishing of the object and the forcing of it into an arbitrary point of view. Philosophical distance, on the contrary, entails freedom from all arbitrariness. It renders possible our allowing ourselves to be borne along in knowledge by the main theme of the object in question.

Above all, in this remoteness of the spiritual position from which philosophy considers the object, there is no "seeing things from without."

We saw, in our analysis of apriori knowledge, that the mind is able to know "from within" only those objects having an essence that can be grasped intuitively. We saw, furthermore, that this knowledge from within is one of the deepest characteristics of philosophical knowledge. The direction toward knowledge of this kind is an essential characteristic of philosophical knowledge alone. By this same feature the above-mentioned dimension of depth, proper to philosophical inquiry and knowing, accredits itself. For philosophy not only seeks the deepest stratum of being, namely, the essences of objects, but also aims at a completely different knowledge-penetration of the object — at the *intus legere*.

All the empirical sciences, as we have already seen, approach the object only "from without," whether in single observations, whereby they grasp their data descriptively or whether through observation and induction whereby they disclose the such-being.

Natural science in our day, especially physics, is not restricted to the strict empirical procedure mentioned above. Besides using observations and inductions, and thus being strictly empirical, physics makes use of explanations, "guesses," and the like, which are not empirical in the strict sense.

In most of the sciences to some extent, but especially in physics, the hypotheses offered as explanations of the physical world have the character of constructions in which imagination and speculation play a predominant role. The role of hypotheses in natural science is highly important. Moreover, the different kinds of hypotheses and their respective natures are a fascinating topic in epistemology. It would be a worthwhile philosophical task to analyze the nature of scientific hypotheses and show how they differ from mere induction and observation. In this context, however, we wish to pass over this difference. For our task here is the distinction between science and philosophy. This distinction is not altered by the fact that the hypotheses of science are not empirical in the strict sense. For even so, they remain instances of knowledge "from without," and in this way they clearly differ from philosophical knowledge.

Scientific hypotheses differ not only from empirical inductions but also from philosophical hypotheses. Both possess the common note of being plausible speculations, but imagination plays a greater role in the scientific than in the philosophical hypothesis. The scientific hypothesis has more the character of a construction, of a possible explanation, whereas a good philosophical hypothesis restricts itself to elaborating the implications of the given. There is less room, consequently, for highly imaginative constructions which *might* happily explain a given fact. A second point of difference is that the scientific hypothesis always calls for a confirmation by empirical means — for a verification.

Whether, therefore, we look at the inductive side of science or the less empirical side of the use and verification of hypotheses, it remains true that science is a knowledge "from without." Philosophical knowledge, on the other hand, drawing from the intuitive givenness of necessary and intelligible essences, understands states of facts as necessarily grounded in the essence. Here the knowing mind stands in a contact of ultimate fruitfulness with the inner essence of the object. The mind moves out from the core and penetrates into the single elements and necessary components of the essence. From this enviable standpoint, the mind perceives the state of facts grounded therein, and, with each enlightened insight, it penetrates more deeply into the essence of the object so that this essence glows with more and more light.

We speak, for example, about "love" as something entirely familiar. We casually regard it as a self-evident, familiar thing. As soon, however, as we delve deeply into the essence of love, in a philosophical direction, a completely new and enlightened contact begins. We place ourselves in a close contact with the object and we are touched by its breath; simultaneously, we stand on a level remote from all contingencies — the de-actualized philosophical stand mentioned above. It is just in this manner that we glance into the interior of this essence instead of glancing, as before, alongside or around it. In looking at this essence we grasp certain constitutive elements of it, as well as states of facts necessarily grounded in it. We grasp, for example, the ordination of love to a being possessing a value, and also the essence of love as a value response. We understand that its two basic components, namely, the *intentio unionis* and the *intentio benevolentiae*, are constitutively grounded in its essence. All this takes place neither in going around the object and observing it from without, nor by reaching through induction facts or features hidden to our immediate approach, but in an intuitive penetration of the object "from within," from the very core of its essence.

Obviously this type of knowledge possesses another level of rational light and intelligibility than observation and induction. This "insight" has a character of understanding which the mere stating of something "from without" lacks completely. Here our mind is supported and embraced by the very meaning of the object, a real "preestablished harmony" between our intellect and the object.

The natural sciences are often considered as the model of criticism. In that they accept nothing unless it is a tangibly verifiable fact, they possess an admirable exactness. Of course, as we saw before, there are also some nonempirical elements in the sciences which cannot be verified in the same way as can inductive conclusions. Such are hypotheses, explanations, and interpretations. Even though there is some room for controversy in this area of hypotheses and interpretations, even though for a limited time there may be actual battles waged over conflicting results in science, medical science, for example, as happened in the Jenner affair over the smallpox vaccine, nonetheless, in general it remains true that the results in science are not controversial. This is in sharp contrast to philosophy, which seems to offer no result that is not scarred and seared by persistent and often violent controversy.

Thanks to the fact that science is exact, that it offers the possibility of tangible verification, and most of all, that its results are for the most part noncontroversial, the opinion is common that science is much more "critical" than philosophy. This opinion is false. Even though philosophy may not be able to boast of an exactness of the kind found in mathematics or the natural sciences, yet philosophy is pervaded by the critical spirit to the highest degree. This is linked to the depth-dimension character of philosophy and also to the higher degree of certitude that philosophy offers.

We saw before that another kind of "wondering" is found in philosophy than in science. The mere fact that epistemology plays such a great role in philosophy is ample and clear testimony that the philosopher still questions and probes where the other sciences already are silently presupposing and taking certain things for granted. In analyzing the various possibilities of knowledge, their validity and certainty, philosophy goes into a deeper stratum than science ever does and is as such more critical. The critical "spirit" which moves Descartes in his methodical doubt is a typical example of this higher criticism in philosophy. And the fact that philosophy can be satisfied only when it has grasped its object with absolute certitude, only when the questioned states of facts are either brought to evidence or ascertained by deduction based on evident premises, again discloses a greater criticism and, in another sense of the term, a greater exactness. True philosophy has, as it were, a much greater self-consciousness than any science. The philosopher is more conscious not only with respect to his object but also with respect to his own procedure and action.

True philosophy must exhibit greater cautiousness, and must never accept the slightest nonevident or unproved silent presupposition. It can never be satisfied with a vague or artificial conception.

That the results of philosophy are much more controversial is no argument against the greater criticism in philosophy nor against its higher type of exactness. We shall understand this after a brief look at the reasons for the controversial character of philosophical systems.

First, philosophical systems include to a great extent hypotheses and possible explanations which surpass the frame of classical philosophical insights. Because unshakable and indubitable insights are interwoven in these systems with constructions and hypothetical explanations, they unjustly share the fate of these constructions. They are dragged into the infinitely prolonged controversies to which the constructions and hypothetical explanations are naturally exposed. Insights like Augustine's *si fallor, sum*, or Plato's distinction in the *Meno* between apriori and empirical knowledge, or the Cartesian insight into the nonspatial character of the spiritual, or Kant's distinction between analytic and synthetic propositions, or Aristotle's distinction between efficient and final causes, are objectively and in themselves absolutely uncontroversial. They are evident and endowed with a higher certitude than any scientific result. But to be appreciated, philosophical insights require in us another intellectual organ than the one which operates by tangible verification. For someone who approaches them in an intellectual attitude which aims at a type of tangible verification, even absolutely evident philosophical truths will be veiled. He acts like the man who wants to hear colors and to see tones. Moreover, the actualization of the philosophical organ presupposes, besides a specific intellectual gift, many general attitudes of the person, such as reverence, spiritual élan, and many others.

Finally, we must not forget that there is a subconscious moral resistance against many philosophical truths, which does not exist with respect to scientific truths. We have dealt with this factor in knowledge in another work.[2] The question of the existence of absolute truth, and many metaphysical and ethical problems, have obviously a different bearing on the depths of our personal life than have scientific facts. They have an existential bearing and imply consequences for our moral life. The subconscious reluctance to accept them thus plays another role here than in the acceptance of the fact that "heat expands bodies," or that "water is composed of hydrogen and oxygen," or that "cosmic rays exist." Apart from these reasons for the more controversial character of philosophy, we must realize that in the sciences also there is controversy, only it manifests itself in a different direction. There have been innumerable scientific theories of former times which are now reversed and abandoned. The immanent and, as it were, automatic progress which is proper to many sciences, especially natural sciences, entails a continuous rhythm of replacing one theory by another. We need only think of medicine and compare the theories in the eighteenth century, concerning the cause of certain diseases,

---

[2] *The New Tower of Babel*, "Catholicism and Unprejudiced Knowledge."

with our present medical doctrines in order to see how one theory in the course of scientific progress dethrones a former one.

Philosophy, on the contrary, does not possess a similar immanent automatic progress. It is in no way an anachronism to encounter a Platonist or an Aristotelian in the twentieth century. Although there undoubtedly exists a hidden "movement" in philosophy, which brings certain problems to the fore in a certain epoch and gives to this epoch the character of *the hour* for this new insight, this rhythm has in no way the character of a continuous replacing of one doctrine by another. This intrinsic movement in philosophy, at which Hegel hints in his "thesis, antithesis, synthesis" doctrine is, first of all, something hidden and not obvious as is the progress in science. It is consequently a great and difficult task to trace this development in philosophy. It is, moreover, not continuous as in science, but exhibits many aberrations and interruptions. Above all, it never dethrones the real philosophical conquests. It never even makes them obsolete or superannuated. The great philosophical truths remain equally new and inspiring for any new epoch to come. This latter feature of philosophy is connected with the fact that sciences can be "learned," whereas philosophy requires a full co-operation, and a real direct grasping of truths on the part of the one who reads a great work in philosophy, e.g., a Platonic dialogue or the Augustinian *De Libero Arbitrio*.

The transmission of philosophical truths presupposes a specific philosophical gift on the part of the receiver. Philosophical truths cannot simply be accepted, as many parts of science can, but they must be understood in a direct contact with the object in question. And this also accounts for the fact that philosophical truths are more controversial in one and the same epoch than are scientific theories. It also explains why philosophy does not possess the character of science which allows a teacher to say: "Science has proved," whereby one utters a result which is commonly accepted.

Thus the reasons for the more controversial character of philosophy show clearly that it cannot be used as an argument against the eminently critical character of philosophy. The fact of philosophical controversy only proves that philosophers in general are less faithful to the requirements of true philosophy than scientists are to their own requirements.

We now see clearly that the difference separating the philosophical attitude toward knowledge from that of the other sciences is of a much more essential nature than the differences found in the separate sciences themselves; the difference, for example, between the natural sciences and the sciences like history, philology, political science, economics, and the like. The grand difference is based on much more essential and important modifications of knowledge as such.

3. *The positive relation of philosophy and scientific knowledge*

It is not sufficient to point out the characteristics of the philosophical attitude and to distinguish it thereby from that of the other sciences. We must also say a word about the positive relation of philosophy to the other sciences. We must affirm, first of all, that philosophy is as incapable of answering scientific questions as the sciences are of solving philosophical problems. To overstep the boundary from either side is equally fateful. Well-differentiated knowledge-objects exist for philosophy on the one hand, and the sciences on the other. They stand side by side, however, in relation to each other. The objects of philosophy need not always lie beyond those of the other sciences, as indeed happens with respect to ethics, aesthetics, epistemology, and so forth. As we saw before, the objects of philosophy are often the objective ground on which the other sciences move.

Thus, logic and epistemology deal with the presuppositions taken for granted and used by science. The philosophy of history, of language, and of law deal with those questions and facts which are the silent bases for the respective single sciences. They deal, for example, with the *essence* of history, of language, of law, and so forth.

But even where philosophy deals with objects which are basic, in one sense or another, for the other single sciences, its function and importance are never a mere preliminary service for science. It would be completely false to assume that the meaning and importance of philosophy lie in its being a formal methodology of sciences, or even a merely formal basis of them. This assumption overlooks the most important parts of philosophy, whose objects lie beyond science.

What the philosophy of right or of language or of history offers are genuine philosophical insights, which have in no way the character of methodological preludes for the respective sciences.

On the other hand, it must also be said that neither do these sciences depend in their own research upon the related philosophical disciplines. The historian need not know the true results of the philosophy of history in order to be a great historian. If it is true that philosophy is not the handmaid of the sciences, it is also true that philosophy is not the master of sciences. They are in general independent of each other even when they deal with the same topic, in a larger sense of the term "topic."

Historically speaking, philosophical views have had a tremendous influence on the development of science, and scientific discoveries have had a great influence on the views of many philosophers. We are not here concerned, however, with the mutual influences of philosophy and science which *de facto* took place, but rather with whether objectively they depend upon each other. In this respect different sciences vary to a great extent.

There is a scale with respect to the mutual influence between philosophy and science. The scale varies with the specific character of sciences. In considering, first, the question of the dependence of a science upon philosophy, we see that sciences like physics and chemistry do not presuppose a specific philosophy. Whatever may be the philosophical view of a chemist, he may accomplish great achievements in his field.

In sciences like zoology and biology, on the contrary, the philosophical view of a scholar does have an influence on his biological conceptions, naturally not insofar as single observations are concerned, but insofar as it is a question of their interpretation and their general evaluation. In a completely different way, his position on certain philosophical problems will influence the historical conceptions of an historian. A materialist will certainly write history in a different manner than a nonmaterialist, a personalist in a different manner than a collectivist. Here, even the concrete acceptance of a fact as authentically historical may sometimes depend upon the "philosophy" of the historian. If he starts from the thesis, for example, that a miracle is something intrinsically impossible, and if he places it on the level of magic, he will not accept the reality of certain facts even if they are historically authenticated in the most scientific manner. In this context, of course, our topic is the influence, not of a conscious adherence to a philosophy, but of unformulated convictions which a scientist holds with respect to philosophical topics. The question is how far does a given science need to presuppose tacitly certain philosophical truths.

When we turn to certain modern sciences, such as sociology, psychology, or psychiatry, a completely different situation is at stake. Here it is easy to see that the dependence upon philosophy reaches much further. The psychiatrist who does not see the difference between contrition and a guilt complex, or the difference between mere inhibitions and a consciousness of moral prohibitions, will inevitably be greatly frustrated in his own field.

In these "new" sciences, it is even true that a set of philosophical truths is the indispensable basis for any fruitful and adequate scientific research. This does not imply that the psychiatrist, sociologist, or psychologist must start with philosophical research, but rather that he must have the right conception of certain philosophical topics for his own work. Whether he knows it or not, he inevitably presupposes certain philosophical theories. If they are wrong, it will have a fatal bearing on the results in his own field.

What now shall be said of the influence of the sciences on philosophy? As independent as philosophy in general is of science, as little as the results of science can influence the results in ethics, aesthetics, epistemology, logic, or metaphysics, still the influence of science may be great in giving birth to new philosophical problems and new philosophical questions. We have already mentioned in Chapter IV the role of empirical scientific results for certain philosophical problems, in the case of Bergson's *Matter and Memory*. But above all, the very existence of the different sciences, and the very fact of their development, offer to philosophy many interesting epistemological problems.

Thus we see that there is a mutual fecundation between science and philosophy. But this must never allow us to forget the essential difference between both and the value and importance which each possesses on its own.

4. *The method of philosophy*

As we saw previously, only by going beyond observation and induction can we obtain knowledge of the world of essences and the states of facts necessarily grounded in them. We obtain apriori knowledge either by intuition or by deduction.

The term "intuitive" for many people connotes the irrational. One believes that intuitive givenness has its home outside the bounds of philosophical rational penetration. If someone says that he grasps something intuitively, he is interpreted as saying that he has a mysterious and irrational contact with the object, a mystical vision, or at least a contact with it lying beyond rational knowledge. This is a complete misunderstanding. We wish, therefore, to give a brief clarification of the term "intuition."

We have pointed to the nature of intuitive givenness in a broad sense in Chapter VI, when dealing with the three marks of perception. We saw that the intuitive element consists in the full unfolding of a such-being before our mind, which is precisely to be found in perception in contrast to inferring. We also saw that representation is more intuitive than meaning. Since, however, in representation we do not take cognizance of something, but only actualize knowing, by the term "intuitive knowledge" or "intuition," we always imply the further note of a self-present givenness of the object. Intuitive knowledge means here "perception," in the broadest sense of this term. Intuition in this sense plays a fundamental role in all of our knowledge, naïve and scientific, as well as philosophical.

There is no need for us to stress the privileged position of intuition from the point of view of plenitude, fecundity, and intimacy of contact with the object.

Besides the broad sense, whereby intuition means the fully deploying, self-present object, there is a narrower and more specific sense of the term. By intuition or intuitive givenness in this narrower sense we refer to such a thing as "intellectual intuition." This is possible only in the case of the highly intelligible necessary such-being unities, which we have called the genuine essences, and the necessary and intelligible states of facts rooted in these essences. Intuitive givenness of this kind includes not only the self-presence and deployment of the essence of the object, but also a unique intelligibility which is present only in the case of these necessary essences. Here, therefore, "intuition" means that deployment of the essence before our mind which enables us to penetrate the object fully. In an intuition the object becomes luminous to us in its essence. It is, for this reason, the most radical and polar opposite to the case wherein our mind merely "falls externally" upon the such-being when it only bluntly observes it. Much more, this intuitive grasping refers to that knowledge "from within," with which we previously became acquainted, and which makes possible also the fulfillment of the contemplative theme. Intuition in this specific sense possesses all the perfections of intuition in the broad sense in addition to those proper to it. What is more, intuition in the narrower sense does not always require for its accomplishment the self-presence of the object in perception. Thus, we do not require the perception of a concrete person in order to penetrate intuitively the nature of person and grasp states of facts which are rooted in the essence of personal being — its nonspatial character, for instance. Placing a personal being before our mind, and then focusing on its essence is sufficient to allow us to reach an intuitive contact. Again we need not perceive the actual colors of orange, red, and yellow, in order to understand intuitively the essence relation which is affirmed by the proposition: "Orange lies between red and yellow."

We are not concerned at the moment with the fact that we need to perceive a being at least once in order to get acquainted with it. What matters here is not the primal experience of essence, but the fact that the contact with the being which is required for intuitive knowledge of essences may already be granted by placing an example of this being before our mind. The extraordinary fact here is that in the case of a necessary intelligible such-being, which we call a genuine essence, this essence is not simply represented, but is also *self*-given and *self*-present, though the example through which it is given may be only represented. Yet we must pay special attention to the fact that if, for example, we try to become clear about the essence

PHILOSOPHICAL KNOWLEDGE AND INQUIRY 217

of willing, and obtain the essence relation of "No willing without thinking," then what we do is not to analyze the concept willing, but rather to represent spiritually the such-being unity of *willing*, following this with an intuitive penetration into it. We do not look at the *concept* of willing, nor at the meaning of the term "willing" and its characteristics. On the contrary, we turn to the unity of willing, not to its accidental features but to its very essence. We look at the intuitively revealed necessary and essential unity of willing.

In the naïve perceiving of willing, more is already given to us than the mere existence of a such-being. The necessary genuine essence of willing is somehow given, but it is, as it were, still sealed. But when the philosophical question which seeks for the essence is put, the nucleus of the essence is fixed upon and explicitly considered as such. It is only at this time, therefore, that we speak of an intuitive grasping in the strict, narrow sense.

With regard to this strict intuition, it is essentially unimportant whether we proceed by means of a concrete perception or, instead, by a mere spiritual representation. For, even when we employ a concrete perception, the self-givenness of the essence which is implied in the intuitive grasping nourishes itself on the concrete givenness of the necessary unity, and not on the self-presence of the concrete object. We must above all realize that this intuition of a higher kind, possible only in the case of contents with a highly intelligible, necessary such-being unity, is just as direct as intuition in the broad sense and is just as different from indirect, deduced knowledge.

It is not difficult to see that intuition in neither the broad nor the narrow sense implies anything "irrational." Indeed, as we have already seen, intuition in the narrow sense presents us with the ultimate source and climax of all *ratio*. The luminous intelligibility of a genuine essence, the completely spiritual penetration of an object "from within," is on the one hand the basis of all rational knowledge and, on the other, the climax of the knowing contact of our mind with an object. Such an intuition is not limited to the direct grasping of an essence itself. It extends also to the states of facts which are necessarily grounded in the essence; they likewise become luminously intelligible. For example, when in a philosophical attitude we represent to ourselves an act of willing in its concrete essence, not only is willing itself intuitively given to us, but also the state of facts that there is "No willing without understanding." The state of facts also is self-present, self-given, and intuitively deployed in its essence before our mind. The mind does not observe it simply from the outside, as it does any empirical fact like "Today the weather is fine." On the contrary, this state of facts becomes luminous. We penetrate it from within. It possesses a lucidity and intelligibility analogous to that of an essence.

After this brief clarification of the broad and narrow sense of intuition, we may ask ourselves in what way philosophical knowledge is possible. We answer as follows: *In most cases intellectual intuition is the only way of acquiring philosophical knowledge.* This is exclusively true, for example, in all ontologies of the different object-territories, as well as in ethics and aesthetics, among others. How else can one intend to understand the difference between substance and accident, the nonspatial quality of psychical beings, the difference between motivation and mechanical causality, the difference between an efficient and a final cause, and the grounds and *ratio* of knowledge, if not by intuitive representation of the objects in question? We cannot deduce these differences, these states of facts, from anything else. Much less can we know them inductively. But intuition plays a prominent role even when deduction is both possible and necessary. This is true of deduction proper, and also of those "inferrings" which, as we saw, are involved in what is the most important point in philosophy. Deduction proper is dependent upon the essentially intuitive character of the initial premises. In philosophy, moreover, deduction plays a minor role, not only quantitatively but also according to its importance.

In that unique case, however, wherein we infer from actual facts the fundamental fact of God's existence, not only is there demanded an especially high form of intuition in the broad sense, but also that essence-premise which is the pivotal point of the inference is always grasped intuitively in the strict sense. At any rate, we can affirm as valid this general rule: The sphere of inferring philosophical knowledge may never be entered by any formalization which abandons, *more geometrico*, as it were, the intuitive contact with the object in question and operates purely in a formal way with the premises. Whenever we deal with deductive knowledge we must always hold firmly to the living, concrete contact with being that is given in the premises which have been directly grasped. We should never leave our feet dangling in the air, basing all our deductions merely on a formalization of a state of facts which is present in the meaning-unity of a proposition. On the contrary, we must base them on states of facts nourished and sustained by the intuitive givenness of the premises.

An all-essential difference between mathematical and philosophical knowledge is present here. As soon as one sees in mathematical knowledge an ideal, and tries to proceed with an analogous formalization in philosophy, the philosophical knowledge becomes sterile and fruitless. At times this attempt even leads to false results because, without the correction of a living contact with the object, one easily falsifies the proper meaning of a premise by an artificial formalization.

Finally, a direct understanding, that is to say, an intuition, is demanded for the ultimate laws which are the tacit presuppositions in any deductive knowledge and which make it possible for the conclusion to identify itself as really existing.

We saw that philosophy does not resort to blunt observation and induction, that it is independent of experience in this sense, and that it presupposes only the such-being experience of its object.

Someone might object: "Do we not also in philosophy, when we analyze a being, look at many examples of it, at various situations, in order to reach its authentic nature? For instance, in analyzing the nature of courage, do we not take several examples, do we not consult different types of courageous people: the temperamentally courageous, the rash, the morally courageous, and so on? Do we not also observe the different examples, and do we not formulate inductive conclusions from our several repeated observations in order to find our way to a clear understanding of the nature of courage and the different types of courage? Do we not find such a way of proceeding in the dialogues of Plato, for instance in *Lysis*, *Laches*, or *Protagoras*?"

In answer we say that philosophy must indeed always consult reality, must again and again in different examples intuit the essence, and listen to the information which the object alone can grant us. But this consultation radically differs from "observation" in the sense in which we use the term. And the function of the *example* in the process of grasping necessary intelligible facts rooted in the essence of a being has nothing in common with the one which the single *observations* have in an inductive process.

The consultation of reality is here a continually repeated *intuitive* contact with the essence of the object. It is pervaded and guided by the light of the intelligible essence of the being. All the different examples here serve, first of all, only to immerse ourselves always anew in the full flavor of the real object, to protect us from any artificial construction, or from any imprisoning of ourselves in concepts; second, to eliminate everything which does not belong to the essence and is only accidentally connected with it. When, for instance, in analyzing the nature of love, we look at such an example as Romeo's love for Juliet, and then again at the love of Heathcliff in *Wuthering Heights*, and again at the love of Dante for Beatrice, the analysis of all these examples is guided by an intuitive contact with the nature of love; it is in the light of this intuitive contact with the nature of love that we clearly grasp the elements of pride, *ressentiment*, and self-assertion in Heathcliff, which are as such incompatible with (though they are here combined with) certain elements of love. In the case of Romeo and Dante, on the other hand, we find an authentic love. In Beethoven's *Fidelio*, however, a full typical embodiment of the essence of love is to be found.

The difference between this and observation and induction is clearly given. In the first place, the examples in philosophical consultation of reality do not necessarily refer to really existing persons, because it is only the such-being which counts, whereas in empirical observation one deals only with really existing facts inasmuch as here the existence counts. Second, philosophical consultation does not look at the example from "without" and pick up every detail which it can find, without the help of the intelligibility of the whole being. On the contrary, in every single case, we have an intuitive contact with the intelligible essence, whether it is an example which has the function of presenting us with a typical embodiment of this essence, or an example with the function of helping us to eliminate all factors which, though coexisting, do not belong to the essence. During the entire process, it is the intuitively given intelligible essence which, embodied in the example, informs us, and which shines forth when we look at it, always granting us new insights, always presenting us from "rushed" statements, always fecundating our mind anew with its plenitude. And again, it is the intelligible intuitively given essence which forms the background against which all the examples are checked to eliminate all elements which only apparently resemble the essence in question. It is continually a consultation of reality whereby the object is grasped "from within." There is no inductive "inferring" in a philosophical consultation of reality. The grasping of necessary intelligible facts rooted in the essence is a purely intuitive process.

Philosophical consultation is not a cautious going-around "from without," whereby only the real experience of a here-and-now existence can support our knowledge, and where the mere fact of existence replaces the intelligibility. It is the always renewed fecundation of our mind with the plenitude of the intelligible essence. It is the step-by-step progress of delving deeper into this essence, always by intuitive insights. And even though philosophical consultation of reality differs from observation, description, and induction, the philosophical intuition which goes with it is in a certain way much closer to reality than is the contact of science. True philosophy is in a certain sense less abstract than science. Certainly, it is a difference which is again determined by the object in question. The highly intelligible necessary essence grants a more intimate contact, a greater proximity to our intellect, than do objects and facts which are the topic of science. But because of this, philosophy is found to observe an intimate contact with the full plenitude of these intelligible beings, and to abstain from an abstract journey from concept to concept. In always going back to concrete examples, philosophy aims to reach the full *sapere*, the full-flavor of the object, and to do justice to its real specific nature in all its mysterious richness and existential flavor. In this sense of the term "empirical," philosophy must be more empirical than the sciences, especially the exact natural sciences.

5. Phenomenology

The term phenomenology has already assumed an ambiguous character today. One meaning of phenomenology is that which Husserl gave to this term after 1913, in his *Ideen*, and all subsequent works. It is this meaning which is the topic of Father Quentin Lauer's *Triumph of Subjectivity*, and which, according to him, leads Husserl to *Transcendental Idealism*. But a completely different meaning of phenomenology is in strict, radical opposition to any idealism. It signifies in fact the most outspoken objectivism and realism. It is this meaning of phenomenology which we find in the writings of Adolf Reinach, Alexander Pfaender, myself, and several others, and which we, at least, identified with the meaning of phenomenology in the first edition of Husserl's *Logische Untersuchungen*. In fact, the historical impact of *this* work of Husserl, attracting students of all countries to Göttingen, was due to its unambiguous refutation of psychologism, subjectivism, and all types of relativism.

The phenomenological approach in this sense is chiefly synonymous with the intuitive analysis of genuine, highly intelligible essences. It is neither a reduction of the world to mere phenomena, nor a mere description of appearances or of subjective experiences. Nor is phenomenology a mere *prise de conscience* of the meaning of our concepts, but it is concerned with the very essence of the object. It is rather the approach which is at the basis of every great philosophical discovery, whether found in Plato's *Meno*, Aristotle's *Organon* or in the *Si fallor, sum* argument of St. Augustine. It is always to be found when a real, intuitive contact with an object having a genuine essence is attained in contrast not only to observation and induction, but to all constructions, speculations, or hypotheses. It is also in contrast to any genetic approach which claims that we understand the object when we know its causes; it is likewise in contrast to the position which sees the climax of intellectual penetration in the definition of the object.

Thus, phenomenology seems not to be something new. And yet, because former philosophers used this arch-method of philosophy only occasionally, and always unsystematically, without being conscious of it as a method, we may say that phenomenology is new and even revolutionary. For phenomenology as a systematic method excludes the confusion of evident insights with mere hypotheses, whereas we see often in former philosophic works real insights placed on the same level as hypotheses.

But that is not all. What is also new in phenomenology is its emphasis on the existential, immediate intuitive contact with the object, in opposition to any abstractionism or any dealing with mere concepts. Finally, what is perhaps especially new in phenomenology is that this method is used, not only *de facto*, but epistemologically founded and legitimated by means of the all-important distinction between genuine essences and mere morphic unities. Obviously, because Father Lauer's book deals only with phenomenology in the sense of the later Husserl, that is, as *Transcendental Idealism*, none of his arguments have any relevance whatever to phenomenology in our sense. Father Lauer says in the same book (p. 142): "The appeal, for example, which we find in the ethics of Max Scheler or of Dietrich von Hildebrand, owes more to its Augustinian foundation than to its phenomenological elaboration." Astonishingly enough, he does not seem to grasp the radically different nature of phenomenology in my works as contrasted to Husserl's phenomenology. Instead of interpreting my ethical work as a hidden Augustinianism which parades under the garb of phenomenology, he might have inferred how much of a phenomenologist St. Augustine truly was in his great philosophical discoveries.

By this we touch on one of the specific features of phenomenology mentioned above, namely, its existential contact with reality, its commerce with the living plenitude and full flavor of being in contrast to any preoccupation with merely abstract concepts.

The phenomenological approach is not, however, restricted to the philosophical analysis of genuine essences, that is, to philosophical apriori knowledge. It is also indispensable for the deeper understanding of many data which play a predominant role in the humanities, such as a great individual personality, or the cultural epoch of baroque, or an individual work of art like *King Lear*, Mozart's *Don Giovanni*, etc.

Besides its existential contact with reality, phenomenology is further characterized by its facing the object itself and by its methodical concern to do justice to the qualitative nature of the object. The true phenomenologist does not believe that he can know the object in its qualitative self-identity simply by gathering information about all those data connected with the object which can be bluntly stated. He sharply disagrees, therefore, with, say, the historian of art who believes that he will attain a real knowledge of a work of art, simply by exploring all sociological influences on an artist and his work, and by minutely analyzing the history of his life. He would charge the historian with proceeding in a typically non-phenomenological way. On the other hand, the one who approaches the work phenomenologically concentrates on the very nature of the work of art itself, its beauty, its atmosphere, and tries to grasp the specific character and individuality of this work by an intuitive delving into it.[3]

Phenomenology is the very antithesis to the anti-qualitative

---

[3] It is obvious that the phenomenological approach presupposes a specific talent which is not always found in a would-be critic or observer. There are many men who are able to grasp the surrounding facts which can be simply stated, but are unable to accomplish understanding of the work itself by an intuitive contact. In our introduction, we spoke of these two basic different capacities in man. Now the fact that specific capacities are presupposed in a man in order to grasp certain truths — capacities which are not granted to every man — is in no way an argument against a proposed method. Nor does it imply any subjectivity whatsoever. It is a great and widespread error to assume that the objectivity and validity of a truth depend upon the fact that everyone and anyone can grasp it or that we can prove it in such a way that everyone must accept it. This assumption itself is not, however, evident, nor has anyone ever attempted to prove it. It is one of the many silent presuppositions which have crept into philosophy during its long history. In certain cases one is not even aware of such presuppositions; in other cases, one deals with them as if they were evident and thus need not be proved. They are anything but evident, however. To this family of illegitimate tacit presuppositions belongs also this extension of *equality* to the domain of knowledge and truth.

trend which we find in some thinkers who are deluded by the prejudice that the more something possesses a qualitative plenitude, the less is it rational and intelligible. Phenomenology, on the contrary, implies a full receptiveness for the essential perfume of spiritual, cultural entities in all their existential and qualitative plenitude. But here again we must emphasize the radical antithesis between the phenomenological sight and any mere description. Even here, where the object does not yield to the cognizance of apriori facts, where there is no question of our reaching necessary and highly intelligible states of facts, the phenomenological sight, because it understands the object in its unity from within, differs essentially from a description. For this consists in merely observing and stating the single features and is, as it were, a going around the object.

In later publications we intend to deal in great detail with the role of phenomenology in understanding important singular objects of history and culture. Here it may suffice to stress first that the phenomenological approach is not restricted exclusively to philosophy; second, that this element of phenomenology just discussed, namely, its intuitive and immediate contact with the given reality in its living plenitude and flavor, clearly reveals the affinity between phenomenology and any serious existentialism, for example, that found in Gabriel Marcel's works.

CHAPTER VIII

THE MEANING OF PHILOSOPHY FOR MAN

We saw what kind of unique knowledge-interest is incorporated into philosophical inquiry and also what a completely new stage of awakening of the human mind is implied by it. As we saw in the beginning, all knowledge is a special form of intentional participation in the objects known. It is, moreover, the presupposition for all other forms of spiritual participation.

Philosophical knowledge is the prototype of knowledge. In it the first perfection of knowledge in general within the natural sphere reaches its high point. As the knowledge of centrally important realities in their essence, and as the penetration of the essence from within with a completely new intelligibility, philosophical knowledge grants a participation in being incomparably higher than all the other types of knowledge as such. The philosophical putting of a question aims at a participation in being which is indescribably deeper and more intimately related to eternity. The philosophical eros, which is incorporated in the Platonic Dialogues and, uniquely, in the works of St. Augustine, aims at a becoming-accepted into the kingdom of truth as such. This is at the base of the solemnity and the ardor characteristic of the striving for true philosophical knowledge. It is found also in the threefold thematicity of philosophical knowledge, namely, the notional theme, the theme of the object itself, and the contemplative theme. Philosophical knowledge is a fundamental position of the human mind. Just as knowledge in general is a basic component of personal life and being, so philosophical knowledge, not only as the highest form of natural knowledge but also as the most classical form of explicit and systematic knowledge, is the basic position of the human spiritual person. It is grounded in the meaning and essence of man as such.

Compared to philosophy, all the other sciences not only have a more special knowledge but also a knowledge which is not centrally grounded in the essence and meaning of man. This is so both because the object of a philosophical inquiry has a more central importance than the objects of the other sciences and because philosophical knowledge, above all other kinds, is the deepest and most classical. In fine, it is the highest fulfillment of natural knowledge in general.

It is no accident that philosophical inquiry stands at the beginning of all systematic theoretical inquiry, and that all sciences are children of philosophy. For philosophical inquiry is the basic position of the awakened and cognizing human mind. The philosophical thirst is of an elementary, classical nature inasmuch as it is very deeply grounded in the metaphysical situation of man in his being ordered toward God, the very Fountain of all being and all truth. The philosophical thirst is grounded in man's task to penetrate, by knowledge, reality as an image of God, which has itself been ordered to God. Man has the task to penetrate reality and then lovingly to embrace it.

The philosophical *eros* is at its very heart a basic form of man's natural longing for God, the absolute truth and the source of all truth. The direction toward philosophical knowledge, therefore, exists in some form in every man, albeit completely covered over and made unconscious, and even despite the fact that only a few possess the intellectual capability to attain to a real and autonomous philosophical knowledge.

THE MEANING OF PHILOSOPHY FOR MAN

Philosophic inquiry is the basic question of the human mind. It is the archcomponent of the spirit turned toward God and a component also of its natural bond to God.

Philosophic inquiry and knowledge is not only the most classical form of theoretical knowledge; in the truest sense of the word, it is also "closer to life" than all the other scientific kinds of knowledge. Nothing is more erroneous and childish than to look upon a philosopher as a man who lives in the clouds and is occupied with abstruse problems, as a man who has lost every living contact with reality. This is an error typical of a pragmatic, shortsighted, banal attitude which sees a content as real and important for life only to the degree that it satisfies an external, even an indispensable practical need. This error is analogous to the one which represents the religious man as one who lives in the clouds and becomes estranged from life and its realities because of religion.

I say an analogous error, for the latter is even more stupid and childish, inasmuch as the religious attitude is indeed the center and the *forma* of the true life. Still, there is an analogy in the misunderstanding which lies at the root of both errors, namely, the failure to grasp the paradox that the glance into eternity deals with the center of the temporal life much more than does the preoccupation with the external needs of life. Analogous also is the attitude of *ressentiment* against the world of the essential and the eternal. It embodies the wrong concept of reality and "nearness to life."

This prejudice against philosophy is nourished by all "practical" and banal minds. They ignore the power of the Idea; they have not the slightest inkling of what unheard-of consequences have resulted from philosophical errors and genuine philosophical knowledge in the political and economic spheres — both of which even they recognize as real and important for life. This prejudice against philosophy is not confined to banal minds, however. It is also found in some of the minds of those who are representatives of the various sciences. Although the latter understand the meaning and value of systematic theoretical knowledge, although they demand such knowledge for their own scientific research and look with contempt upon the banal minds, they nonetheless think that philosophical inquiry is a superfluous intellectual luxury. They regard philosophical inquiry as a vain expedition into an abstract world. They see it as lying beyond the investigation of the "real" world, as an overemphasizing of the theoretical and as foreign to life. We pass over in silence their complaints about the inexactness and unscientific quality which they deem to be bound up with the philosophical method.

In truth, however, philosophy is in many respects much closer to life than are all the other sciences. In the first place, the questions of philosophy are primarily of a deeper and much more universal importance for man and life than those of the other sciences. We need think only of ethics, and philosophy of community, philosophy of law, and, above all, natural theology. But even in those cases where the content of the object in its universal character is not easily grasped as having a direct significance, philosophy yet deals in a way completely different from science with things related to man, his destiny, the position from which his real life as a spiritual person proceeds, and the ground on which he evidently stands with his whole being and in which he is rooted. This difference between philosophical questions and those of the other sciences is still valid even when we consider that, within the sciences themselves, some are directly related to man and his life and others are more distant. History and medicine belong to the first class and mathematics and mineralogy to the second. Logic, which deals with the formal bases of all truth; metaphysics, which deals with the essence and basic forms of being; epistemology, which

THE MEANING OF PHILOSOPHY FOR MAN

investigates the certainty of the foundations of knowledge — all deal with questions treating of the constitutive elements of the spiritual space in which we live and work.

Philosophical knowledge, second, as a prototype of knowledge in general, is a much more linear continuation and fulfillment of the highest form of naïve knowledge than are all the other kinds of scientific knowledge. To be sure, it requires a much more essential awakening, a much sharper eruption from the ordinary attitudes of life than do all the other sciences. This is so because philosophy is completely unpragmatic and proceeds from a nonactual position. Despite this distance from the ordinary attitudes of life, philosophy in its direction toward the essential, substantial content of things yet stands in an incomparably deeper relation to the spiritual life of the person, and especially to the above-mentioned highest form of naïve knowledge.

Third, philosophical knowledge is linked, too, in a manner completely different from that of science to classical "common sense," that is, to the aspect which the world offers in the organic living contact of the mind with reality. Philosophy aims at the intuitively graspable necessary essences of things and does not draw conclusions "from without," from a hidden essence. Consequently, there exists no gap between the naïve worldview and the world-view of true philosophy as there does between physics and the naïve view of the world.

Even as philosophy deals mercilessly with false "common sense," the kingdom of *doxa*, the world-view that results from inorganic theoretical reasoning, so true philosophy is linked respectfully to all that discloses the object to man in a naïve living contact. Thus, the philosophical essence-analysis of beauty or love does not sovereignly disregard what these contents disclose in prephilosophical, living, organic experience. On the contrary, it refers back to these springs of reality, not, however, in order to elevate the aspect given in the naïve experience to a theoretical and systematic consciousness, but rather to proceed from it and to push forward to an essence-analysis of the thing itself. Hence, it not only broadens and deepens but also rectifies the naïve aspect. Never, however, will philosophy treat the naïve aspect disrespectfully or disregard it, as physics does, for example, when it substitutes "vibrations" for colors and tones. No, philosophy fulfills its deepest intentions with regard to the naïve aspect.

We see, therefore, that although philosophical knowing and inquiry proceed from a position which is removed from all the whirl of actuality, they are nevertheless a form of systematic theoretical knowledge which is closer to life than those of the other sciences. Moreover, philosophy requires for its research no physical apparatus and no complicated method. Yet it has the deepest effect on human life.

Here we touch a very difficult problem, which we have already mentioned earlier, namely, the manner in which philosophical results, which are completely directed toward being understood and not merely toward being communicated, can penetrate to the broadest masses, who are unable to grasp philosophical knowledge. Of course, we think here of the results of genuine philosophy and not of popular philosophy, which from the start chooses its level to match the unphilosophical intellect.

We have already seen the unfortunate role that erroneous philosophical attitudes play in false common sense and inorganic reasoning about the world. It represents the illegitimate penetration of false philosophy into the organic, theoretical, prescientific world-view of man. In the recent past, it has resulted in widespread subjectivism, skepticism, relativism, and so forth. But there is also another kind of penetration. This is the legitimate but unconscious and uncritical influence which the prescientific world-view absorbs from the results of pure philosophy. Even from a formal point of view this legitimate influence is completely different from the illegitimate penetration of false philosophies.

First of all, it is not a question of genuine philosophical results being grasped uncritically by the dilettante, by the inorganic spiritual register of a person's mind. On the contrary, the question of a legitimate influence is centered around the penetration of a philosophical truth into that aspect of the world which organically grows out of a naïve living contact, with the result that there forms an orderly, enlightened, purified, and solidified principle.

Let us give examples of this in ethics, logic, and metaphysics. The simple man has a naïve living contact with goods endowed with an ethical value. True ethics does not sovereignly disregard the world disclosed in the naïve grasping of these values. Rather, it elevates the deepest and most correct of the naïve impressions to another stage of consciousness and forms the mind into a lasting conviction. It purifies the impression of all murky elements, all "idols," which combine haughtiness with concupiscence, and it fixes our gaze on the truly ethical elements in the naïve experience. Ethical values, such as generosity, the forgiving of a wrong suffered, self-less love, all of which perhaps flash up in the highest moments of naïve experience, only to be obscured for the most part by idols like "honor," revenge, and so on, are elevated by the basic propositions of genuine ethics to a possession that cannot be lost, to an unchangeable attitude. Nor do logic and true metaphysics pull the carpet from under the naïve world-view by means of abstruse, unclassical constructions. Quite the contrary. They elevate the classical elements of the simple world-view to the sphere of a clear consciousness. They dig out the classical heart of things and present them purified and clear.

Thus we see that philosophy does not act upon the spiritual center of the inorganic reasoning, but rather influences the naïve, living contact itself. It does this through ordering, purifying, and illuminating the impressions obtained in the naïve, organic, living contact. It transforms these impressions into rectified convictions which are permanent. The role of philosophy here is to be a judge that does not eliminate what is presented, but rather deepens and clarifies it.

Again, this legitimate influence of philosophy is by no means the same as the suggestive penetration of fragments from a fashionable philosophy which are then uncritically taken over by the theorizing dilettante as allegedly indisputable starting points. The mediation between genuine philosophical results and the ordinary person is accomplished by the classical man, who not only understands philosophical truths, but also translates their integral ethos and perspective in such a way that the classical nature of the basic philosophical thoughts is intuitively reflected in them. These are the qualified transmitters of basic philosophical truths. From them these truths are then received with a reverent preparedness by the man who remains rooted in the naïve living contact and who, precisely in his innocence and freedom from pseudo criticism, is equipped with a latent sense for truth. Such classical men are not simply formal "authorities." Intuitively mediated, however, the truths they teach bear the stamp of something which comes "from above."

Just this latent sense for truth is authentic common sense, which refuses to accept abstruse and arbitrary theories. It is the sense of those persons who stand in an organic living contact with reality, who are theoretically unwarped, so that they very willingly accept whatever is linked to the objective *logos* of an object insofar as this *logos* has disclosed itself to them in naïve experience. Even when this naïve experience is by far exceeded by the mediated philosophical truth, the latter simply leads deeper into the language of the object and is never completely removed from this language. These naïve people certainly do accept philosophical truths without criticism, without a philosophical examination of them. Nevertheless, unless dilettante, inorganic reasoners, they do not take over such truths in an illegitimate manner. For philosophy appeals not to their minds, which are willing enough to know theoretically and yet which lack the suitable means, but rather to their naïve sense which is much more at home in the truth.

We see, therefore, the profound mission of philosophy with respect to the whole life of man — for philosophers themselves, first of all, but, second, for the people who, although not professional philosophers, are yet full personalities with a classical receptivity for truth. Even though they are incapable of their own philosophical research, such people not only understand philosophical truth, but even embody it in their personality. They, and not the mere theorizing students of a philosopher, are entrusted with the tradition of truth for the unphilosophical masses.[1] Philosophy has its importance also for a third type of man, namely, the naïve person who is unable to gain a theoretical understanding of philosophical truth. He must accept these truths from the mediator personalities just discussed. With regard to all three, the philosopher himself, the mediator, and the naïve man, despite the very different relation of each toward philosophical truth, philosophy possesses the deepest importance for the whole of life. It enlightens, deepens, purifies, and sanely solidifies living contact with the world of objects.

In a negative respect philosophy has the mission to sweep away the fog which comes from inorganic theoretical reasoning and lies like a suffocating cloak over the meaning-content of being as it flashes up in naïve living contact. Philosophy has the task of prohibiting and destroying all the transgressions of the undigested results of different sciences into the metaphysical sphere in an amateurish chatter about them. Philosophy must sweep away the kingdom of *doxa*, just as Socrates did in a unique manner in the field of ethics.

---

[1] Of course, we do not mean to contradict the fact that the inner philosophical tradition actually belongs to the students and disciples of the philosophers.

In a positive respect philosophy has a basic function for the building of a spiritual earthly cosmos. Like a spiritual skeleton, its basic truths must support the flesh of community life, art, poetry, and the whole culture. Philosophy must help form the life of the individual from this point of view. Every cultural epoch has its immanent philosophical basis, and one of the measures for the classicity of an epoch is the truth or falsity of this basis. We think here of philosophical theses which are embodied in a certain culture as such. Let us, therefore, not confuse this immanent philosophical basis with some fashionable philosophy which happens to be the ruling one of an epoch.

The path along which these basic philosophical truths penetrate the lives of those masses who are destined neither for philosophical research and teaching nor for philosophical learning, is not, as we have already seen, an intellectual path. The results of philosophy are not meant to be theoretically understood by every individual in a popularized form. These results have to penetrate the spiritual space of a time-epoch by means of their direct effect upon certain classical personalities who intuitively reflect the philosophy in their ethos, that is, upon great poets, statesmen, and the like. This results in the acceptance of truths by the individual unphilosophical man, not as theoretical but as embodied truths, which can be accepted with a genuine common sense.

It now becomes clear how far removed from a mere unproductive reflection is genuine philosophy. We see what kind of highly classical indispensable mission it possesses for the life of mankind and the individual, not to mention the high meaning and value which philosophical knowledge possesses in itself. But the meaning and importance of philosophical inquiry and knowledge, which it possesses apart from its self-importance and value, as the deepest natural truth-contact with reality, is not yet exhausted.

Philosophy fulfills its highest mission by leveling the way for religion, by preparing for it and serving it. Philosophical knowledge has its climax in the knowledge of the existence of God and of His attributes as grasped by the natural light of reason. Its highest step is the understanding of the existence of the absolute personal Being by whom every being is created, who is imaged by all beings, and toward whom all beings are ordered. The proofs for the existence of God, as previously explained and clarified, are the classical preamble to faith.

Not even this, however, exhausts the importance of philosophy for religion, and still less for theology.

For religion presupposes all basic philosophical truths. What is disclosed by revelation remains beyond what is accessible to philosophy. It lies above philosophy, however, and not aside from it. Religion implicitly presupposes, therefore, basic philosophical truths, such as the objectivity and autonomy of being, the incompatibility of being and nonbeing, the objective validity of values, the existence of personal beings, the freedom of human decision, the fact that every value demands a positive response on the part of the person, the fact that the higher value should be preferred to the lower, and so forth. The permanent solidification, and the explicitly essential bringing to consciousness, of our convictions about these basic truths is, therefore, part of the ground of religion in ourselves and is also a preamble to faith, although in a sense other than that of the proofs for the existence of God. Certainly, God is able to call into being the children of Abraham from stones. He can give a man the grace of the living faith without any philosophical preparation, and then the one to whom such grace has been given possesses all basic philosophical truths per *eminentiam*. Even so, and in this sense also, philosophy has objectively the mission of being a preamble to faith, and this in such a way that the degree of clearness and solidification of explicit convictions, engendered by basic philosophical truths, create a proportionately favorable situation for the reception of faith. In this sense, the Platonic-Aristotelian philosophy was looked upon as a preparation for the truths of the Christian Revelation, however little the philosophy itself could say about the truth and reality of Revelation.

Finally, philosophical inquiry as such means a longing for philosophical knowledge, for a contemplative gaze upon the thing known. As we have already seen, this is a significant counterpart to the religious longing for God. In turning toward the centrally important contents of the world, the philosophical eros leads the human mind into the depths of reality. As Plato says, it leads man "to his true home." It directs his glance away from the world of perishing things, of things accidental, and fixes it on the world of the eternal, on the meaning of things in themselves which they possess as images of God and as things ordered to Him. In such a way does philosophy prepare the soul for the acceptance of the revelation of God.

The philosophical eros with its contemplative goal, its consideration of being from a position of an eternity, removed from the whirl of actuality, its respectful sense of listening and allowing things to unfold themselves in their proper content and importance in themselves, its freedom from all pragmatic elements — this acts in an important way upon the growth of those spiritual organs which are indispensable for a truly deep and full religious life.

It is clear, therefore, what rank rightly belongs to philosophical inquiry. True philosophizing carries man into recollection and frees him from all alleged autarchy. In it mankind becomes, like Daniel, the "man of longing," of that longing which St. Augustine expressed when he said: "Our hearts are restless until they rest in Thee." The true philosopher is, like Plato, *paidagogos eis Christon*, the preparer of the way to Christ.

INDEX

Abstraction, degrees of, 129; nature of, 113; third degree of, 130
Aesthetic appearance, 98
Analytic propositions, 77
Appearance such-being, 103
Apriori, the, distinguished from presuppositions, 92 ff; and experience, 96 ff; and philosophical knowledge, 63 ff
Apriori knowledge, absolute certainty of, 70 ff; characteristics of, 63 ff; criterion of, 130 ff; incomparable intelligibility of, 69 ff; possibility of, summary, 99 f; range of, 129; refutes all skepticism, 140; strict necessity, 64 ff
Aristotle, discoveries in logic, 137; distinction between final and efficient causes, 208 f
Augustine, St., on knowledge and contemplation, 182; "Si fallor, sum," 74, 124, 146 f, 208

Beatific Vision, 182
Being, architectonic structure of, 92
Bergson, Henri, 8; distinction between technical and intellectual memory, 32 n; on memory, 150, 214
Blind familiarity, 200
Blondel, Maurice, 8
Body-soul relation, 151
Bracketing, of existence, 97, 99 n, 128
"By definition," 80

Cartesian doubt, 73
Certainty, of apriori knowledge, 70
Certitude, about recollection, 35; proper to knowing states of facts, 35
Chaotic unity, 100 ff
"Cogito, ergo sum," 74, 124, 146; as one premise in proof of God's existence, 150
Cognizance, see Taking cognizance
Colors, existence of, 121
Common sense, 231; authentic, 234
Contact, existential, lived, 202
Contemplative "dwelling-in," 179 f
Contemplative theme, of knowledge, 178; in religion, 182
Controversy, in philosophy, 208
Conviction, a theoretic response different from taking cognizance, 19 f
Cosmological proof, 149
Creation, message-character of, 162 n
Criterion, of apriori knowledge, 130 f
Criticism, lack of, in inorganic knowledge, 59; lack of, in theoretical prescientific knowledge, 57 f

Deactualized standpoint, of philosophy, 194
Deception, based on sense-structure, 160
Deduction, 74; confused with source of intelligibility as such, 138; in philosophy, 218 f
Depragmatization, of philosophical knowledge, 191 ff
Depth, in certain objects, 143; in philosophy, 189, 191; of the universe, 199
Descartes, critical spirit, 208; see also "Cogito, ergo sum"
Description, empirical way of knowing, 105
Dilettantism, of inorganic theoretical prescientific knowledge, 56
Discovery, philosophical and scientific, 136
Distortion, 116
Doxa, and inorganic theoretical knowl-

edge, 231; realm of, 235
Dream, possibility of, 73

Ego, reality of, 148
Eidos, reality of, 132; and unity, 101
Empirical, blunt observation, 96
Empiricism, denies the apriori, 77
Entia rationis, 118
Eros, philosophical, 188, 227, 238
Essences, aesthetic, 108 f; constitutive, 98; genuine, 116; genuine, epistemological characteristics of, 131 ff; genuine, intuitive grasp of, 97 ff; genuine, source of all *ratio*, 132; as self-given, 216; *see also* Such-being
Eternal verities vs. idealism, 158
Euclidean geometry, not tautological, 78
Existential closeness, of philosophy, 199
Experience, and the apriori, 96 ff; meanings of, 86 ff

Familiarity, blind, 200
Fictions, reality of, 170
Formal, concept of, 93
Frui, Augustinian, 180 n, 181

Gap, between a conclusion and the given, 71 f
Generality, degree of, 130
Given, the, 58
Givenness, of a such-being, 77
God, as Creator and Lord, 162; man's longing for, 228; necessary existence of, 126; our knowledge of, 149; proof of existence of, 219

Hallucination, no threat to apriori, 75; possibility of, 73
"Having knowledge of," different from knowing in limited sense, 34
Hegel, G. F. W., dialectics, 210
Heidegger, Martin, 8
History, objects of, 194
Hume, David, skepticism, 2
Husserl, Edmund, 8; on bracketing of existence, 99 n, 128; Lauer's criticism of, 99 n, 224; on phenomenology, 223
Hypotheses, in philosophy, 150; in science and philosophy, 205

Ideal existence, of essences, 114; two kinds of, 119 f
Idealism, on the meaning of truth, 158; misinterpretation of taking cognizance, 24; refutation of, 140; summary of its differences from author's position, 167 ff; transcendental, self-contradictory claim that taking cognizance is a producing of the object, 16
Ideas, Platonic, and genuine essences, 116
Immediacy, of perception, 174
Induction, fate of, 72
Innate ideas, in Descartes, 88
Inorganic theoretical knowledge, 53 f
Insanity, as related to grasp of necessary essences, 115
Insight, 69
Intelligere, meaning of, 69 f, 134
Intelligibility, of apriori knowledge, 69 ff; of apriori states of facts, 69 f; frontiers of, 144
Intuition, of genuine essences, 97 ff; intellectual, 113, 183, 215; in philosophy, 214 f
Intuitive "having," of necessary essences, 139
Inventions, 110

Judging, not the same as taking cognizance of something, 16
Judgment, marks by which it is distinguished from taking cognizance, 18 ff

Kant, Immanuel, on discrepancy between appearance and reality, 169; distinction between analytic and synthetic propositions, 208; extent of his subjectivity, 166 f; on knowledge of things-in-themselves, 147; meaning of subjective, 157 f; on the noumenon as inaccessible to man, 157; on phenomena, 152 f; on the possibility of experience, 93; on presuppositions, 92; on the role of intuition, 84; on tautology, 77
Kantian categories and forms of intuition, 88
Kennen, having knowledge of, 33; as opposed to *wissen*, 33
Kierkegaard, S., on subjectivity, 158 n

INDEX

Knowing, in broad and in narrow sense, 34; static, as distinct from taking cognizance, 26 ff

Knowledge, basic forms of, 26 ff; contemplative theme, 178; general discussion of, 13 ff; notional theme, 177; a primary datum, 13 ff; a spiritual possession of an object, 14; superactual form of, 28 ff; two basic themes of, 172 ff; as a "wedding" with object, 177 f; see also Prescientific knowledge, Naïve prescientific knowledge, Philosophical knowledge, Taking cognizance

Knowledge-thematicity, 43

Lauer, Quentin, critique of Husserl, 99 n; on meaning of phenomenology, 224

Learning, the dynamic process that leads to static knowing, 27

Logical positivism, 147 n

Lying, 146

Man, as a questioner, 11
Marcel, Gabriel, 226
Material, concept of, 93
Meaning, distinguished from perception, 175
Meaningfulness, stages of, 100
Memory, knowledge subsists as potential, 32
Message-character, of creation, 162 n f; of some sense images, 161
Message objectivity, 163
Metaphysics, definition of, 126
Method, of philosophy, 214 ff
Moral values, existence of, 122
Morphic unity, 141 f, 192

Naïve prescientific knowledge, 38 ff; six types of, 48 ff
Nature, constitutive, 104
Necessary unity, 110 ff
Necessity, of apriori knowledge, 64 f; of essence, 68; formal, 66; of "laws of nature," 68; structural, 67
Noncontradiction, principle of, 84 f
"Nothing else but" formula, 5
Notional theme of knowledge, 36 f, 177
Numbers, existence of, 120; as object of philosophy, 142

Object, of philosophical knowledge, 63 ff, 140 ff, 185 ff; pragmatic deformation of, 42
Objective existence, 152
Object-thematicity, 43; in philosophical knowledge, 185 ff
Ontology, object of, 145
Opaque facts, 192
Organ, for philosophical knowledge, 5
Organs, various intellectual, 3
Oughtness, of moral values, 122

Perception, nature of, 172 f; starting point for experience, 87; three characteristic features of, 172 ff; two perfections of, 176 f
Person, reality of, 124
Pfaender, Alexander, phenomenology, 223
Phenomena, in Kant's sense, 152 f, 157
Phenomenology, existential character, 224; meaning of, 222 ff; as transcendental idealism, 224
Philosophical knowledge, basic difference from theoretical prescientific knowledge, 61; contrasted with prescientific knowledge, 38 ff; depragmatization of, 191 ff; depth of, 189 f; distance from the object, 197 f; distinguishing mark of, 188 ff; object of, 63 ff; summary of differences from naïve knowledge, 48 ff
Philosophic inquiry, dominant themes of, 185 ff
Philosophy, concern for existence, 146; deactualized standpoint, 194; meaning for man, 227 ff; method, 214 ff; object of, 140 ff; object of, apriori nature, 63 ff; object-thematicity in, 185 ff; rehabilitation of, 10; and science, 186 ff, 204 ff; and science, positive relation, 211 ff; subconscious moral resistance to, 204; see also Philosophical knowledge
Physics, character of, 204 f
Plato, achievement of, 64; on direct grasp of species, 113 f; on distinction between apriori and empirical knowledge, 208; on the theory of reminiscence, 91
Positivism, knowledge as blunt observation, 4 f; main feature of, 6; on

the role of philosophy, 1
Possible, meaning of, 101, 125
Pragmatic attitude, in knowledge, 42
Pragmatic character, of some naïve knowledge, 40
Pragmatic interest, nature of, 186
Prescientific knowledge, naïve, 38; organic and inorganic, 52; theoretical, 50 ff; theoretical, inorganic, 53 f
Presuppositions, 60; distinguished from the apriori, 92 ff
Prise de conscience, 83, 136 f
Propositions, analytic, 77; being of, 118 f; synthetic, 77
Psychologism, error of, 15

Recall, authentic, 181
Reinach, Adolf, distinction between affirmation and conviction, 17; phenomenology, 223
Religion, and philosophy, 229; role of philosophy for, 236 f
Reminiscence, in Plato, 88
Representation, in contemplation, 181; how distinct from perception, 173

Scheler, Max, 8
Science, and philosophy, 186 ff, 404 ff; and philosophy, positive relation, 211 ff
Self-evidence, 84
Semblances, 160; distinguished from subjectivity, 166
"*Si fallor, sum*," 74, 124, 146, 208; analyzed, 147
Skepticism, contemporary, 1; of Greek Sophists, 1; of Hume, 2
Soul-body relation, 151
States of facts, definition of, 33; as object of an assertion or judgment, 17
Status viae, man's earthly situation, 11
Subject, concept of, 80
Subjective, several meanings of, 153 f
Subjectivity, 154 n; idealistic, 157; of valid aspects, 166

Such-being, experience of, 87 ff
Superactual subsistence, of knowing, 28 ff
Synthetic propositions, 77

Taking cognizance, active component in, 22 ff; active elements in, 24 f; differs from conviction, 19 f; distinguished from judging and other theoretical acts, 16 f; distinguished from static knowing, 26 ff; dynamic appropriation of some new object, 26 ff; marks whereby it differs from judgment, 18 f; philosophical, distinctly thematic, 38; philosophical, twofold distinction from pragmatic knowledge, 41 f; a "receiving," 15; specific features of, 15 ff
Tautology, distinguished from fruitful statements, 77 f
Thematicity, of object and of knowledge, 43
Theme, of both taking cognizance and knowing, 36; of knowledge, 172 ff; notional, 36 f
Thomas Aquinas, St., on contemplation, 183; on *intelligere*, 134 n
Transcendental idealism, self-contradictory claim that taking cognizance is a producing of the object, 16
Transcendentals, of being, 130
Transparency, confused with intelligibility, 133

Unity, of appearances, 104 f; chaotic and accidental, 100 ff; of genuine types, 102 ff; morphic, 192; necessary essential, 110 ff; types of, 100 ff

Verities, eternal, 117

"Wedding" with object, 178
Wissen, knowing, 33; as opposed to *kennen*, 33
Wonder, a mark of philosophy, 189, 197